FROM PERIPHERY TO CENTRE STAGE

AMBEDKAR, AMBEDKARISM & DALIT FUTURE

From Periphery to Centre Stage

Ambedkar, Ambedkarism & Dalit Futue

Edited by

K.C. YADAV

MANOHAR
2025

First published 2000
Reprinted 2025
First eBook edition 2025

ISBN 978-81-7304-276-8 (hardbound)
ISBN 978-93-6080-508-1 (eBook)

Published by
Ajay Kumar Jain for
Manohar Publishers & Distributors
4753/23 Ansari Road, Daryaganj
New Delhi 110 002

Printed and bound by CPI Group (UK) Ltd, Croydon, CR0 4YY

For
Mahatma Jotiba Phule,
the first great rebel against
social injustice and inequality
in modern India
and
Shri Ramraj,
who has been waging his struggle
in present times.

Contents

Preface

This book has grown out of a national seminar on the life and work of Babasaheb Dr Bhimrao Ramji Ambedkar (1891-1956) held at Kurukshetra University (India) in May 1992. Many eminent scholars from various disciplines participated in the seminar and presented thought-provoking papers. Later, some write-ups were added to make the work as comprehensive and full as was practically possible.

Like many other great men, Dr Ambedkar is a much misunderstood person. Both his admirers and critics have contributed a great deal to this situation. The former have raised him to a height that it becomes almost impossible to view him from as to what really he is like. On the other hand, hostile critics have spared no pains to reduce him to a naught—invisible naught, to be precise. Happily, in the early 1990s, especially after the V.P. Singh government celebrated Ambedkar's centennial, some really serious work began to be done by scholars with right academic credentials and scholarly background to understand him and his monumental effort to improve the lot of the plundered, profaned and disinherited section of Indian humanity. But before things could improve to any appreciable extent, they again began to drift along a wrong way: organizations, outfits and establishments from right to left, from conservative to liberal, and so forth vied with each other in glorifying the Dalit Messiah to serve their vested interests. This has confused our understanding of the great man and obscured the spirit and identity of his movement for making Dalit future safe and secure.

The eleven essays presented here remove the confusion and show things in their real form and taste. They explain, though briefly, many things relating to Dr Ambedkar and his movement which have remained unexplained so far.

In doing this work many persons have helped me in a number of ways. I am specially greatful to Prof. Upendra Baxi, Dr Gail Omvedt, Prof. Raosaheb Kasbe, Prof. Gopal Guru, Mr Yogendra Yadav, Dr Anand Teltumbde, Dr S.K.Gupta and Dr Eleanor Zelliot for allowing me to share their researches with the readers. My thanks are also due to the following personal friends and colleagues who lent me moral support as well as expertise: Mr R.C. Rao, Mr Satyaprakash Singh Yadav, Thiru D. Nagendhiran and Dr S.S. Nehra. I am also thankful to Dr M.L. Ranga, Health Minister, Haryana, for taking keen interest in this project, Mr S.K. Chahal for preparing the bibliography, and my son, Dr Neeraj Yadav for reading the proofs and my wife Shashipriya for editorial assistance.

K.C. YADAV

Introduction

The abolition of slavery has gone on for a long time. Rome abolished slavery. America abolished it, and we did, but only the words were abolished, not the thing.[1]

Perhaps there is no other man in the annals of our history who could equal Dr Ambedkar in waging a relentless struggle in our part of the world to accomplish the undone task referred to above by Tolstoy. This 'colossus of rebellion' coming from the terribly depressed and disadvantaged section of our society, completely devoid of material means and other resources, fought long-drawn battles against the most powerful foes almost single-handedly. And, surprisingly, achieved success, and joined, as Lord Justice Bingham of England has justly said, 'the most select company in history, that of the great liberators and emancipators, along with Abraham Lincoln, Wilberforce, The tsar Alexander II (perhaps) and very few others.'[2]

It is but natural that some such questions should arise here as: How did Ambedkar do this seemingly impossible work? Where did he get his strength from? And resources? Then, can we follow him in future to fight the vested interest? How? The present book deals with these and other such questions at length.

II

The book consists of eleven chapters in all. Chapter 1 is an autobiographical note where one gets an answer in so many words to some such difficult but important questions as: Why Ambedkar was Ambedkar? He had great qualities and qualifications to become a great national leader—a Nehru, a Patel or somebody else. Why did he not try to do that? And why did he elect to choose a narrow, sectarian space for himself, instead? Why was he always a man in hurry? Why was he tense, angry and anguished?

This is followed by an interesting account (Chapter 2) by Beverley Nichols, a foreigner—British, to be precise—who has looked at

Babasaheb from a distance—not for the reason that he considered, like the orthodox Hindus, the Dalit leader ' a creature whose touch would make him precipitate himself into the nearest bath-tub, to soap and pray, and pray and soap,and soap and pray, so that the filth of Dr Ambeddkar (M.A. London), the shame of Dr Ambedkar (high honours at Columbia University), the plague and scourge of Dr Ambedkar (special distinction at Heidelberg) should be washed for ever', but for the reason that he should be maximally objective in his assessment of the man and his flock—the Dalits.

In what follows (Chapter 3), Prof. Upendra Baxi gives a faithful portrait of Ambedkar and the formative context of his struggle for emancipation of Dalits. And also a sane word of advice for getting maximum benefit from the Dalit Messiah: Choose your Ambedkar carefully, for there is not one but many Ambedkars. And 'celebrate' the right one, for

> I think that, whether we are conscious of it or not, we are celebrating the Ambedkar whose spirit was domesticated for all practical purposes by the Mahatma and whose presence was marginalized by his political heir. We are celebrating the 'Modern Manu', not the iconoclast or the rebel. By this, we diminish the historical significance and contemporary relevance of Babasaheb and reconstruct him only as a memory of a Mahar whose appearance the gracious galaxy of Gandhi, Nehru and others tolerated; we are celebrating the tolerance and appropriation of Ambedkar which is, on all counts, opportunisitically vandalist in ways carefully calculated to remove from the Dalit memory the incandescent luminosity of the real Ambedkar, lest it might give a precious contemporary insurrectionary identity to Babasaheb and threaten the hegemonic empires of present-day political managers by the revival of the Ambedkar of the thirties and forties.[4]

Our second concern is comprehending the phenomenon called Ambedkarism. It is a pretty difficult task. For, as rightly pointed out by Dr Gail Omvedt, 'Dr Ambedkar's thought was not always consistent and it did not (and the same of course can be said for Marx) fully resolve the problems he grappled with'. But, as she rightly observes later, some themes stand out with the help of which we can go about this work. These themes, in brief, are:

> First, an uncompromising dedication to the needs of his people, the Dalits which required the total annihilation of the caste system and the Brahmanic superiority it embodied;
>
> Second, an almost equally strong dedication to the reality of India whose historical-cultural interpretation he sought to wrest from the imposition of a 'Hindu' identity to understand it in its massive, popular reality;

Third, a conviction that the eradication of caste required a repudiation of 'Hinduism' as a religion, and adoption of an alternative religion, which he found in Buddhism, a choice which he saw as not only necessary for the masses of Dalits who followed him but for the masses in India generally;

Fourth, a broad economic radicalism interpreted as 'socialism' ('state socialism' in some versions; 'democratic socialism' in others) mixed with and growing out of his democratic liberalism and liberal dedication to individual rights;

And finally, a political orientation which linked a firmly autonomous Dalit movement with a constantly attempted alliance of the socially and economically exploited (Dalits and Shudras, 'workers' and 'peasants' in call terms) projected as an alternative political front to the Congress party he saw as the unique platform of 'Brahmanism' and 'capitalism'.[5]

The six write-ups (Chapters 4-9), 'The Ambedkarian Ideology: A Perspective' by Dr Raosaheb Kasbe; 'The Man who Thought Differently: An Inquiry into the Political Thinking of Dr Ambedkar' by Dr Gopal Guru; 'Dr Ambedkar's Perception of the Indian Society and his Egalitarian Vision' by Dr S.K. Gupta; 'Undoing the Bondage: Dr Ambedkar's Theory of Dalit Liberation' by Dr Gail Omvedt; 'Empowering the Powerless: Dr Ambedkar's Contribution to the Ideology of Dalit Protest' by Dr K.C. Yadav; and 'The Process of Securing Places of Power for Dalits: A Note on Dr Ambedkar's Contribution' by Dr Eleanor Zelliot, help us understand the complex processes governing the above six themes. In other words, they give us, though in brief, what 'Ambedkarism' really is in most of its aspects.

In the end, the question of Dalit future is discussed. A general notion persists—thanks to the efforts of the vested interest—that in free India all is well with Dalits; and their future is bright. The reasons for such a happy situation are not far to seek. They say: 'The republican constitution of the land provides for reservations of seats for them in its legislatures. A definite percentage of the jobs is reserved for them. Article 17 has made untouchability a cognizable offence. And the statute book has law against atrocities against Dailts on it.'[6] There is a provision, both at central and state levels, to help these poor people to get over their educational deficiency, economic deprivation and so forth.[7]

What is the reality? Put bluntly, over fifty years of freedom have hardly made any appreciable change in the Dalit life.[8] Take, for instance, untouchability, history's most flagrant example of man's inhumanity to man. Despite the constitutional ban, the monster still exists almost everywhere, in every state, in some measure or the other. A survey conducted by a social organization some time ago, covering 1,155 villages in 12 states, has shown that 'untouchability is practiced in some way or the other in the rural areas in terms of denial of access to the Dalits to wells, temples, hotels and restaurants, barbershops, laundries, and so on'.[9] In Gujarat, the land hallowed by Gandhiji, Dalits are not being allowed to become members of some cooperative societies, banks, etc. According to another survey conducted recently, 'the Scheduled Caste milk producers had to find customers in their own community as the Patels and Kshatriyas refused to buy milk from 'untouchables'.[10] The story was no way different in the adjoining state of Maharashtra. The Dalits 'have been given fair price shops here against reserved quotas for them under the Essential Commodities Act. The upper castes do not come to these shops for the reason that the Dalits who were once begging food now control the food distribution system'.[11]

Worse, they still continue to be treated atrociously almost everywhere, in every state (Table 1).[12] The government reports do not give a comprehensive account of the crimes against them. They give only a few cases which could somehow attract the attention of the government and press. Many more such cases did not reach there.

The situation is equally bad, if not worse, in the economic sphere. There have been land reforms in the past, but land has not reached Dalits as promised. Industries do not belong to them. They are nothing short of strangers in the field of trade and commerce. They are not absorbed to any satisfactory measure even in the 'labour pool' in these sectors. There is reservation of jobs for them in state services. But they are not provided for jobs there fairly and speedily. All sorts of excuses are extended for not filling up their reserved seats. Recently even such cases have come to light that qualified Dalit candidates selected by competent selection committees were not given appointment orders without any rhyme or reason. Had deceptions, frauds and feints not been employed, the SCs, STs, should have got their due share of jobs (22.5 per cent) by now. But the way things are moving, they will have to wait for a considerably long time to reach even half the limit.[13]

The position in the sphere of education is even worse. There is a lot of noise about Dalits being given special facilities there, but there is hardly any big improvement in the situation—especially in the rural areas where the vast majority of them live.

TABLE 1: STATEWISE CASES OF ATROCITIES AGAINST DALITS, 1996-8.[14]

	Crimes (IPC)							
State	Murder	G.H.	Rape	Arson	IPC	PCR	C&R	Total
Andhra Pradesh	41	1	53	2	20	3	90	210
Arunachal Pradesh	–	–	–	–	–	–	–	–
Assam	–	–	1	–	1	–	1	3
Bihar	17	1	–	2	–	2	64	86
Goa	–	–	–	–	–	–	2	2
Gujarat	–	2	4	–	1	–	10	17
Haryana	9	–	7	1	2	–	81	100
Himachal Pradesh	3	–	1	–	–	–	3	7
Jammu & Kashmir	–	–	–	–	–	–	2	2
Karnatka	1	1	–	–	2	–	19	23
Kerala	–	–	1	–	1	–	11	13
Madhya Pradesh	9	–	6	–	3	1	42	61
Maharashtra	5	1	–	–	3	–	32	41
Manipur	–	–	–	–	–	–	1	1
Meghalaya	–	–	–	–	–	–	–	–
Mizoram	–	–	–	–	–	–	1	1
Orissa	2	–	–	–	1	–	17	20
Punjab	5	–	3	–	1	–	17	26
Rajasthan	11	–	4	1	2	–	119	137
Sikkim	–	–	–	–	–	–	–	–
Tamil Nadu	4	–	–	1	6	1	51	63
Tripura	1	–	–	–	1	–	1	3
Uttar Pradesh	17	5	22	5	14	4	467	587
Andman & Nicobar	–	–	–	–	–	–	–	–
Chandigarh	–	–	–	–	–	–	–	–
Dadar & Nagar Haveli	–	–	–	–	–	–	–	–
Daman & Diu	–	–	–	–	–	–	–	–
Delhi	6	1	3	2	1	-	200	213
Lakshdweep	–	–	–	–	–	–	–	–
Pondicherry	–	–	–	–	–	–	–	–
Total	187	12	110	14	59	11	1258	1651

In short, Dalits still continue to suffer a great deal in many ways in almost every walk of life. Yet some people, who are out to teach the world that 'black is white and yes is no, down is up and stop is go', paint an altogether different picture. In the fifty years of Freedom, the Dalits, they say, have got 'a lot in life'. Far from it: Dalits, as noted above still continue to suffer injustice, deprivation and disinheritance. They are still very much on the margin.

Nor are there any surer indications that their future is going to be anyway better soon. Where do we go, then, to effect improvement in the situation? To Ambedkar, says Yogendra Yadav, in his write-up (Chapter 10: 'On the Relevance of Dr Ambedkar's Ideology'). But, cautions the author, Ambedkar should be taken objectively. Especially, he should not be judged from any given doctrine. For

> he had the courage—he thought he also had good reasons—to reject all the available ideological packages; it would be less than fair to evaluate him from a standpoint he knowingly rejected unless special reasons can be given for that. Nor would it be quite appropriate to use an artificially large category (e.g. the poor, the nation) as the measuring rod; Dr Ambedkar addressed himself largely to the question of the Depressed Classes and it is from the point of view of their interest and upliftment—howsoever defined—that the relevance of his ideas should be examined.[14]

Contextually, the question, then, is: Does Ambedkar's ideology show us the way for effecting meaningful changes in the status and conditions of Dalits? What and how can a Dalit activist learn from Dr Ambedkar's ideology? And how can he transform it into a reality? Dr Anand Teltumbde answers these and other such questions in the last write-up (Chapter 11, 'Beyond the Torturing Times: Dr Ambedkar and the Dalit Future'). To begin with, the author comes very heavily on, and admonishes, as Dr Ambedkar would himself have done, his followers very harshly: 'While there is so much noise being made in eulogy of Babasaheb, all that he lived and died for are being trempled upon by the very people who claim to carry on his legacy.' It is high time, he says, that we understand Ambedkarian essense and concentrate on it adequately,

> through a genuine empathy for the cause he chose to be his life objective. It is then alone that one could comprehend why his concern for landless peasants and workers had to be subdued in favour of his wider community, why he had to go against the Communists or Gandhi, why he had to sit as Labour member of the Viceroy's Executive Council, accept the law ministership in Nehru's cabinet or write India's Constitution and also later disown it.

In Dr Ambedkar's apparent inconsistencies, Dr Teltumbde adds,

> one would probably find more valuable material than may appear at first sight. He would be more understandable by the questions he raised than by the answers he seemed to provide. The antithesis might hold forth more promise than the thesis. The unsaid might prove more truth-bearing than

what is said, or, if not by anything else, his expressions were constrained by his own familiarity.[15]

III

The long and short of the story is that not lip eulogy but hard, sincere efforts are the crying need of the hour to rescue Babasaheb from obscuration and to liberate Ambedkarism from the clutches of vested interest, for no serious discussion of Dalit future is, and will be possible, without reference to Dr Ambedkar and Ambedkarism for many centuries to come.[16]

NOTES

1. Quoted in Justice V.R. Krishna Iyer, 'Social Justice to Dalits' in *Dr Ambedkar Birth Centenary Souvenir*, London, 1992, vol. IV, p. 27.
2. Ibid., p. 107.
3. Beverley Nicholas , 'Below the Bottom Rung', pp. 39-48.
4. Upendra Baxi, 'Emancipation as Justice: Legacy and Vision of Dr Ambedkar', pp. 49-74.
5. Gail Omvedt, 'Undoing the Bondage', pp. 113-46.
6. Article 17 declares that 'untouchability is abolished and its practice in any form is forbidden. The enforcement of any disability arising out of 'untouchability' shall be an offence punishable in accordance with law'.
7. For details pertaining to the issue, see the annual *Reports of the Commission for Scheduled Castes and Scheduled Tribes*, Government of India, New Delhi.
8. Ibid.
9. For details see *Economic and Political Weekly*, vol. XXVI, no. 33, 17 August 1991, pp. 1913-15.
10. *The Times of India*, 6 December 1993.
11. Ibid., 20 December, 1993.
12. These cases are for the years 1996-97. See *Report of the Commission for Scheduled Castes and Scheduled Tribes*, 1996-97, New Delhi, 1988, vol. 1, pp. 245.
13. See K.C. Yadav, *India's Unequal Citizens: A Study of OBCs*, Delhi, 1994, p. 199.
14. Yogendra Yadav, 'On the Relevance of Dr Ambedkar's Ideology', pp. 175-82.
15. Dr Anand Teltumbde, 'Beyond Torturing Times: Dr Ambedkar and the Dalit Future', pp. 183-92.
16. Ibid.

[illegible] were constructed by his own Constitution.[illegible]

III

The long and short of the story is that [illegible] efforts are the [illegible] to rescue Babasaheb from [illegible] Ambedkar [illegible] from the clutches of vested interest [illegible] serious discussion of Dalit [illegible] possible without reference to Dr Ambedkar and Ambedkarites [illegible]

NOTES

[illegible]

1
Ambedkar on Ambedkar: What does it mean to be a Dalit?

Foreigners of course know of the existence of untouchability. But not being next door to it, so to say, they are unable to realize how oppressive it is in its actuality. It is difficult for them to understand how it is possible for a few untouchables to live on the edge of a village containing a large number of Hindus, go through the village daily to free it from the most disagreeable of its filth and to carry the errands of all and sundry, collect food at the doors of the Hindus, buy spices and oil at the shops of the Hindu Bania from a distance, regard the village in every way as their home, and yet never touch nor be touched by any one belonging to the village. The problem is how best to give an idea of the way the untouchables are treated by the caste Hindus. A general description or a record of cases of the treatment accorded to them are the two methods by which this purpose could be achieved. I have felt that the latter would be more effective than the former. In choosing these illustrations I have drawn partly upon my own experience and partly upon the experience of others. I begin with events that have happened to me in my own life.

II

Our family came originally from Dapoli Taluka of Ratnagiri District of the Bombay Presidency. From the very commencement of the rule of the East India Company my forefathers had left their hereditary occupation for service in the army of the Company. My father also followed the family tradition and sought service in the Army. He rose to the rank of an officer and was a subedar when he retired. On his retirement, my father took the family to Dapoli with a view to settling down there. But for some reason he changed his mind. The family left Dapoli for Satara where we lived till 1904.

The first incident, which I am recording as well as I can remember, occurred in about 1901 when we were at Satara. My mother was then dead. My father was away on service as a cashier at a place called Goregaon in Khatav Taluka in the Satara District, where the Government had started the work of excavating a tank for giving employment to famine-stricken people who were dying in thousands. When my father went to Goregaon he left me, my brother, who was older than myself and two sons of my eldest sister who was dead, in charge of my aunt and some kind neighbours. My aunt was the kindest soul I have ever known, but she was of no help to us. She was somewhat of a dwarf and had some trouble with her legs which made it very difficult for her to move about without the aid of somebody. Often times she had to be lifted. I had sisters. They were married and were away living with their families. Cooking our food became a problem with us, especially as our aunty could not, on account of her helplessness, manage the job. We four children went to school and we also cooked our food. We could not prepare bread. So we lived on pulav, which we found to be the easiest dish to prepare, requiring nothing more than mixing rice and mutton.

Being a cashier, my father could not leave his station to come to Satara to see us, therefore he wrote to us to come to Goregaon and spend our summer vacation with him. We children were thoroughly excited over the prospect, especially as none of us had up to that time seen a railway train.

Great preparations were made. New shirts of English make, bright bejewelled caps, new shoes, new silk-bordered dhoties were ordered for the journey. My father had given us all particulars regarding the journey and had told us to inform him on which day we were starting, so that he would send his peon to the railway station to meet us and to take us to Goregaon. According to this arrangement, myself, my brother and one of my sister's sons left Satara, our aunt remaining in charge of our neighbours who promised to look after her. The railway station was 10 miles distant from our place and a tonga (a one-horse carriage) was engaged to take us to the station. We were dressed in the new clothing specially made for the occasion, and we left our home full of joy but amidst the cries of our aunt who was almost prostrate with grief at our parting.

When we reached the station my brother bought tickets and gave me and my sister's son two annas each as pocket money to be spent at our pleasure. We at once began our career of riotous living and each ordered a bottle of lemonade at the start. After a short while the train whistled in and we boarded it as quickly as we could for fear of being left behind. We were told to detrain at Masur, the nearest railway station for Goregaon.

The train arrived at Masur at about 5 in the evening and we got down with our luggage. In a few minutes all the passengers who had got down from the train had gone away to their destination. We three children remained on the platform looking out for my father or his servant whom he had promised to send. Long did we wait but no one turned up. An hour elapsed and the station-master came to enquire. He asked us for our tickets. We showed them to him. He asked us why we tarried. We told him that we were waiting for father or his servant to come but that neither had turned up and that we did not know how to reach Goregaon. We were well-dressed children. From our dress or talk no one could make out that we were children of the untouchables. Indeed the station-master was quite sure that we were Brahmin children and was extremely touched at the plight in which he found us. As is usual among the Hindus, the station-master asked us who we were. Without a moment's thought, I blurted out that we were Mahars. (Mahar is one of the communities that are treated as untouchable in the Bombay Presidency.) He was stunned. His face underwent a sudden feeling of repulsion. As soon as he heard my reply he went away to his room and we stood where we were. Fifteen to twenty minutes elapsed; the sun was almost setting. The father had not turned up; nor had he sent his servant and now the station-master had also left us. We were quite bewildered and the joy and happiness which we felt at the beginning of the journey gave way to the feeling of extreme sadness.

After half an hour, the station-master returned and asked us what we proposed to do. We said that if we could get a bullock-cart on hire we would go to Goregaon and if it was not very far we would like to start straightaway. There were many bullock-carts plying for hire. But my reply to the station-master that we were Mahars had gone round the cartmen and not one of them was prepared to suffer being polluted and to demean himself carrying passengers of the untouchable classes. We were prepared to pay double the fare but found that money did not work. The station-master who was negotiating on our behalf stood silent, not knowing what to do. Suddenly a thought seemed to have entered his head and he asked us, 'Can you drive the cart?' Feeling that he was finding a solution to our difficulty we shouted, 'Yes, we can.' With that answer he went and proposed on our behalf that we were to pay the cartman double the fare and drive the cart and that he should walk on foot along with the cart on our journey. One cartman agreed as it gave him an opportunity to earn his fare and also saved him from being polluted.

It was about 6.30 p.m. when we were ready to start. But we were anxious not to leave the station until we were assured that we would reach Goregaon before it was dark. We, therefore, questioned the cartman as to the distance and the time he would take to reach Goregaon. He assured us that it would be not more than three hours. Believing in his word, we put our luggage in the cart, thanked the station-master and got into the cart. One of us took the reins and the cart started with the man walking by our side.

Not very far from the station there flowed a river. It was quite dry except at places where there were small pools of water. The owner of the cart proposed that we should halt there and have our meal as we might not get water on our way. We agreed. He asked us to give a part of his fare to enable him to go to the village and have his meal. My brother gave him some money and he left, promising to return soon. We were very hungry and glad to have an opportunity to have a bite. My aunty had pressed our neighbour's women into service and had got some nice preparation for us to take on our way. We opened the tiffin basket and started eating. We needed water to wash the things down. One of us went to the the pool of water in the river basin nearby. But the water really was no water. It was thick with mud and the urine and excreta of the cows, buffaloes and other cattle who went to the pool for drinking. In fact, that water was not intended for human use. At any rate, the stench of the water was so strong we could not drink it. We had therefore to close our meal before we were satisfied and wait for the arrival of the cartman. He did not come for a long time and all that we could do was to look for him in all directions. Ultimately, he came and we started on our journey.

For some four or five miles we drove the cart and he walked on foot. Then he suddenly jumped into the cart and took the reins from our hands. We thought this to be rather strange conduct on the part of a man who had refused to let the cart on hire for fear of pollution, to have set aside all his religious scruples and to have consented to sit with us in the same cart but we dared not ask him any questions on the point. We were anxious to reach Goregaon, our destination, as quickly as possible. And for some time we were interested in the movement of the cart only. But soon there was darkness all around us. There were no street lights to relieve the darkness. There were no men or women or even cattle passing by to make us feel that we were in their midst. We became fearful of the loneliness which surrounded us.

Our anxiety was growing. We mustered all the courage we possessed. We had travelled far from Masur. It was more than three hours. But there was no sign of Goregaon. There arose a strange thought within us. We suspected that the cartman intended treachery and that he was taking us to some lonely spot to kill us. We had a lot of gold ornaments on us and that helped to strengthen our suspicions. We started asking how far Goregaon was, why we were so long reaching it. He kept on saying, 'It is not very far, we shall soon reach it.' It was about 10 at night when finding that there was no trace of Goregaon we children started crying and abusing the cartman. Our lamentations and wailings continued for long. The cartman made no reply. Suddenly we saw a light burning at some distance. The cartman said, 'Do you see that light? That is the light of the toll-collector. We will rest there for the night.' We felt some relief and stopped crying. The light was distant, but we could never seem to reach it. It took us two hours to reach the toll-collector's hut. The interval increased our anxiety and we kept on asking the cartman all sorts of questions, as to why there was delay in reaching the place, whether we were going on the same road, etc.

Ultimately, by midnight the cart reached the toll-collector's hut. It was situated at the foot of the hill but on the other side of the hill. When we arrived we saw a large number of bullock carts there all resting for the night. We were extremely hungry and wanted very much to eat. But again there was the question of water. So we asked our driver if it was possible to get water. He warned us that the toll-collector was a Hindu and that there was no question of our getting water if we spoke the truth and said that we were Mahars. He said, 'Say you are Mohammedans and try your luck.' On his advice I went to the toll-collector's hut and asked him if he would give us some water. 'Who are you?' he inquired. I replied that we were Musalmans, I conversed with him in Urdu which I knew very well so as to leave no doubt that I was a real Musalman. But the trick did not work and his reply was very curt, 'Who has kept water for you? There is water on the hill, if you want, go and get it, I have none.' With this he dismissed me. I returned to the cart and conveyed to my brother his reply. I don't know what my brother felt. All that he did was to tell us to lie down.

The bullocks had been unyoked and the cart was placed sloping down on the ground. We spread our beds on the bottom planks inside the cart, and laid down our bodies to rest. Now that we had come to a place of safety we did not mind what happened. But our minds could not help turning to the latest event. There was plenty of food with us. There was hunger burning within us; with all this we were to sleep without food; that was because we could get no water and we could get no water because we were untouchables. Such was the last thought that entered our mind.

I said we had come to a place of safety. Evidently my elder brother had his misgivings. He said it was not wise for all of us to go to sleep. Anything might happen. He suggested that at one time, two should sleep and one should keep watch. So we spent the night at the foot of the hill.

Early at 5 in the morning our cartman came and suggested that we should start for Goregaon. We flatly refused. We told him that we would not move until 8 o'clock. We did not want to take any chance. He said nothing. So we left at 8 and reached Goregaon at 11. My father was surprised to see us and said that he had received no intimation of our coming. We protested that we had given intimation. He denied the fact. Subsequently, it was discovered that the fault was of my father's servant. He had received our letter but failed to give it to my father.

The incident has a very important place in my life. I was a boy of nine when it happened. But it has left an indelible impression on my mind. Before this incident occurred, I knew that I was an untouchable and that untouchables were subjected to certain indignities and discrimination. For instance, I knew that in school I could not sit in the midst of my class students according to my rank but that I was to sit in a corner by myself. I knew that in school I was to have a separate piece of gunny cloth for me to squat on in the class room and the servant employed to clean the school would not touch the gunny cloth used by me. I was required to carry the gunny cloth home in the evening and bring it back the next day. While in school I knew that children of the touchable classes, when they felt thirsty, could go out to the water tap, open it and quench their thirst. All that was necessary was the permission of the teacher. But my position was separate. I could not touch the tap and unless it was opened for me by a touchable person, it was not possible for me to quench my thirst. In my case the permission of the teacher was not enough. The presence of the school peon was necessary, for he was the only person whom the class teacher could use for such a purpose. If the peon was not available I had to go without water. The situation can be summed up in the statement—no peon, no water.

At home I knew that the work of washing clothes was done by my sisters. Not that there were no washermen in Satara. Not that we could not afford to pay the washermen. Washing was done by my sisters because we were untouchables and no washerman would wash the clothes of an untouchable. The work of cutting the hair or shaving the boys including myself was done by my elder sister who had become quite an expert barber by practising the art on us. Not that there were no barbers in Satara, not that we could not afford to pay the barber. The work of shaving and hair cutting was done by my sister because we were untouchables and no barber would consent to shave an untouchable. All this I knew. But this incident gave me a shock such as I never received before, and it made me think about untouchability which, before this incident happened, was with me a matter of course as it is with many touchables as well as the untouchables.

III

In 1918, I returned to India. I had been sent to America by His Highness the Maharaja of Baroda for higher education. I studied at Columbia University in New York from 1913 to 1917. In 1917 I came to London and joined the postgraduate department of the School of Economics of the University of London. In 1918 I was obliged to return to India without completing my studies. As I was educated by the Baroda State I was bound to serve the State. Accordingly, on my arrival I straightway went to Baroda.

My five years stay in Europe and America had completely wiped out of my mind any consciousness that I was an untouchable and that an untouchable wherever he went in India was a problem to himself and others. But when I came out of the station, my mind was considerably disturbed by a question: 'Where to go? Who will take me?' I felt deeply agitated. Hindu hotels, called Vishis, I knew, there were. They would not take me. The only way of seeking accommodation therein was by impersonation. But I was not prepared for it because I could well anticipate the dire consequences which were sure to follow if my identity was discovered, as it was sure to be. I had friends in Baroda who had come to America for study, 'Would they welcome me if I went?' I could not assure myself. They may feel embarrassed by admitting an untouchable in their household. I stood under the roof of the station for some time thinking, where to go, what to do. It then struck me to enquire if there was any place in the camp. All passengers by this time had gone. I alone was left. Some hackney drivers who had failed to pick up any traffic were watching and waiting for me. I called one of them and asked him if he knew if there was a hotel in the camp. He said that there was a Parsi inn and that they took paying guests. Hearing that it was an inn maintained by the Parsis, my heart was gladdened. The Parsis are followers of the Zoroastrian religion. There was no fear of my being treated by them as an untouchable because their religion does not recognize untouchability. With a heart glad with hope and a mind free from fear I put my luggage in a hackney carriage and asked the driver to drive me to the Parsi inn in the camp.

The inn was a two-storey building on the ground floor of which lived an old Parsi with his family. He was the caretaker and supplied food to tourists who came there to stay. The carriage arrived and the Parsi caretaker showed me upstairs. I went up while the carriage driver brought up my luggage. I paid him and he went away. I felt happy that after all I had solved the problem of finding a sojourn. I was undressing as I wanted to be at ease. In the meantime the caretaker came in with a book in his hand. Seeing as he well could see from my half-dressed state that I had no Sadri and Kasti, the two things that prove that one is a Parsi, in a sharp tone he asked me who I was. Not knowing that this inn was maintained by the Parsi community for the use of Parsis only, I told him that I was a Hindu. He was shocked, and told me that I could not stay in the inn. I was thoroughly shocked by his answer and was cold all over. The question returned again: 'Where to go?' Composing myself, I told him that though a Hindu I had no objection to staying there if he had no objection. He replied, 'How can you? I have to maintain a register of all who stay here in the inn.' I saw his difficulty. I said I could assume a Parsi name for the purpose of entering it in the register. 'Why do you object if I do not object, you will not lose, you will earn something if I stay here.' Evidently he had not had a tourist for a long time and did not like to forego the opportunity of making a little money. He agreed on condition that I pay him a rupee and a half per day for board and lodging and entered myself as a Parsi in his register. He went downstairs and I heaved a sigh of relief. The problem was solved and I felt very happy. But alas! I did not know then how short was to be this happiness. But before I describe the tragic end to my stay in this inn, I must describe how I passed my time during the short period I stayed therein.

The inn on the first floor had a small bedroom and adjoining it was one small bathroom with a water tap in it. The rest was one big hall. At the time of my stay, the big hall was filled up with all sorts of rubbish, planks, benches, broken chairs, etc. In the midst of the surroundings I lived, a single solitary individual. The caretaker came up in the morning with a cup of tea. He came again at about 9.30 with my breakfast or morning meal. A third time he came up at about 8.30 in the evening with my dinner. The caretaker came up only when he could not avoid it and on these occasions he never stayed to talk to me. The day was spent somehow.

I was appointed a probationer in the Accountant General's Office by the Mahraja of Baroda. I used to leave the inn at about 10 a.m. for the office and returned late at about 8 in the evening, contriving to while away outside the inn as much time in company of friends as I could. The idea of returning to the inn to spend the night therein was most terrifying to me and I used to return to the inn only because I had no other place under the sky to go for rest. In this big hall on the first floor I was quite alone. The whole hall was enveloped in complete darkness. There were no electric lights nor even oil lamps to relieve the darkness. The caretaker used to bring up for my use a small hurricane lamp. Its light could not extend beyond a few inches. I felt that I was in a dungeon and I longed for the company of some human being to talk to. But there was none. In the absence of the company of human beings I sought the company of books and read and read. Absorbed in reading I forgot about my lonely condition. But the chirping and flying about of the bats, which had made the hall their home, often distracted my mind and sent cold shivers through me, reminding me of what I was endeavouring to forget, that I was in a strange place under strange conditions. Many a time, I must have been angry. But I subdued my grief and my anger by the feeling that though it was a dungeon, it was a shelter and some shelter was better than no shelter. So heart-rending was my condition that when my sister's son came from Bombay bringing my remaining luggage which I had left behind and saw my state, he began to cry so loudly that I had to send him back immediately.

In this state I lived in the Parsi inn impersonating as a Parsi. I knew that I could not long continue this impersonation as I would be discovered some day. I was, therefore, trying to get a State bungalow to stay in But the Prime Minister did not look upon my request with the same urgency. My petition went from officer to officer and before I got the final reply, the day of my doom arrived. It was the 11th day of my stay in the inn. I had taken my morning meal and was about to step out of my room to go to the office. As I was picking up some books which I had borrowed overnight for returning them to the library, I heard the footsteps of a considerable number of people coming up the staircase. I thought they were tourists who had come to stay and was therefore looking out to see who these friends were. Instantly I saw a dozen angry-looking, tall, sturdy Parsis, each armed with a stick, coming towards my room. I realised that they were not fellow tourists and they gave proof of it immediately. They lined up in front of my room and fired a volley of questions: 'Who are you? Why did you come here? How dare you take a Parsi name? You scoundrel ! You have polluted the Parsi inn!' I stood silent. I could give no answer. I could not persist in impersonation. It was in fact a fraud and the fraud was discovered, and I am sure if I had persisted in the game I was playing I would have been assaulted by the mob of angry and fanatic Parsis and probably doomed to death. My meekness and my silence averted this doom. One of them asked when I thought of vacating. At that time my shelter I prized more than my life. The threat implied in this question was a grave one. I, therefore, broke my silence and implored them to allow me to stay for a week at least, thinking that my application to the Minister for a bungalow would be decided upon favourably in the meantime. But the Parsis were in no mood to listen. They issued an ultimatum. They must not find me in the inn in the evening. I must pack off. They held out dire consequences and left. I was bewildered. My heart sank within me. I cursed all and wept bitterly. After all I was deprived of my precious possession—namely my shelter. It was no better than a prisoner's cell. But it was to me very precious.

After the Parsis were gone, I sat for some time engaged in thinking to find a way out. I had hopes that I would soon get a State bungalow and my troubles would be over. My problem was therefore a temporary problem and I thought that going to friends would be a good solution. I had no friends among the untouchables of Baroda State. But I had friends among other classes. One was a Hindu, the other was an Indian Christian. I first went to my Hindu friend and told him what had befallen me. He was a noble soul and a great personal friend of mine. He was sad and also indignant. He, however, let fall one observation. He said, 'If you come to my home, my servants will go.' I took the hint and did not press him to accommodate me. I did not like to go to the Indian Christian friend. Once he had invited me to go and stay with him. But I had declined, preferring to stay in the Parsi inn. My reason was that his habits were not congenial to me. To go now would be to invite a rebuff. So I went to my office but I could not really give up this chance of finding a shelter. On consulting a friend I decided to go to him and ask him if he could accommodate me. When I put the question his reply was that his wife was coming to Baroda the next day and that he would have to consult her. I learnt subsequently that this was a very diplomatic answer. He and his wife came originally from a family which was Brahmin by caste and although on conversion to Christianity the husband had become liberal in thought, the wife had remained orthodox in her ways and would not have consented to harbour an untouchable in her house. The last ray of hope thus flickered away. It was 4 p.m. when I left the house of my Indian Christian friend. Where to go was the supreme question before me. I must quit the inn and had no friend to go to! The only alternative left was to return to Bombay.

The train to Bombay left Baroda at 9 p.m. There were five hours to be spent. Where to spend them? Should I go to the inn? Should I go to my friend? I could not buck up sufficient courage to go back to the inn. I feared the Parsis might come and attack me. I did not like to go to my friend. Though my condition was pitiable I did not like to be pitied. I decided to spend the five hours in the public garden which is called the Kamathi Bagh, on the border of the city and the camp. I stayed there partly with a vacant mind, partly with sorrow at the thought of what had happened to me, and thought of my mother and father as children do when they are in a forlorn condition. At 8 p.m. I came out of the garden, took a carriage to the inn, brought down my luggage. The caretaker came out but neither he nor I could utter a word to each other. He felt that I was in some way responsible for bringing him into trouble. I paid him his bill. He received it in silence.

I had gone to Baroda with high hopes. I had given up many offers. It was war time. Many places in the Indian Educational Service were vacant. I knew very influential people in London. But I did not seek any of them. I felt that my duty was to offer my services first to the Maharaja of Baroda, who had financed my education. And here I was driven to leave Baroda and return to Bombay after a stay of only eleven days.

The scene of a dozen Parsis armed with sticks lined up before me in a menacing mood and myself standing before them with a terrified look imploring for mercy is a scene which so long a period of 18 years has not succeeded in fading away. I can now vividly recall it and can never recall it without tears in my eyes. It was then for the first time that I learnt that a person who is an untouchable to a Hindu is also an untouchable to a Parsi.

IV

The year was 1929. The Bombay Government had appointed a Committee to investigate the grievances of the untouchables. I was appointed a member of the Committee. The Committee had to tour all over the Province to investigate into the allegations of injustice, oppression and tyranny. The Committee split up. I and another member were assigned the two districts of Khandesh. My colleague and myself after finishing work parted company. He went to see some Hindu saint. I left by train to go to Bombay. At Chalisgaon, I got down to go to a village on the Dhulia line to investigate a case of social boycott which had been declared by the Caste Hindus. The untouchables of Chalisgaon came to this station and requested me to stay for the night with them. But as they were keen I agreed to stay overnight. I boarded the train for Dhulia to go to the village, went there and informed myself of the situation prevailing in the village and returned by the next train to Chalisgaon.

I found the untouchables of Chalisgaon waiting for me at the station. I was garlanded. The Maharwada, the quarters of the untouchables, is about 2 miles from the railway station and one has to cross a river on which there is a culvert to reach it. There were many horse carriages at the station plying for hire. The Maharwada was also within walking distance from the station. I expected immediately to be taken to the Maharwada. But there was no movement in that direction and I could not understand why I was kept waiting. After an hour or so a tonga (one-horse carriage) was brought close to the platform and I got in. The driver and I were the only two occupants of the tonga. Others went on foot by a short cut. The tonga had not gone 200 paces when there could have been a collision with a motor car. I was surprised that the driver who was paid for hire every day should have been so inexperienced. The accident was averted only because on the loud shout of the policeman the driver of the car pulled it back.

We somehow came to the culvert on the river. On it there are no walls as on a bridge. There is only a row of stones fixed at a distance of five or ten feet. It is paved with stones. The culvert on the river is at right angles to the road we were coming by. A sharp turn has to be taken to come to the culvert from the road. Near the very first side-stone of the culvert the horse, instead of going straight, took a turn and bolted. The wheel of the tonga struck against the side-stone so forcibly that I was bodily lifted up and thrown down on the stone pavement of the culvert and the horse and cart fell down from the culvert into the river. So heavy was the fall that I lay down senseless. The Maharwada is just on the other bank of the river. The men who had come to greet me at the station had reached there ahead of me. I was lifted and taken to the Maharwada amidst the cries and lamentations of the men, women and children. As a result of this I received several injuries. My leg was fractured and I was disabled for several days. I could not understand how all this had happened. The tongas pass and repass the culvert every day and never has a driver failed to take the tonga safely over the culvert.

On enquiry I was told the real facts. The delay at the railway station was due to the fact that the tongawalas were not prepared to drive with a passenger who was an untouchable. It was beneath their dignity. The Mahars could not tolerate that I should walk to their quarters. It was not in keeping with their sense of my dignity. A compromise was therefore arrived at. That compromise was to this effect: the owner of the tonga should give the tonga on hire but not drive. The Mahars may take the tonga but find someone to drive it. The Mahars thought this to be a happy solution. But they evidently forgot that the safety of the passenger was more important than his dignity. If they had thought of this, they would have considered whether they could get a driver who could safely conduct me to my destination. As a matter of fact, none of them could drive because it was not their trade. They therefore asked someone from amongst themselves to drive. The man took the reins in his hand and started thinking there was nothing in it. But as he progressed, he felt his responsibility and became so nervous that he gave up all attempt to control the tonga. To save my dignity the Mahars of Chalisgaon had put my very life in jeopardy. It is then I learnt that a Hindu tonga-wala no better than a menial has a dignity by which he can look upon himself as a person who is superior to all untouchables, even though the untouchable in question may be a barrister-at-law.

V

In the year 1934 some of my co-workers in the movement of the depressed classes expressed a desire to go on a sight-seeing tour if I agreed to join them. I agreed. It was decided that our plan should at all events include a visit to the Buddhist caves at Verul. It was arranged that I should go to Nasik and the party should join me there. To go to Verul we had to go to Aurangabad. Aurangabad is a town in the Mohammedan State of Hyderabad and is included in the dominion of His Exalted Highness, the Nizam. On the way to Aurangabad we had first to pass another town called Daulatabad, which is also in the Hyderabad State. Daulatabad is a historical place and was at one time the capital of the famous Hindu king by the name of Ramdeo Rai. The fort of Daulatabad is an ancient historical monument and no tourist while in that vicinity should omit a visit to it. Accordingly our party had also included in its programme a visit to the fort of Daulatabad.

We hired some buses and touring cars. We were about 30 in number. We started from Nasik to Yeola as Yeola is on the way to Aurangabad. Our tour programme had not been announced, and quite deliberately. We wanted to travel incognito in order to avoid difficulties which an untouchable tourist has to face in outlying parts of the country. We had informed our people at those centres only at which we had decided to halt. Accordingly on the way although we passed many villages in the Nizam State none of our people had come to meet us. It was naturally different at Daulatabad. There our people had been informed that we were coming. They were waiting for us and had gathered at the entrance to the town. They asked us to get down and have tea and refreshment first and then to go to see the fort. We did not agree to their proposal. We wanted tea very badly but we wanted sufficient time to see the fort before it was dusk. We therefore left for the fort and told our people that we would take our tea on our return. Accordingly we told our drivers to move on and within a few minutes we were at the gate of the fort.

The month was Ramjadan, the month of fast for the Mohammedans. Just outside the gate of the fort there is a small tank of water full to the brim. There is all around a wide stone pavement. Our faces, bodies and clothes were full of dust gathered in the course of our journey and we all wished to have a wash. Without much thought some members of the party washed their faces and legs on the pavement with the water from the tank. After these ablutions we went to the gate of the fort. There were armed soldiers inside. They opened the big gates and admitted us into the archway. We had just commenced asking the guard the procedure for obtaining permission to go into the fort. In the meantime an old Mohammedan with white flowing beard was coming from behind shouting, 'The Dheds (meaning untouchables) have polluted the tank.' Soon all the young and old Mohammedans who were near about joined him and all started abusing us: 'The Dheds have become arrogant. The Dheds have forgotten their religion (i.e. to remain low and degraded.) The Dheds must be taught a lesson.' They assumed a most menacing mood. We told them that we were outsiders and did not know the local custom. This turned the fire of their wrath against the local untouchables who by that time had arrived at the gate. 'Why did you not tell these outsiders that this tank could not be used by untouchables?', was the question they kept on asking them. Poor people! They were not there when we entered the tank. It was really our mistake; it was not their fault. But the Mohammedans were not prepared to listen to my explanations. They kept on abusing them and us. The abuse was so vulgar that it had exasperated us. There could easily have been a riot and possibly murders. We had however to restrain ourselves. We did not want to be involved in a criminal case which would bring our tour to an abrupt end.

One young Muslim in the crowd kept on saying that every one must conform to his religion, meaning thereby that the untouchables must not take water from a public tank. I had grown quite impatient and asked him in a somewhat angry tone, 'Is that what your religion teaches? Would you prevent an untouchable from taking water from this tank if he became a Mohammedan?' These straight questions seemed to have some effect on the Mohammedans. They gave no answer and stood silent. Turning to the guard, I said, again in an angry tone, 'Can we get into the fort or not? Tell us, if we can't, we don't want to stop.' The guard asked for my name. I wrote it out on a piece of paper. He took it to the Superintendent inside and came out. We were told that we could go into the fort but we could not touch water anywhere in the fort and an armed soldier was ordered to go with us to see that we did not transgress the order.

I gave one instance to show that a person who is an untouchable to a Hindu is also an untouchable to a Parsi. This will show that a person who is an untouchable to a Hindu is also an untouchable to a Mohammedan.

VI

The next case is equally illuminating. It is a case of an untouchable school teacher in a village in Kathiavar and is reported in the following letter which appeared in the *Young India*, a journal published by Mr Gandhi in its issue of 12th December, 1929. It expresses the difficulties he had experienced in persuading a Hindu doctor to attend to his wife who had just delivered and how the wife and child died for want of medical attention. The letter says:

> On the 5th of this month a child was born to me. On the 7th, she fell ill and suffered from loose stools. Her vitality seemed to ebb away and her chest became inflamed. Her breathing became difficult and there was extreme pain in the ribs. I went to call a doctor—but he said he would not go to examine the child. Then I went to Nagarseth (mayor) and Garasia Darbar (local head man) and pleaded them to help me. The Nagarseth stood surety to the doctor for my paying his fee of two rupees. The doctor came but on condition that he would examine them only outside the Harijan colony. I took my wife out of the colony together with her newly born child. Then the doctor gave his thermometer to a Muslim, he gave it to me and I gave it to my wife and then returned it by the same process after it had been applied. It was about eight in the evening and the doctor on looking at the thermometer in the light of the lamp said that the patient was suffering from pneumonia. Then the doctor went away and sent the medicine. I brought some linseed from the bazaar and used it on the patient. The doctor refused to see her later, although I gave the two rupees fee. The disease is dangerous and God alone will help us. The lamp of my life has

gone out. She passed away at about two o'clock this afternoon.

The name of the untouchable school teacher is not given. So also the name of the doctor is not mentioned. This was at the request of the untouchable school teacher who feared reprisals. The facts are indisputable.

No explanation is necessary. The doctor, who in spite of being educated, refused to apply the thermometer and treat an ailing woman in a critical condition. As a result of his refusal to treat her, the woman died. He felt no qualms of conscience in setting aside the code of conduct which is binding on his profession. The Hindu would prefer to be inhuman rather than touch an untouchable.

VII

There is one other incident as telling as this. On 6 March 1938, a meeting of the Bhangis was held at Kasarwadi (behind Woollen Mills) Dadar, Bombay, under the Chairmanship of Mr Indulal Yajnik. In this meeting, one Bhangi boy narrated his experience in the following terms:

'I passed the Vernacular Final Examination in 1933. I have studied English up to the 4th standard. I applied to the Schools Committee of Bombay Municipality for employment but I failed as there was no vacancy. Then, I applied to the Backward Classes Officers, Ahmedabad, for the job of a Talati (i.e. revenue officer, village Patwari) and I succeeded. On 19th February, 1936, I was appointed a Talati in the office of the Mamlatdar (senior revenue officer) of the Borsad Taluka in the Kheda District.

Although my family came originally from Gujarat, I had never been in Gujarat before. This was my first occasion to go there. Similarly, I did not know that untouchability would be observed in the Government Offices. Besides, in my application the fact of my being a Harijan was mentioned and so I expected that my colleagues in the office would know beforehand who I was. That being so, I was surprised to find the attitude of the chief clerk of the Mamlatdar's office when I presented myself to take charge of the post of the Talati.

The Karkun contemptuously asked, "Who are you?" I replied, "Sir, I am a Harijan." "Go away, stand at a distance. How dare you stand so near me? You are in this office, if you were outside, I would have given you six kicks, what audacity to come here for service!"

Thereafter, he asked me to drop on the ground the certificate and the order of appointment as a Talati. He then picked them up.

While I was working in the Mamlatdar's office at Borsad I experienced great difficulty in the matter of getting water for drinking. In the verandah of the office there were cans containing drinking water. There was a water-man in charge of these cans. His duty was to pour out water to clerks whenever they needed it. In the absence of the water-man they could themselves take water out of the cans and drink it. That was impossible in my case. I could not touch the cans, for my touch would pollute the water; I had therefore to depend on the mercy of the water-man. For my use there was a small rusty pot. No one would touch it or wash it except myself. It was in this pot that the water-man would dole out water to me. But I could get water only if the water-man was present. This water-man did not like the idea of supplying me with water. Seeing that I was coming for water he would manage to slip away, with the result that I had to go without water and the days on which I had no water to drink were by no means few.

I had the same difficulties regarding my residence. I was a stranger in Borsad. No caste Hindu would rent a house to me. The untouchables of Borsad were not ready to give me lodgings for fear of displeasing the Hindus who did not like my attempt to live as a clerk, a station above me. Far greater difficulties were with regard to food. There was no place or person from where I could get my meals. I use to buy 'bhajhas' morning and evening, eat them in some solitary place outside the village and come and sleep at night on the pavement of the verandahs of the Mamlatdar's office. In this way, I passed four days. All this became unbearable to me. Then I went to live at Jentral, my ancestral village. It was six miles from Borsad. Every day I had to walk eleven miles. This I did for a month and a half.

Thereafter the Mamlatdar sent me to a Talati to learn the work. This Talati was in charge of three villages, Jentral, Khapur and Saijpur. Jentral was his headquarters. I was in Jentral with this Talati for two months. He taught me nothing and I never once entered the village office. The Headman of the village was particularly hostile. Once he had said, 'You fellow, your father, your brother are sweepers who sweep the village office and you want to sit in the office as our equal? Take care, better give up this job.'

One day the Talati called me to Saijpur to prepare the population table of the village. From Jentral I went to Saijpur. I found the Headman and the Talati in the village office doing some work. I went, stood near the door of the office and wished them "good morning" but they took no notice of me. I stood outside for about 15 minutes. I was already tired of life and felt outraged at being thus ignored and insulted. I sat down on a chair that was there. Seeing me seated on the chair, the Headman and the Talati quietly went away without saying anything to me. A short while after, people began to come and soon a large crowd gathered round me.

This crowd was led by the Librarian of the village library. I could not understand why an educated person should have led this mob. I subsequently learnt that the chair was his. He started abusing me in the worse terms. Addressing the Ravania (village servant) he said, "Who allowed this dirty dog of a Bhangi to sit on the chair?" The Ravania unseated me and took away the chair from me. I sat on the ground. Thereupon the crowd entered the village office and surrounded me. It was furious crowd raging with anger, some abusing me, some threatening to cut me to pieces with dharya (a sharp weapon like a sword). I implored them to excuse me and have mercy upon me. That did not have any effect upon the crowd. I did not know how to save myself. But an idea came to me of writing to the Mamlatdar about the fate that had befallen me and telling him how to dispose of my body in case I was killed by the crowd. Incidentally, it was my hope that if the crowd came to know that I was practically reporting them to the Mamlatdar they might hold their hands. I asked the Ravania to give me a piece of paper, which he did. Then with my fountain pen I wrote the following on it in big bold letters, so that everybody could read it:

To

The Mamlatdar, Taluka Borsad.

Sir,

Be pleased to accept the humble salutations of Parmar Kalidas Shivram. This is to humbly inform you that the hand of death is falling upon me today. It would not have been so if I had listened to the words of my parents. Be so good as to inform my parents of my death.

The Librarian read what I wrote and at once asked me to tear it off, which I did. They showered upon me innumerable insults: "You want us to address you as our Talati? You are a Bhangi and you want to enter the office and sit on the chair?" I implored them for mercy and promised not to repeat this and also promised to give up the job. I was kept there till seven in the evening when the crowd left. Till then the Talati and Mukhiya (headman) had not come. Thereafter, I took fifteen days' leave and returned to my parents in Bombay.'

2

'Below the Bottom Rung': A British Estimate of Dr Ambedkar, 1944

Beverley Nicholas

'A man of about fifty. Waiting for me in a wicker chair on the verandah of his house. Bulky, dynamic. Very charming manners, but nervy, inclined to fiddle with his shoelaces. Seemed to be on his guard, as though ready to parry taunts from all directions. Well, after all it's only to be expected. ...'

So runs an extract from my diary.

The man is Dr Ambedkar. And in a moment we shall see why it is 'only to be expected'.

Ambedkar is labour member in the Government of India, and one of the six best brains in India. He is of the Cavour school of statesmen—an implacable realist. When he speaks in public he is galvanic, creative, and almost embarrassingly to the point. To compare the average oration of a Congress politician with a speech by Dr Ambedkar is like comparing a Hindu chant with a fusillade of pistol shots. As a result, he is one of the best hated men in India.

And why is it 'only to be expected' ... this nervousness, this suggestion that he would be ready to take offence? Because Dr Ambedkar, in the eyes of most of the 180 million caste Hindus, is 'untouchable'. A person to bring pollution if his Mayfair dinner-jacket should happen to brush against their dhotis. A creature from whose touch the extreme orthodox must fly as though he were a leper, a monster whose slightest contact compels them to precipitate themselves into the nearest bath-tub, to soap and pray, and pray and soap, and soap and pray, so that the filth of Dr Ambedkar—(M.A. London)—the shame of Dr Ambedkar—(high honours at Columbia University)—the plague and scourge of Dr Ambedkar—(special distinction at Heidelberg)—should be washed for ever from their immaculate and immortal souls.

We are not talking of the past, but of the year 1944. These are not legends, fairy-tales, gypsy songs; they are news paragraphs, stop-press.

Untouchability—history's most flagrant example of man's inhumanity to man—is still deeply rooted in the Hindu social system; nearly all attempts to abolish it have met with failure. If a 10 per cent improvement has occurred in the last fifty years, that is an optimistic estimate. A large number of people in England and America are deluded by Gandhi's denunciations of it. They have seen photographs of him with his arm round the shoulders of the out-castes, and they know that he gave the title of 'Harijan'[1] to his own newspaper, which circulated among the high and mighty of the land. 'Surely', they say to themselves, 'such a powerful example, in these enlightened days, must be having some effect?' It is not. As for Gandhi being the untouchables' friend, let us listen to Dr Ambedkar, who is their indisputed leader. He said to me: 'Gandhi is the greatest enemy the untouchables have ever had in India.' A little knowledge of recent history is necessary in order to understand this accusation. But first let us refresh our memories with the theory of untouchability, and then illustrate that theory with a few facts.

II

As Macaulay's schoolboy would tell you, there are four main castes in the Hindu religion. At the top come the Brahmins, the hereditary holy persons. The stormy and brilliant Nehru, whose autobiography was a best-seller on both sides of the Atlantic, is a Brahmin, and it is wise never to forget it. It weighs a great deal more heavily with him than the fact that he was educated at Harrow and Cambridge. C.R. Rajagopalachari, ex-President of Congress, and the chief link between the Extremists and the British, is also a Brahmin. So is Pandit Malaviya, the leader of the extreme right wing of Hinduism. So are most of the Congress bigwigs.

The Brahmins might be said to play the same role in India's political life as the old Etonians in Britain, the main difference is that they have no organized labour to keep them in order. By and large, they are masters of all they survey—except when they turn round and take a look at the Muslims.[2]

The three other castes are the *Kshatriyas* or warriors, the *Vaishyas* or traders—(Gandhi is a *Vaishya*)—and the *Shudras*, or cultivators and menials. Way off in the outer darkness, sunk deep in the mind, are the casteless ones, the untouchables, nearly 60 million of them.

This classification is drastically simplified. There are actually 2,500 castes, all with their taboos, their social restrictions, and their almost incredible ingenuity in complicating the most simple process of life. These castes split the Hindu fabric into a sort of crazy quilt, lacking all homogeneity, held together only by fear—fear of each other, fear of the Muslims, fear of British law. Over and over again it must be emphasized that these castes are a matter of modern, not ancient history.

A homely little instance may sometimes make a point more vivid than any amount of statistics; here is one. Not long ago I spilt a bottle of iodine on the floor of a flat where I was staying. I had nothing to wipe it up with, and I called for a servant to ask him if he would kindly get a rag and remove the stain. There were five servants in the flat and they had nothing to do. And though a reasonable request, it was not granted. One after another they came in, regarded the stain, and departed, with blank looks. Losing my patience, I went to the kitchen, found a rag, and wiped the thing up myself. 'What is the matter with you all?' I demanded, when I handed back the rag. They explained that Dido, the sweeper, the untouchable, was out having his lunch, and only *he* could wipe up the stain. They would be degraded if they did it themselves, and he—Dido—would lose respect for them if he heard about it.

Heaven knows, this may sound a trivial instance, but when you multiply it by millions it ceases to be trivial; it becomes a major problem, not only for India but for the whole democratic world.

III

Very briefly, let us consider the life of the untouchables. It is largely a matter of negatives. They may not use the public wells, which means that they are condemned to drink any filthy liquid they can find. Their children may not enter the schools; they must sit outside, whatever the weather, even in the monsoon. They may not go near the bathing places. Hence, through no fault of their own, they are usually unutterably filthy. The temples are closed to them. This is the unkindest cut of all, for if you take away faith from people so sunk in misery, you take away the only consolation they have. Admittedly, one or two dramatic gestures have been made in the past few years, by enlightened rulers and statesmen, who have thrown open temples to all comers. But what happens? As soon as the untouchables flock in, the orthodox flock out. The temple becomes an 'untouchable' temple, it is tainted, unholy, and as such it ceases to be an object of reverence even to the untouchables themselves.[3] Among other restrictions, the barbers may not cut their hair, nor the washermen wash their clothes.

One thing they *can* do is to tend the earth closets and carry away the night soil from the villages. This they do in large wicker baskets, which they put on their heads. The baskets leak, and the untouchable is not a pretty sight when he, or she, has finished the job.

Still—say the Hindus—it is their own fault; they are paying for the sins of a previous incarnation; why should we have any pity for them? A convenient doctrine, if you happen to have been born in the right bedroom.

'Ah, this is very old stuff,' you may say. 'Of course it is', we answer. 'And it is also very new. It is as old as the history and as new as the morning dew. It is a long way BC and it is also AD 1944.'

Let us have a few more examples from personal experience. Slight though they are, they may help us to realize the bitter struggle which these 60 million must make for the most elementary decencies, a struggle which is being carried on as you read these words.

SCENE ONE. A bungalow on a small island lying a few miles off the west coast. We have just finished dining on the verandah and a British subaltern joins us for a drink. He has walked up the hill from the seashore, where he is in charge of a training camp for young Indian engineers. He looks tired and depressed.

'Had a trying day?'

'Pretty sticky.' He flings himself into a chair. 'Trouble with recruiting.'

'Aren't they coming in fast enough?'

'Oh—they're coming in all right. But I have to send them away again. Look over there.'

He jerks his thumb over his shoulder. We see two young Indians standing in the shadow of a eucalyptus tree, staring at the dust. They are of exceptional physique, and they are spick and span as though they were dressed for a party.

'See those chaps? Well, they're two of the best who've ever come my way, physically and mentally. Well above standard. They want to join my lot; I want to have them; and I can't.'

'Why on earth not?'

'Untouchable. Sweeper class.'

'But that's preposterous!'

'Of course it is. But it's India. My men would just down tools if I took 'em on.'

'But surely', I exclaimed, 'you've got some authority as their commanding officer?'

'No, I haven't. Not in a thing like that. Why, the very rumour of those chaps coming has caused a hell of a row all day—desertions, insolence, insubordination. I had to give in. I don't want to start another Indian Mutiny.'

He swallowed his drink, and sighed.

'Sounds silly, I know', he said, 'but the worst of it was that one of the chaps *cried*. Said I'd broken his heart. *Me!* It's pretty grim when a chap like that starts crying.' He laughed uneasily. 'Maybe I'm well shot of him—maybe he was a sissy. Oh what the hell, anyway.'[4]

SCENE TWO. A village in a remote part of the south-west. I have come to see a temple which is reputed to be of great beauty. The expedition is not a success; the temple is devoid of any architectural interest and is only notable for the astonishing obscenity of the Phallic scenes which are carved round its base.

Having digested the obscenities, I came to a big mud hut. It was the village school. I peered through the window. About a hundred little boys squatting on the floor, gazing at a blackboard on which a young man was tracing letters in Canarese. They made the prettiest picture—the rows of dusky faces and the snow-white eyes turning from right to left, like marbles rolling on a dark cloth.

I drew back my head from the window and strolled round the corner of the building. And there, to my surprise, were twelve little boys, sitting on a bench, huddled together as though they were frightened of something.

'What are those little boys doing? Are they in disgrace or something?'

The young Hindu guide answered me. 'They are of the Scheduled Classes', he said curtly.

I stared at the little boys, who had huddled themselves closer together. They were thin and almost naked and none too clean, but they *were* little boys, after all. Each of them was 'somebody's bairn', as one might say, if one were sentimental and Scotch.

Perhaps one should have kicked up a row about it. Those kids were supposed to be allowed into the schools. They had passed all sorts of laws for their protection in this State. But what could one do? If one reported the matter it would only get the teacher into trouble, and it probably wasn't the teacher's fault. He looked a decent sort of chap even though he was half starved on his 25 rupees a month. It was more likely due to the parents of the children inside.

So I walked away and left the little outcasts to their fate, straining their ears towards the window, listening to the teacher's voice. Now and then one of them would scribble something in a tattered note-book. Young India, getting education.

SCENE THREE. A dinner table in Peshawar. Dramatis personae, Pandit Malaviya and B—, one of the leaders of the opposition in the legislative council. The year is 1933, and Peshawar is full of bustle and excitement, for there is a great conference in full swing, which will settle the fate of the Hindu-Sikh minorities. The venerable old Pandit is being entertained by B—, and they are both anxious to please each other. But the dinner party is not a success. Why? Because the Pandit cannot eat. Why? We shall see.

B—had taken a great deal of trouble about this dinner. He knew that the Pandit was a vegetarian, and so he provided only fruit; moreover, he chose only such fruits as Nature had ensured from outside pollution, such as oranges and bananas. And he had been even more careful than that. *He had bought an entirely new dinner service;* for he was aware that if the Pandit were asked to eat off a plate which might once have had meat on it, the worst would happen. The Pandit would be horrified beyond measure; he would never feel clean again.

So here we are. Fresh fruit, covered with thick skins. New plates, never used before. An old gentleman, anxious to please host, staring at banana or whatever it is. All to no avail. He *cannot* eat the banana. Sometime, somewhere, somehow, somebody might have touched something, and made it unclean. He dare not risk it. He is a brave old man but he is not as brave as all that. So the demands of courtesy must be set aside. The dinner, we repeat, was not a success.

This story has been told flippantly, because at first sight it falls into the category of farce. But is it entirely farcical? Malaviya, at the time, was leader of Congress. He was, and still is, one of the most powerful personalities in India. He is the sort of man who, if and when India gains independence, will help to represent his country at international conferences. To put it mildly, his extreme orthodoxy may tend to slow up the business of the day.

Supposing that we translate this situation into Western terms. Imagine a conference between Churchill, Roosevelt, Stalin and Chiang Kai-Shek on orthodox Hindu lines. What would happen? Well—most of them would be popping in and out of the bathroom during the greater part of the proceedings. Churchill would sign a document with the same pen as Roosevelt and would rush to have a shower. Stalin would inadvertently drink a cup of tea handed to him by Chiang Kai-Shek and hurry away to gargle. Roosevelt would constantly be calling for a flit spray, and if anybody ever got any business done it would be such a miracle that half the war debt would have to be sacrificed on the altar of Krishna.

Nevertheless, Malaviya, in spite of these foibles, is entitled to our respect. Extreme Hindu as he is, he has fought the battle of the untouchables, and admitted hundreds of them into the Hindu fold. That proves that his heart is very much in the right place, for only a deep love of his fellow-men could make him challenge the faith of his fathers. He starves himself for that faith, and yet he takes up the cudgels for those whom the faith has made pariahs. It would be ungenerous to deny that he comes out of this story pretty well.

IV

We left Dr Ambedkar, leader of the 60 million untouchables, proclaiming that ... 'Gandhi is the greatest enemy the Untouchables have ever had in India.' This will come as a violent shock to most people. Gandhi has ceaselessly proclaimed his detestation of untouchability. He has untouchables in his ashram, he has adopted an untouchable child, and he has declared, 'I would rather see that Hinduism die than untouchability live'. This often-quoted remark, by the way, does not really make sense. Untouchability is as integral a part of the Hindu faith as anti-semitism of the Nazi; begin by destroying untouchability and you will end in destroying all caste. And caste is the only cement which saves the incredibly complicated Hindu structure from collapse. None the less, Gandhi was probably sincere when he spoke.

So what did Ambedkar mean? We can best explain it by a parallel. Take Ambedkar's remark, and for the word 'untouchables' substitute the word 'peace'. Now, imagine that a great champion of peace, like

Lord Cecil, said, 'Gandhi is the greatest enemy of peace the world has ever had'. What would he mean, using these words of the most spectacular pacifist of modern times? He would mean that passive resistance—which is Gandhi's form of pacifism—could only lead to chaos and the eventual triumph of brute force. That to lie down and let people trample on you (which was Gandhi's recipe for dealing with the Japanese) is a temptation to the aggressor rather than an example to the aggressed; and that in order to have peace you must organize, you must be strong, and that you must be prepared to use force.

Mutatis mutandis, that is precisely what Ambedkar meant about the untouchables. He wanted them to be organized and he wanted them to be strong. He rightly considered that the best way of gaining his object was by granting them separate electorates; a solid block of 60 million would be in a position to dictate terms to its oppressors. Gandhi fiercely opposed this scheme. 'Give the untouchables separate electorates', he cried, 'and you only perpetuate their status for all time.' It was a queer argument, and those who were not bemused by the Mahatma's charm considered it a phoney one. They suspected that Gandhi was a little afraid that 60 million untouchables might join up with the 100 million Muslims—(as they nearly did)—and challenge the dictatorship of the 180 million orthodox Hindus. When such irreverent criticisms were made to him, Gandhi resorted to his usual tactics; he began a fast unto death. (As if that altered the situation by a comma, or proved anything but his own obstinacy!) There was a frenzy of excitement, ending in a compromise on the seventh day of the fast. The untouchables still vote in the same constituencies as the caste Hindus, but a substantial number of seats are now reserved for them in the provincial legislatures. It is better than nothing, but it is not nearly so good as it would have been if Gandhi had not interfered. That is what Dr Ambedkar meant. And I think that he was right.

V

What of the future? It depends very largely on the British. If we knuckle under the Congress demands, the state of the untouchables will remain either stationary or deteriorate. And it cannot be too often emphasized that even if it remains stationary it will still be quite intolerable.

In spite of the much vaunted 'new approach', in spite of Gandhi's soulful proclamations, how many untouchables have managed to obtain university degrees? Five hundred ! Five hundred, in the whole history of Indian Education, in a country with a population of nearly 400 million!

Congress, dominated by the Brahmins, has no intention of changing this situation. It is highly significant that by far the most sweeping measures to improve the lot of the untouchables have been made in the States where the Congress writ does not run. Mysore, for instance, could set an example to the whole of India.[5] If we give way to Congress, the untouchables might as well run to the nearest village well and hurl themselves into it *en masse.* They are forbidden to use it in life; they might as well use it in death.

Ambedkar said to me that Cripps proposals 'would have dealt a death blow to our interest'.

Some people challenge Ambedkar's right to leadership. They would not do so if they had ever attended any of his meetings, such as the great rally at Nagpur where 75,000 untouchables acclaimed him with a fervour that even Gandhi might have envied. Besides, even if he had any competitors—which he has not—his clear-cut, creative ideas demand the support of all men of decency and sense. We will end this random survey by a few sentences from my diary which throw light on those ideas. Ambedkar said to me: 'The keynote of my policy is that we are *not* a sub-section of the Hindus but a separate element in the national life.'

'Gandhi says to us "Trust us—trust the caste Hindus!" I reply, "We will not trust you, for you are our hereditary enemies".'

'In every village there is a tiny minority of untouchables. I want to gather those minorities together and make them into majorities. This means a tremendous work of organization—transferring populations, building new villages. But we can do it, if only we are allowed.'

'We are as staunchly nationalist as any of the Congress. But we do not want the British to quit India till our rights are safeguarded. If they do, our fate will be more terrible than the fate of any of the oppressed people of Europe.'

Can any sane man doubt to whom we ought to give our support? To Gandhi, the caste Hindu, who would fast unto death rather than grant these 60 million outcasts the right of uniting into an independent organization which might challenge him? Or to Ambedkar, who has himself risen from the depths, and fought his way through a ceaseless barrage of insult and superstition, to emerge triumphant as the champion of his people?

It is not always, in British history, that the path of honour is identical with the path of self-interest, but that is the situation in India today. There is only one path that we should tread, for our own sake, and for the sake of the underdog. Let us hope that we tread it.

NOTES

1. Harijan really means 'Child of God'. It has come to be associated with the untouchables. The Government of India's official designation for them is 'Scheduled Castes'.
2. The Brahmins, in spite of their lofty position, have not attracted much love to themselves in the long history of India.
3. The classic example of this tendency was afforded by the great temple at Madurai, 300 miles south of Madras. Premier Rajagopalachari went so far as ordering a government official to lead a group of untouchables into the temple. The great majority of Brahmins have refused to set foot in it ever since.
4. This story could be multiplied *ad nauseam*. However, it is worth noting that the Army, once it has got hold of a man, is proving a powerful instrument in undermining the extreme caste system. Discipline, comradeship, and above all a common mess for dining, have worked wonders in the present war.
5. The student who would like to know what *can* be done by a benevolent and enlightened ruler should read *Harijan Uplift in Mysore,* published by the Government Press, Bangalore.

3
Emancipation as Justice: Legacy and Vision of Dr Ambedkar

Upendra Baxi

I should begin this oration by a testimonial to a lack, an absence. The Indian social science landscape has disarticulated Babasaheb Ambedkar by studious theoretical silence. Even on the eve of his birth centenary, we do not have a complete corpus of his writings. Comparisons are odious, but we have organized corpus of texts of Mahatma, Nehru, Rajendra Prasad, and Patel (to mention a few examples). But Ambedkar's corpus has just begun to emerge and that too, on the initiative of the Government of Maharashtra. If the market for knowledge is also operated on the laws of supply and demand, we have to ruefully conclude that Ambedkar's construction of the Hindu society, nationalist movement, and resurgent post-colonial India, are cognitive commodities for which there is no organized demand either from epistemic entrepreneurs or by cognitive consumers in India.

Further, neither the autonomous academia nor the substantially funded monopoly of governmental knowledge industries (the Indian Council of Social Science Research, the Indian Council of Historical Research, the Indian Council of Philosophical Research, the UGC, etc.) provide spaces—curricular or research—for Ambedkar. Ambedkar remains a totally forgotten figure. In the circumstances, the centenary celebrations will only generate hagiographic works, enriching the quality of national neglect of Babasaheb's evolution both as an ideological thinker and as political activist.

This complete disregard by the academia of Ambedkar poses a critical question concerning the modes of production of knowledge through the formal educational and research systems in India. How is it that these knowledge systems have produced a near total annihilation of the very author of *Annihilation of Caste System?* How is it that the most contemporary proselytizer of the Depressed Classes does not figure even as a representative of heretical thought, worthy even of preliminary scientific discourse? How is it that after four decades of reservations, emergent communities of the Depressed Classes research scholars have also felt inhibited in organizing the discourse around Ambedkar's life and contribution? Even the *Subaltern Studies* have to pause after six volumes, to acknowledge Ambedkar! How do we characterize this lack or absence? Do we explain this by saying that Ambedkar does not redeem any theoretical labour? Or do we say that the lack betrays a collective conspiracy of silence on the part of Indian scholarship? Or do we recourse to a benign class based explanation that the lack merely represents inadvertence by the communities of knowledge? Or do we say that the contemporary scientific mind is unable or unwilling to come to terms with what Jacques Lacan called the structures of 'paranoid knowledge?' Ambedkar's discourse represents, archetypically, the pervasive 'fear of anonymous prosecutors' typical of the structures of paranoid knowledge.[1]

In any case, the communities of knowledge and communities of power in India are united in their marginalization of Babasaheb. Neither politics nor knowledge discovers in him a vision towards which India may move. Is this due to the possibility that practices of power and of knowledge in India are incoherent before a heretical discourse, especially when it emanates from an untouchable?

These questions must be taken seriously if the centenary is to have any significance in terms of collective self-understanding of the making of a modern India. I might add that this pursuit has already been hampered by the organized neglect of Babasaheb's thought and work in the sense that our understanding of leading historic figures like Gandhiji or Nehru is bound to remain incomplete, both in the sense of biography and history, in the absence of the grasp of their relation with Ambedkar. Babasaheb was the Other of the nationalist thought and practice which was being forged by Gandhiji and Nehru. The absence of such understanding has flawed and fractured our grasp of the making of modern India.

II

In the absence of a corpus, and of any inaugural discourse, it is difficult to recall and represent to ourselves the image of Ambedkar. But, certainly, this much is clear: there is not one but there are many

Ambedkars or there are many kaleidoscopic images. When we presume to celebrate the centenary of Babasaheb, it becomes crucially relevant to ask *which* Ambedkar we now choose to recall. And what is the moral logic of our preference?

True, what I hereafter describe as seven Ambedkars merely represent successive steps in the lived experience of Babasaheb. And there is some danger in presenting an 'evolutionary' sequence of a life-history in terms of different persona. But all of us, in one way, or the other, represent a repertoire of many mixed identities. To unravel each distinct identity as a *persona* need not to entail a methodological sin. Centenary celebrations are organized political events having distinctive ideologies of recall and distinctive modes of appropriating a historic figure for the purposes of the present. In India, centenary celebrations simultaneously function as instruments of organizing memory and forgetfulness; the Ambedkar that we choose to remember now entails organized oblivion about other Ambedkars.

The *first* Ambedkar that we may recall is the young student who bore the full brunt of the practices of untouchability—a young boy, who with his brother, was denied on his way home in a bullock cart a drop of water from evening till midnight; a young boy who was made to know that the razor of the barber would be defiled by contact with his hair while it could be used without fear of pollution in shaving buffaloes; a young school boy whose teachers would not touch his notebooks; a foreign-returned Ambedkar, required to serve Baroda State for ten years, being denied any accommodation in Baroda, and denied minimum dignity even from peons in the office who thought it morally wrong to hand over office papers and files to him, which they simply flung at him! This is the Ambedkar who understood existentially what it meant to be an untouchable in India. We tend to believe that conditions in India since independence have so substantially changed that we need not recall this Ambedkar. But without this Ambedkar there would have been *no* other Ambedkars. And no other Ambedkars have followed the Babasaheb after his death, simply because no one has been fully privileged by history and by power as was Ambedkar to articulate the horrors of untouchability which still prevail on a wide scale.

There is the *second* Ambedkar; the student-scholar Ambedkar. This Ambedkar worked for eighteen hours a day in Columbia University to obtain the M.A. degree in 1916 and published his thesis eight years later on the *Evolution of British Provincial Finance in British India* for which he obtained his doctorate; an Ambedkar who grew into a bibliophile and purchased about 2,000 books in the city of New York; an Ambedkar who for years went to London Museum and toiled there from dawn to dusk till the watchman had to seek him out to leave; an Ambedkar who lived on frugal diet so that he could use his savings for buying books; an Ambedkar who then went to London School of Economics to complete his D.Sc. and enrolment at the Bar. The second Ambedkar is a voracious reader, a hardworking student, and a polymath. This Ambedkar is almost altogether forgotten; this ideal model of a first generation learner; this incomparable learner and an exalted figure in the nationalist movement has been robbed of his exemplarship. Even as opportunities for university education have grown very substantially, the methods of study and dedication which Ambedkar displayed as a student do not provide any more for the bulk of Scheduled Caste students any model of excellence; they only emulate models of mediocrity furnished by their reference groups among the urban middle class Indians. Privations and deprivations did not deter this fourteenth child of humble Mahar parents; indignities and humiliations inflicted on him only spurred him to achieve high levels of academic excellence; he took self-consciously to learning and education as instrumentalities for the eminent leadership of the depressed classes of India or the *Atishudras* (the 'social and economics proletariat') as he was to later call him. Ambedkar the gentleman scholar has been all but erased. Is this a planned erasure?

To allow him to be thus forgotten is to deprive ourselves of the notion that education can be a means of empowering the dis-empowered. To organize the oblivion of the second Ambedkar is to deny access to the best and brightest of scheduled communities students access to an epic Indian narration, testifying the critical relevance of the growth of powers of the mind for the maturation of the struggle for emancipation and equality. Not just this; by forgetting this Ambedkar we have also encouraged the growth of traditions of learning and teaching in our campuses, and made most of our teachers and students indolent, impertinent and incontinent.

The *third* Ambedkar is a militant Ambedkar who emerges as an editor and a journalist with the publication of the fortnightly paper as early as 1920, entitled the *Mukanayak*, the Leader of the Silent. The very first issue, we recall with Dhananjay Keer, compared the Hindu society with a tower 'which has several storeys without a ladder or an entrance' in which one 'was to die in the storey in which one was born'.[2] This was the Ambedkar who in another article categorically articulated that 'it was not enough for India to be an independent country', that Indian freedom meant guarantees of equal status to all classes 'offering every man an opportunity to rise in the scale of life and creating conditions favourable to his advancement.' Ambedkar stated that 'the Swaraj wherein no fundamental rights guranteed for the Depressed Classes would not be a Swaraj to them'. It would, indeed, 'be a new slavery for them'. And indeed, he asserted vigorously that even that 'despicable man' did not exist who 'would object to the statement that if the Brahmins were justified in their attack upon an opposition to the unjust power of the British Government, the Depressed Classes were justified a hundred times more so in their opposition to the rulership of the Brahmins in case the transfer of power took place'.[3] This was the same Ambedkar who wrote in his editorial of the *Bahiskrit Bharat* on the 29 July 1927: 'If Tilak had been born among the untouchables, he would not have raised the slogan "Swaraj is my birthright", but he would have raised the slogan "Annihilation of Untouchability is my birthright".'[4] By organizing oblivion of this Ambedkar, a scholar-journalist-activist, modern India has also organized oblivion of his message; in the process it has robbed the vibrant concept of Swaraj of its emancipatory plenitude.

The *fourth* Ambedkar is the young boy who was denied access to drinking water led the first ever *satyagraha* of the *Atishudras* on access to minimum basic human needs—an initiative which should rightly have been one to be seized by the Mahatma! The events of 24 December 1927 have not been vividly recalled if compared in courage equally with the Mahatma's finest hour in the Dandi march. The Mahar Conference which Ambedkar addressed demanded that Hindu society 'should be reorganized on two main principles—equality and absence of casteism'. The conference adopted a declaration of human rights: an innovative enunciation proclaiming that 'all men were born equal and continued to be so till death'. The *Manusmriti*, which was denounced by Ambedkar and his compatriots on 24 December 1927, as a monumental historic repudiation of human equality in India, was actually set to fire on 25 December 1927; Dhananjay Keer is not far off the mark when he describes this event as 'one of the greatest sacrilegious blows ever since the days of Luther upon the egoistic bigots, custom-mongers and no-changers on the earth'. Keer was to describe this event in 1954 by the statement: 'Mahad thus became the Wittenberg of India.'[5] Keer forgets that while there is something in the Christian traditions which allows its own Luther and Wittenberg, the Hindu tradition has a way of organizing amnesia of heretical discourse, even of the most daring variety that Ambedkar manifested at Mahad.

There was no occupation of the Chowdar Tank in December 1927; in fact, the protest was silenced by the British rule of law. Ambedkar, even so ready to believe in the British as having the better potential to ameliorate the plight of *Atishudras,* yielded to the District Magistrate's request not to storm the Tank in view of a stay order obtained from the Court at the behest of the Mahad caste notables. The historic and symbolic significance of the Mahad satyagraha lies in four features. *First,* it establishes the emergence of Babasaheb Ambedkar as a leader of the *Atishudra* masses. *Second,* it symbolizes protests at the worst aspect of Hindu hegemony which denies access to the basic human needs to the untouchables; access to drinking water. Ambedkar thus inaugurates the discourse of equality in access to satisfaction of the most minimum basic needs in the history of Indian jurisprudence. *Third,* the Mahad satyagraha testifies to Ambedkar's submissiveness to the concept of the rule of law, even when he perceives what the rule of law does is no flaming sword to liquidate any of the manifold existential horrors and tragedies affecting his people. *Fourth,* the Mahad satyagraha innovates a tradition of protest (more cogently than the temple entry protests) of challenging the very foundations of the Hindu hegemony. As compared with temple entry, which only affect the spiritual sentiments of the priests as the keepers of the deity and of the devotees as emaciated spiritual beings, the Mahar satyagraha strikes at the very root of temporal power of caste Hinduism which denies to untouchables the right to be recognized as human beings.

This Ambedkar, who is in a sense a pre-Gandhian Ambedkar, who puts to innovative uses the technique of *satyagraha* and civil disobedience to versatile uses for the emancipation of the untouchables. He is pre-Gandhian in the sense that he has not come into authentic contact with the deep structure of Gandhian thought and practice in adversarial and polemical ways which later led him to denounce Gandhi as an adversary of the *Atishudras* in India.

The *fifth* Ambedkar is in a mortal combat with the Mahatma on the issue of legislative reservations for the depressed classes. The story of the Poona Pact terminating Gandhi's spiritual coercion over

Ambedkar, needs its own narration and renarration. I attempt a narration in what follows. Suffice it to say that this Ambedkar is at the end of the day, a Gandhized version of Babasaheb. In a curious, and even perverse way, the Mahatma who thought (before he came to know Ambedkar) that Ambedkar was an earnestly compassionate Hindu, animated by the desire to ameliorate the plight of the *Atishudras,* made Ambedkar fit his own image! Ambedkar's rhetoric remained radical; his denunciation of the Mahatma and the Congress continued; but post-Poona Pact Ambedkar became a precursor to many a latter-day Congress scheduled caste leaders.

The *sixth* Ambedkar is a continuation of the fifth. Increasingly involved in the discourse on transfer of power, he was drawn into the processes of Constitution-making. So pre-eminent was his role that, in a deep irony, the man who made a bonfire of *Manusmriti* was hailed as a 'Modern Manu'. But even this modern Manu was ultimately reduced to a backroom boy. When the Constitution he helped make and move for adoption was acclaimed (as Eleanor Zelliot reminds us) by the Constituent Assembly, the incantation was '*Mahatma Gandhi Ki Jai*' (Zelliot, 1972: 69).

The process of co-option of a radical Dalit leader was historically now complete. He was no longer relevant and useful. For full four years and fifty-six days, he remained as the Law Minister in Nehru's cabinet. I urge you to read in full his statement (released on 10 October 1951 on the eve of his resignation from the cabinet.[7] This poignant statement reveals his own sense of humiliation as not being treated as an equal. Not merely did he feel misled and betrayed by Nehru on the movement for Parliamentary deliberation of the Hindu Code Bill, he also articulated his anguish and indignation at the 'neglect of the Scheduled Castes by the Government'. The Nehru Government did not merely betray the promises of urgent ameliorative action for the *Atishudras;* it also treated Babasaheb with historic nonchalance. Indeed Babasaheb not merely complains that the Scheduled Castes are exposed to the 'same old tyranny, the same old expression, the same old discrimination which existed before' existing 'now and perhaps in a worst form'; but he also complains of reproduction of marginalization of their leader of three decades. He complains bitterly that he was given only the law portfolio—a portfolio of no administrative importance, 'an empty soap-box, only good for old lawyers to play with'. He desired labour and planning portfolios or at least some association with planning, given his excellent economics background (and the prerogative of influencing allocation of resources for the betterment of the weaker sections). But he complained that he was 'always left out of consideration'; when his colleagues were given additional portfolios, he was denied even a temporary charge! In character with this marginalization when Ambedkar breathed his last in Delhi, the Prime Minister sent an emissary with a wreath; and was absent at his funeral in Bombay.

The *seventh* Ambedkar is a renegade Hindu, not just in the sense of the man who let aflame the *Manusmriti* in Mahad in 1927 but in the symbolic statement on conversion in 1935 and his actual conversion to Buddhism in late 1954. The scholar in him stood by him in the last hour of life. At 11.15 p.m. on 5 December 1956 he asked his secretary to place on his bedside table the typescript of the Preface and Introduction of the *Buddha and his Dhamma;* he was found dead the next morning by Savita Ambedkar. In his finitude, he recombined his emancipation from Hinduism with scholarly solitude in the hour of his dying.

Which Ambedkar are we celebrating thses days ? Which ought we to celebrate? I think that, consciously or otherwise, we are celebrating the Ambedkar whose spirit was domesticated, for all practical purposes, by the Mahatma and whose national presence was marginalized by his political heir. We are celebrating the 'Modern Manu', not the iconoclast, nor the rebel. By this we diminish the historic significance and contemporary relevance of Babasaheb; and reconstruct him only as a memory of a Mahar whose presence on the scene was tolerated within limits by the gracious galaxy of Gandhi, Nehru and others. We are celebrating the tolerance of hegemonic nationalist leadership. We are celebrating an appropriation of Ambedkar which is, on all counts, opportunistically vandalist in ways carefully calculated to remove from the Dalit memory the incandescent luminosity of the real Ambedkar, lest it might give a precious contemporary insurrectionary identity to Babasaheb and threaten hegemonic empires of present day political managers by the revival of the Ambedkar of the thirties and the forties.

In this zodiac, the only way to combat the centenary-monger merchants of the Ambedkar icon is to reinstate and reappropriate Ambedkar's vision of emancipatory politics for the *Atishudras.* This is the historic challenge posed, though inadvertently, by the centenary celebrations.

III

The conflict between Ambedkar and Gandhi on the issue of separate electorates for untouchables and the depressed classes, and the way in which it was resolved, has affected very fundamentally the nature of political participation by the scheduled castes and tribes in contemporary India. That is my justification for revisiting a somewhat forgotten chapter of the History of independence movement. An addition and equally fundamental justification, for focusing on this matter in some details is that in the matter of amelioration of the lot of scheduled groups, Indian leaders have chosen a middle path, or an amalgam, which has contributed to a situation of a crisis of credibility and a crisis of justice, both for the depressed classes and the upper classes.

Ambedkar's participation in the Round Table Conference in 1930 was really responsible for the ultimate policy announcement by Premier Ramsay McDonald. In nutshell, the British proposal was that there will be a number of special seats for the depressed classes which will be filled by election from special constituencies in 'which only the members of the "depressed classes" electorally qualified will be entitled to vote.' Depressed classes would also be entitled to vote for the general constituencies. The select constituencies were to be formed only in areas where 'the depressed classes were most numerous' and except in Madras 'they should not cover the whole area of the Province'. The British Prime Minister further clarified in a letter to Gandhi that the 'number of special seats' thus created 'will be seen to be small' and was just not intended to 'provide a quota numerically appropriate for the total representation of the whole of the depressed class population'. The arrangement was temporarily limited to twenty years. The Prime Minister emphasized that this proposal was different from the idea of 'a communal electorate for the depressed classes'. The entire purpose of this transitional arrangement was to 'place them in a position to a peak for themselves'. He further clarified that the method of creating legislative reservation of seats was not considered by the British Government as helpful since it was unlikely to produce members who could genuinely represent the depressed classes 'because in practically all cases, such members would be elected by a majority consisting of higher caste Hindus'.

Gandhi responded to this reasoned proposal by the simple threat, which he carried out, to 'resist with my life the grant of separate electorate to the depressed classes'. He began his fast, in Yervada Prison, on 20 September, ending it only on 24 September, upon the signing of the Poona Pact. He undertook this fast 'as a man of religion' and also a leader of 'numberless men and women who have childlike faith in my wisdom'. (This is not exactly the language of humility.) Gandhi, at no stage, attempted to give reasons or counter arguments to the British proposals, which Ambedkar—wholeheartedly, supported. But his main objection to the arrangement was that the separate electorates were 'harmful' for the depressed classes and for Hinduism; the separate electorate would simply 'vivisect and disrupt' Hinduism. The mere fact that depressed classes had two votes, under the proposals, said Gandhi 'does not protect them or Hindu society in general from being disrupted'. Such a system was tantamount to 'the injection of poison that is calculated to destroy Hinduism and do no good whatever to the depressed classes'. A 'statutory separation even in a limited form, from the Hindu fold', will be harmful for them 'as it would arrest the marvellous growth of the work of Hindu reformers who have dedicated themselves to the uplift of their suppressed brethren in every walk of life'. Gandhi disputed the claim of the British, however sympathetic they might be, to 'come to a correct decision on a matter of such vital and religious importance of the parties concerned'. Gandhi made it crystal clear that for him the matter was entirely a religious one. Let us listen to this statement:

> For me the question of these classes is predominately moral and religious. The political aspect, important though it is, dwindles into insignificance compared to the moral and religious issue.

Ambedkar reacted violently to Gandhi's fast. He was able to point out that the Mahatma's arguments were strange and incomprehensible and complained 'he has staked his very life in order to deprive them of little they have got'. He counselled Mahatma that his 'determination to fast unto death is worthy of a far better cause'. He urged the Mahatma to freely consult the members of the depressed classes in the full confidence that if they were given a choice, 'between Hindu faith and possession of political power', they would choose the latter and thus 'save the Mahatma'. He charged him with releasing uncontrollable reactionary forces and widening the 'gulf between the depressed classes and the Hindus'.

Ambedkar maintained that the untouchables were an element separate from Hinduism and went to great lengths to prove it. He went to the root of the matter when he said that the Hindus had much to lose by the abolition of untouchability, though they had nothing to fear from political reservations leading to this abolition. The matter was economics rather than religious. His resounding words need to be quoted extensively:

> The system of untouchability is a gold mine to the Hindus. In it the 240 millions of Hindus have 60 millions of Untouchables to serve as their retinue to enable the Hindus to maintain pomp and ceremony and to cultivate a feeling of pride and dignity befitting a master class, which cannot be fostered and sustained unless there is beneath it a servile class to look down upon. ... In it the 240 millions of Hindus have 60 millions of untouchables to be used as forced labourers. ... In it the 240 millions of Hindus have 60 millions of Untouchables to do the dirty work of scavengers and sweepers which the Hindu is debarred by his religion to do and which must be done by non-Hindus who could be no others than untouchables. In it the 240 millions of Hindus have 60 millions of Untouchables who can be kept to lower jobs. ... In it the 240 millions of Hindus have the 60 millions of Untouchables who can be used as shockabsorbers in slumps and dead-weights in booms, for in slumps it is the Untouchables who is fired first and the Hindu is fired last and in booms the Hindu is employed first and the Untouchable is employed last.

Untouchability is not a religious system but an 'economic system which is worse than slavery'.[8]

As to Gandhi's claim that the proposals for limited electoral separation would arrest that 'marvellous work' of Hindu reformers, Ambedkar's response was blunt and cold, but true and memorable. He said:

> There have been many Mahatmas in India whose sole object was to remove Untouchability and to elevate and absorb the Depressed Classes, but every one of them has failed in this mission. Mahatmas have come, Mahatmas have gone. But the Untouchables have remained as Untouchables.[9]

But the fact that Gandhi had undertaken the fast was in itself a refutation of everything that Ambedkar said and could have said. It was not refutation on reason but on sentiment and moral coercion. The result was inevitably a compromise. Gandhi won on separate electorates; there were to be none. The rest of the terms of the Poona Pact show that Ambedkar made the best of a bad bargain.

Ambedkar accepted a total of 148 reserved seats in all legislatures. Gandhi agreed to a collegiate procedure for election to reserved seats whereby a panel of four candidates belonging to the depressed classes will be 'the candidates for election by a general electorate': a kind of 'primary' election procedure. This system was to continue until ten years, unless 'terminated by mutual agreement'. The pact also provided that there shall be no disabilities to anyone, by reasons of his being a member of the Depressed Classes, for 'election to local bodies or appointment to public services'. There was further agreement that an adequate sum shall be made available 'for providing educational facilities to the members of the Depressed Classes' in every province.

The Poona Pact no doubt gave more seats to the depressed classes: the Award had given them only 78 separate electoral seats while they had in 1937 as many as 151 seats. As Ambedkar himself put it, its increase in seats could never compensate for the priceless privilege of the second vote given to the untouchables. The value of such a vote 'as a political weapon was beyond reckoning'. The 1937 elections, under the Poona Pact, 'disliked by the Hindus and disfavoured by the untouchables', in effect gave only 73 victorious candidates, 'the true and independent representatives', since 78 untouchable candidates elected were Congress Party members. Ambedkar could not help saying that the Congress made, through the Poona Pact, 'a handsome profit on its political transaction'.[10]

Ambedkar repented this decision bitterly all through his remaining life. Although he had appealed to the Mahatma not to drive 'me to the necessity of making a choice between his life and the rights of my people', this is what the Mahatma did. And although Ambedkar ended his comments on Gandhi's fast by valiantly declaring that 'I can never consent to deliver my people bound hand and foot to the Caste Hindus for generations to come' this is what he was constrained to do. The Indian Constitution, of which he was the principal architect, merely reserves seats for the Scheduled Castes for separate electorates. He did not have the strength of purpose to urge the continuation of the 'primary' system for such constituencies, which was the second best. He himself could not, in one of the most enigmatic electoral reversals in India, return from Bombay in opposition to the Congress nominee. Ambedkar received 1,23,576 votes against Kajorokar who secured 1,37,950 votes. It is said that more than 50,000 votes, to be cast for the reserved constituency were 'purposely wasted'.[11]

Indian history would have been written differently, and with it, the destinies of the downtrodden untouchables, if Ambedkar had responded to Gandhi's threat to fast unto death, by himself offering similar self-immolation as a strategy of persuading the Mahatma. Instead, he chose the strategy of compromise and denunciation. He derived satisfaction in calling Gandhi's fast as unheroic and as an 'adventure', saying there was 'nothing noble about it' and that it was a 'foul and a filthy act'.

These angry and bitter words of Ambedkar reveal the depth of his anguish and also outright frustration. Ambedkar found himself at the bitter end of a stick. He must have foreseen that if Gandhi died at the critical juncture, he and the Untouchables will never be forgiven, not just by the caste Hindus, but a majority of Indians. He also apprehended that Gandhi's departure on this issue will invite unpredictable violence over the depressed classes and their prospects of orderly amelioration would be further deferred. He must also have realized that his own leadership would be liquidated. This picture of extreme consequences might have inhibited him even from thinking about a counter-fast. Had he thought about these, he might have been persuaded otherwise. He might have reckoned with a climb down by Gandhi; he might have mobilized quite effectively the political consciousness and even allegiance of the Depressed Classes. It is idle to speculate for there is no indication that such thoughts ever crossed his mind.

Gandhi knew that, all said and done, Ambedkar was a political liberal. And Gandhi knew *par excellence* how to deal with liberals. Through his experience, Gandhi had acquired the shrewd insight that the mainstream political liberals do not usually know strategies of handling or coping with non-violently manufactured crisis other than those of procrastination or of compromise. Liberals, unlike revolutionaries, cannot comfortably face the opponents who undertake to die for a manifest cause; nor could they easily offer to self-immolate themselves in a like fashion or assume moral responsibilities for potential violence which might thus ensue. Gandhi knew his opponent well. During his public speech in London, defending his position on Untouchables, Gandhi complimented Ambedkar in following terms: 'I have the highest regard for Dr Ambedkar. He has every right to be bitter. That he does not break our heads is an act of self restraint on his part'. Gandhi 'gambled' on Ambedkar's self-restaint and won.

The costs of the victory would have to be recorded by an untouchable historian of future India. But this much is clear that whatever be the merits of the actual electoral proposals, Gandhi's victory represented, for him and others, the victory of idea that the problem of Untouchability was a social problem, not a political one. It was a problem of Hindu religion and not of the Hindu economy. Subsequent evolution of the regime shows variations on this theme. One sincerely hopes that Gandhi was right, despite increasing evidence to the contrary, as otherwise historians in the coming centuries might deprive him of the cherished title of social reformer gifted with unique vision of the authentic India. In the meantime, much though one may deplore this, just as Ambedkar denounced Gandhi, Ambedkar too may come to be denounced by the present and coming generations of untouchables for having yielded to Gandhi and Nehru.

To avert this possibility, or at any rate to provide a perspective, it is necessary briefly to say that many distinguished students of the period have praised Ambedkar for his humanism and wisdom in yielding to Gandhi. And Gandhi himself stands condemned for what he did to Ambedkar. 'Condemned' may not take kindly to Gandhi's intransigence on the issue of separate electorate for untouchables. For example, it has recently been observed that the communal award, as it related to the depressed classes, was in itself 'reasonable and fair' and 'the alleged separatist tendency in it was more the result of sentimental apprehensions than a reality'. It has been observed: 'How the occasional act of voting in a separate constituency, that too after voting in a general constituency, by a depressed class voter would take him away from the Hindu fold passes one's comprehension.' Not merely was the act of fast a 'drastic step' but also it is 'clear beyond any doubt to even a casual observer that while Gandhi's leadership of the untouchables was "sentimental" and "assumed", the leadership of Ambedkar was natural and real'.[13]

Similarly in a vivid account of the five days which produced the pact, Appadorai recalls that the 'situation was getting explosive'; letters threatening Ambedkar's life 'came in showers'. Furthermore, 'murderous looks were cast on him in the street and some of the leaders insanely reviled him behind his back'. But 'even in these frightful circumstances he continued to press for an honourable agreement'. When Gandhi said that the primary system should continue for five years ('Five years or my life'), Ambedkar who had intially pressed for fifteen years and reduced the period to ten, yielded to a formula which would defer the specification of the period in order to save Gandhi's life. Appadorai says that in doing this, Ambedkar 'showed a great respect for conventional morality and humanist value'.[14]

It has also been suggested persuasively by Namboodiripad that Gandhi's interest in 'constructive work' and 'Harijans' was more as aspect of political tactics 'with a view to meeting a concrete political situation' than an aspect of conscientious struggle to fundamentally change the social structure of Hinduism.[15] Namboodiripad suggests persuasively that Gandhi's

> interest in Harijan cause and activities ... should be considered as nothing but an effort on his part to disengage the Congress from the situation in which it had been placed following its break with the Government. It was an effort to find out points of contact with the British, to pursue the negotiations on constitutional reforms started and temporarily broken at the Second Round Table Conference, and to reorganize the Congress with a view to enabling it to meet this new situation.[16]

In other words, the problem was one of disengaging the Congress from the mass civil disobedience movement and cultivating legitimation for this decision. In 1933-4 period, Gandhi used the tactics of fast, and consequent release from prison, for intensive tours ostensibly for Harijan welfare work but really for informal consultations on the future of civil disobedience.[17]

Though not wholly complementary to Gandhi (particularly when Namboodiripad describes him as an 'astute political leader of a class—the bourgeoise in whose class interests he always acted') this explanation of the events is certainly plausible in the light of contemporary events and subsequent analysis of the Indian independence movement. One can not deny Gandhi's unquestioned commitment to the cause of 'eradication' of untouchability or his moral integrity, in order to understand and accept Namboodiripad's analysis. But only some such analysis can help explain Gandhi's fast. The British were clearly surprised that Gandhi who had championed the cause of depressed classes at the conference should resort to such tactics; so was Ambedkar whose life work was suddenly and rudely shaken by Gandhi. But always, Gandhi shrewdly combined concern for the legitimation of his leadership, integration of the Congress Party and 'constructive' work for the untouchables. In the ultimate result, the untouchables, so history may record, were the immediate and perhaps long-term losers.[18]

The Constitution, as it emerged through the Herculean labours of the Constituent Assembly, promised an all-out war against untouchability. It abolished, as a matter of fundamental right, untouchability and bonded labour. As far as I know the Indian Constitution is the only document which creates offences in its Bill of Rights provisions. This only underlines the mood of commitment to total abolition of untouchability. Discrimination of any kind on the basis of caste, religion or birth was made unconstitutional. Special solicitude for the 'weaker sections' was the distinctive theme of the Directive Principles. Government was given power to ameliorate the plight of 'other backward classes'. Reservations in education and employment were made possible. A Commissioner for Scheduled Castes and Tribes was provided.

It was in this context that the Constituent Assembly debated the question as to whether there should be any reservations at all for scheduled castes and tribes. There was some suggestion that the system of separate electorates be considered but this was pressed only feebly, since all other communities had agreed to dispense with 'communal' or separate electoral quotas. However (in consultation with and in deference to the wishes of the scheduled group leaders), it was decided to provide for an interim system of legislative reservations for a period of ten years. No doubt, there were voices against this arrangement and Ambedkar himself who had earlier canvassed tentatively the idea of separate electorates, was later in favour of electoral integration. But he, and others, yielded to the transitional system. Apprehensions were, of course, voiced that the transitional system may, in course of time, become permanent. But somehow people were persuaded to believe that it would not be so since in Independent India there would occur swift and thorough-going ameliorative changes in the plight of the scheduled groups. People also felt reassured, particularly the scheduled castes, by the *reapproachment* between the Congress and Ambedkar, manifest in the leading role he was assigned in the formulation of the Constitution and in his nomination as the First Law Minister of Independent India.

However, all this was short-lived. Ambedkar resigned from the Nehru cabinet. Although he resigned on the issue of the Hindu Code Bill, his publicly stated reasons concerned the slow progress in the amelioration of the plight of the scheduled castes. The Untouchability Offences Act was enacted only in 1955. Reservations in education and employment did not seem adequate. Ambedkar's fear of Hindu domination was further nurtured by the fact that in all elections to reserved constituencies his own Scheduled Caste Federation (later the Republican Party of India) lost overwhelmingly to the Congress backed candidates. Ambedkar himself was defeated, as noted, in a by-election in 1954 from a Bombay constituency by a Congress nominee.

IV

We have surveyed the formative context of Babasaheb's struggle for emancipation of Dalits. Obviously, a more sustained discursive analysis is needed to formulate responses to many theoretical/ideological questions which necessarily arise. Some of these questions are:

1. What conception of 'freedom', 'rights' and 'justice' animate Ambedkar's thought and action?
2. What are the conceptions of *Swaraj* in Ambedkar's corpus? And how, in what precise ways, did they differ from the Mahatma's and the Congress ideological mutations?
3. What are the cultural/historical roots or matrices of these conceptions in Ambedkar's thought?
4. Did Ambedkar have an implicit theory of colonial state and law?
5. How did Ambedkar view the complexity and contradiction in the nationalist movement? To what extent he innovated the theory of representation both in terms of legislative representation and participation of disadvantaged people in bureaucracy?
6. What kinds of theories/ideologies informed Ambedkar in his Herculean labours to sculpt the endless normativity of the Constitution and the apparatuses of governance?
7. What role did Ambedkar perceive and endow to the movement of the depressed classes in India's democratic future?
8. Did Ambedkar have a theory of relationship between state and religion?
9. Did Babasaheb have a distinctive approach to women's oppression and gender justice? This question assumes importance when we recall that Dalit women are doubly oppressed; First as *Women* and next as *Dalits*.
10. How did Ambedkar view the problematic issue of 'minority rights' in general? How did, if at all, this relate to a special solicitude in his world-view concerning the 'scheduled castes'?

These ten questions are distinct, though related, they need a more careful and imaginative formulation which may even expand the number. It must be said at the outset that I know of no work on Ambedkar which even formulates these types of agenda for scientific/theoretical labour. Clearly, the centenary should provide a fertile theoretical provocation for the reconstruction of Ambedkar's thought. In what follows, I examine briefly the first two questions. But before that I must pause to narrate Ambedkar's critique of Hindu law and jurisprudence.

V

Ambedkar emerges as a most articulate archivist of atrocities against the *Atishudras.* His corpus is full of contemporary testament of Dalit suffering, whereas much of the nationalist discourse is bloodless. Mahatma Gandhi's discourse, for example, on the 'removal of untouchability' is not *haunted* by a single lynched *Dalit* corpse, or a single raped and bloodied *Dalit* woman. The apostle of non-violence sanitized the here-and-now violence against untouchables, and, remarkably, succeeded in making the issue of untouchability an agendum of reform of Hindu social organization. The Mahar Mahatma had no such sublimating options, he portrays, anguishingly, Hinduism (with apologies to Tennyson's Nature), red tooth and claw.[19]

Even as an incomparable archivist of human suffering, Babasaheb's solitary place in modern Indian history is assured. But he proceeds to unravel the structural sources of production of misery in Hindu ideology, religion and social organization. In the process (as concerns my tiny jurisprudential domain) Dr Ambedkar raised for the first time in Indian Jurisprudence the problematic of '*lawless laws*'.[20] Drawing scorchingly from the 'sacred' law-texts of Manu, Yagnavalkya, Narada and Vishnu, Ambedkar presents the full horrors of the 'classical' Hindu law and jurisprudence. This not only denied 'equality before the law' as a principle to the Untouchables, erecting permanent edifice of legitimated subalternity over them down the ages, but also inscribed, what Georges Bataille terms as 'heterogeneity'. That is, the extra territorialization of whole communities of human beings and their castigation as being outside the pale of humanity. In terms of what Bataille calls a science of heterology that 'would permit us to foresee the effective social reactions that convulse the super-structure—perhaps even to manipulate them to a certain degree. ...'[21]

Ambedkar's characterization of the Hindu law as a code of lawlessness is, by itself, a heterological practice.

The classical lawless law of Hindu celebrates the 'illegality of rights' as Michael Foucault was to describe the phenomenon in his *Discipline and Punish.*[22] But the terroristic 'sacred' law at every point aims to achieve its coercible political economy through unmitigated bloody-mindedness. It would be instructive to list Ambedkar's narration in a tabular form:[23]

The very act of enunciation of these punishments suggests the plenitude of law as an act of terror. In characterizing these laws as

Offence	Punishment	Organ
1. mentioning names of high caste 'with contempt'	an iron nail, ten fingers long shall be inserted in mouth	mouth
2. teaching 'arrogantly' the Brahmin or the King of his duty	hot oil to be poured in his mouth and ears	mouth ears
3. hurt to high caste	offending limb to be cut off	indeterminate
4. raising of hand or a stick to a high caste	cutting off of the offending limb	hand foot
5. sitting or trying to place oneself on the same level as high caste	branding on his buttock; buttock to be gashed	buttock
6. spitting on a superior	cutting off both the lips	lips
7. urination on a superior	cutting off penis	penis
8. 'breaking wind' before a superior (farting)	cutting off the anus	anus
9. laying hold of a hair of superior	cutting of hands	hands
10. taking a superior by feet	decapitation	beard, neck, or the scrotum (as the case may be)
11. reading *Vedas*	blinding	gorging out of the eyes
12. hearing *Vedas*	imposition of deafness	hot oil put in both ears
13. reciting *Vedas*	cutting off his tongue	tongue*

*Ambedkar does not specifically mention the last three categories: On the, 'refined' Kautilyan notion of Vakparushyam (verbal violence) see Ranajit Guha, 1983: 45-8, see also Prabhavati Sinha, 1982: 74–84.

'lawless laws', Ambedkar may appear anachronistically to subject the 'classical' Hindu jurisprudence to contemporary standards of liberal jurisprudence. But an alternate reading is surely open. Ambedkar may be seen here as narrating 'tradition of the oppressed' which teaches us (in the striking words of Walter Benjamin) that 'the "state of emergency" in which we [i.e. the oppressed] live is not an exception but the rule'.[24] Or, put another way, the *rule of law* always coexists with a *reign of terror.*[25] *A la'* Benjamin, Ambedkar here educates us into thinking that the 'cultural treasure' called 'Hinduism' has an origin which cannot be contemplated 'without horror'. As Benjamin says, 'There is no document of civilization which is at the same time not a document of barbarism'.

If the tradition of Hindu Law is a mark of civilized jurisprudence, it is also at the same time a testament to barbarism.

Ambedkar failed to initiate the nationalist leaders in the 'traditions of the oppressed' so much so that their successors in celebrating Ambedkar's memory as a 'Modern Manu' have also reduced his historic project of emancipation of the *Atishudras*—the Constitution of India—also into a code of 'lawless laws'.

Ambedkar's deeper point of critique of Hinduism is simply this: the jurisprudence of the *dvija* is a jurisprudence of (what Ranajit Guha has termed in the context of colonial state in India) dominance without hegemony. But, Ambedkar seems to insist, that the law cannot be reduced to pure dominance, that it is conceivable only as a hegemonic phenomenon in exposing the lawlessness of the Hindu Law. He is implicitly committing himself to reading the history of dalit India as one in which the necessary effort of manufacturing the consent of the depressed classes in the justice of their millennial oppression is simply improbable. Subaltern history should assuredly, be able to sustain, refine and enrich this position, as and when its benign historiography becomes animated by contact with Ambedkar's corpus.

But from a purely jurisprudential standpoint, Ambedkar is the first, and the only major Indian thinker to have so frontally posed the problematic of the 'lawless laws'. And what distinguished him from radical naturalist thinkers like Gustav Redbruch and post-modernist Jean Francois Lyotard (who made Auschwitz the metaphor for a radical rethinking of political and legal theory) is that Ambedkar interrogates the organized millennial lawlessness structured through the 'sacred' law of an ancient civilization. The daring of this enterprise is simply unmatched in contemporary times.

VI

In a certain sense, Ambedkar's conception of 'freedom' and 'justice' is derived from the liberal vision and tradition. The figure of human rights is pre-eminent in many a text of Ambedkar's (available) corpus. But, given the horrible context of destitution, deprivation and disadvantage systematically haunting the depressed classes, and given the context of a colonial state, Ambedkar innovates thinking about justice, freedom and rights in a remarkable way. From today's standpoint, this may not sound original, but in terms of the history of ideas, it may well be acknowledged as pioneering.

Departing fundamentally from the liberal paradigm of rights and justice, Ambedkar sought to accomplish two unusual results. First, his theory of rights was addressed more to civil society than to the state. Rights do not appear as constraints and limits on the power of the state, rather, they emerge as legal entitlements casting corresponding obligations on the members of civil society. They atypically, in Ambedkar's thought legitimize an interventionist state, even the dominant colonial formation. In Hohfeldian terms, Ambedkar's essential juristic strategy was to innovate jural relations. According to him, the state has a power coupled with duty to which the rights of the depressed classes corresponded.

This remarkable detourement of the classical model of right anticipates many a later-day development in thinking about rights. Ambedkar had the happy gift of consistency which is reflected in Articles 17 and 23 of the Indian Constitution which forbid discrimination on the ground of untouchability and exploitation of labour (trafficking in human beings, bonded and forced labour, etc.) and declare them to be offences. The Constitutional articulation is remarkable in that it, in a chapter on fundamental rights, creates specific offences and that the rights themselves are limitation on the *power* of civil society rather than that of the state.

Put yet another way, Ambedkar converts rights as instrumentalities of 'negative' liberties (that is requiring specific action by the state so that the liberty may be availed by the depressed classes). The majority communities' 'rights' to cultural and religious freedom stand fully curtailed, normatively by the enunciation of the right of social equality of the depressed classes. The juristic phrases pregnant with possibilities of history—such as 'equality before the law', 'equal protection of the law' and the 'rule of law'—transform themselves from being shields against state power to swords of sovereignty.

Second, Ambedkar *persistently* posed the problem of 'rights' and 'basic needs'. The basic human needs of the *Atishudras* were both material and non-material. The latter comprise a variety of needs for dignity and fraternity or respect for the *Atishudra's* right to be human; the former include a whole set of material needs such as access to basic need—for example, immunity from bodily and psychic aggression, access to public facilities, access to resources such as drinking water and access to participation in government employment. Animating this last identification results in a very distinctive theory of representation: political representation goes beyond legislative reservations and extends to reservations in administration. The bare catalogue of needs thus identified and the sustained campaign to transform needs into rights is an astonishing facet of Ambedkar's achievement.

Babasaheb does not develop a theory of representation in general. But he does offer some insights. For example, in *Mr. Gandhi and Emancipation of the Untouchables* he meets the Hindu contention against untouchable representation in the executive on the ground that 'the Executive must represent the majority of the Legislature'. Ambedkar argues that legislative 'majorities' and 'minorities' and 'fluid' categories are subject to the processes of party formation and electoral practices. The Hindu and Untouchable relationship cannot be encapsulated by these categories. Their difference is not one 'in the point of views'. Rather, they are 'separated by a fundamental and deadly antagonism'; Hindus/Untouchables are not 'fluid' categories but they are 'fixed as permanent communities'.[26]

Obviously, Ambedkar does not believe that liberal democratic politics in its future Indian evolution will have the transformative potential of dissolving history into politics—or in other words, he does not believe that power politics will redeem the 'deadly antagonism' between these 'fixed permanent communities'.

Given the intransigence of Hindu culture and civilization, without representation in the legislature, the executive and public services, even 'good government' in India (from a *Dalit* standpoint) will always be a 'communal government'.[27] In public services, he urges, untouchables possessing minimum qualifications should have a preference over Hindus who possess 'qualifications higher than minimum qualifications'. For, such qualifications can only be claimed, ordinarily by Hindus. Fulfilment of minimum qualifications would provide for 'efficient' governance and also ensure good government because it would ensure 'self-government'.

It is sure that for this jurisprudential feat Babasaheb does not offer any theoretical framework. Partly, he treats the needs as self-evident and their redressal also morally natural. Partly, he appeals to millennia old practices of denial of humanity to the *Atishudras*, for basic entitlement. Both Nature and (Hindu) History furnish unproblematic grounds justifying conversion of needs into rights.

But, of course, his caste opponents perceived nothing in history or nature to legitimate this conversion. What is more, Ambedkar's opponents marshalled a theory of illegitimacy of colonial state as a powerful argument militating against transformation of needs into rights as this only enhanced the Lieviathan of the British high colonial state.

Confronted by such view, Ambedkar seems to have mostly been content with the response that imposition of slavery on the depressed classes through religion, as a means of social control, is an incontestable feature of the history of evolution of the Hindu caste system. This history cannot be gainsaid. The surviving question then is: is slavery justified? Ambedkar seems to have maintained two mutually reinforcing stances on this question: *first,* slavery is in principle never morally justifiable; *second,* by the standards of early and mid-twentieth century, even if agruably justifiable in other periods and modes (of production), it is wholly unjustified now.

But what if slavery finds religious sanction? What if religion and ethic both assign moral standing to the master and slave united in a cosmic *dharmic* relation? To such questions, Ambedkar's response was not necessarily that no true religion can justify slavery as just, but that Hinduism, which has been appropriated by Brahminism, must be reformed or abandoned through conscientious *acts* of conversion to religions which valorize equality and dignity of all human beings.

As practical reasoning in aid of struggle for equality and emancipation, Ambedkar's positions are catalytically cogent. But an appeal to self-evident moral truths works best when preaching, to the converted or about-to-be converted. With 'ethical' adversaries one needs a morally reasoned discourse refuting justification of slavery to be found in Aristotle's *Nichomachean Ethics.* Widely read as he was, Ambedkar possessed talent to refute Aristotle; it is rather sad that he never did find (except through sharp polemical attacks on the absurdities and cruelties of a fossilized Hinduism) time to inaugurate an ethical discourse on liberation.

Ambedkar's conception of emancipatory politics proceeded beyond a comprehensive delegitimation of slavery, which was but another name of untouchability. It proceeded to a wide-ranging programme of equality and equity measures aimed at fulfilment of a wide variety of material and non-material needs. It is this total programme of societal transformation which constituted his conception of *swaraj*. *Swaraj* was *not* just freedom (from the British); it was a *just* freedom.

In contrast, the Mahatma's (and the Congress's) core conceptions of *swaraj* vacillated in a variety of ways: participation in governance, dominion status, *purna swaraj (azadi)*. *Swaraj*, in the latter sense, signified both political and economic liberation from the British hegemony and domination. At the highest, *Swaraj* was the restoration of sovereignty of an *Indian* nation state in the making; at the lowest, it was simply (and we *still* use this phrase artlessly) a mere *transfer of power*.

It is this creation of a morally vacuous (from the standpoint of depressed classes) space and time for a new nation-state which Ambedkar opposed with all his moral might. He foresaw that transition from the British to Hindu masters signified no emancipatory potential for the masses of *Atishudras*. Indeed, it might mean the reincarnation of horrors of casteist history even in 'worse forms'. From a *Dalit* standpoint, this poignant and pathetic prophecy has almost wholly come true.

To dare to recall, Babasaheb invites vigorous confrontation with the question: does Liberal democratic politics in a society like India have any *redeeming* emancipatory potential for the *Atishudras?* If it has, how has this potential been so systematically deactivated for four long decades? And how does the recovery and reappropriation of Ambedkar assist the release of this potential? More concretely put: were Babasaheb with us today and beyond, how would *he* have responded to the promise and the peril of the present day politics of reservational equality conducted under the auspices of his name? And how would he have confronted, at the levels of ideology and action, the construction and reconstruction of backwardness for re-legitimation of practices of power, wholly threatened with erosion of performative legitimacy? What *symbolic* and deconstructive politics would he have engaged in? (Would he have, for example, accepted a belated Bharat Ratna, in an Age of Atrocity against *Atishudras?*)

For those who (perhaps vainly in the eye of history) believe in the possibilities of emancipatory politics, there is no escape from rediscovering Ambedkar. Perhaps, in that lies the prospect of a Discovery of India—an un-Nehruvian 'discovery', for a change, for the real *Atishudras* of India.

NOTES

1. J. Lacan, *Structures des psyochosos paranoiaques, Somain des Paris*, 1931.
2. Dhananjay Keer, *Dr. Babasaheb Ambedkar: Life and Mission*, Bombay, 1954, p. 41.
3. Ibid., p. 41.
4. Ibid., p. 81.
5. Ibid., p. 101.
6. E. Zelliot, 'Gandhi and Ambedkar: A Study in Leadreship', in *The Untouchables in Contemporary India*, p. 69.
7. Bhagwan Das, *Selected Speeches of Dr Babasaheb B.R. Ambedkar*, Jalandhar, 1963, pp. 71-83.
8. B.R. Ambedkar, *The Cabinet Mission and the Untouchables*, Bombay, 1947, pp. 196-7.
9. Ibid., p. 326.
10. Ibid., p. 95.
11. Dhananjay Keer, op. cit., p. 437.
12. B.R. Ambedkar, *What Congress and Gandhi have done to Untouchables*, Bombay, 1945, p. 261.
13. A.M. Rajashekhariah, *B.R. Ambedkar: The Politics of Emancipation*, 1971, p. 62, 103.
14. Ibid.
15. E.M.S. Namboodiripad, *The Mahatma and the Ism*, 1958, p. 63.
16. Ibid., p. 62.
17. Ibid., p. 63.
18. Upendra Baxi, 'Legislative Reservations for Social Justice: Some Thoghts on India's Unique Experiment', in *Independence to Statehood: Managing Ethnic Conflict in Five African and Asian States*, London, 1984, pp. 221-3.
19. B.R. Ambedkar, *Slavery and Untouchability: Which is Worse*, Jalandhar, 1989, pp. 34-62.
20. Ibid., pp. 62-74.
21. Bataille Georges, *Die psychologische Structure des Faschimus. Die Souveranitat*, Munich, 1978, pp. 42ff quoted in J. Habermas, *The Philosophical Discourse of Modernity, Five Lectures*, 1987, p. 221.
22. Michael Faucault, *Discipline and Punish*, 1977, pp. 271-82.
23. Ranajit Guha, *The Elementary Forms of Peasant Insurgency*, 1983, pp. 45-8; Prabhavati Sinha, *Smriti: Political and Legal System*, 1982, pp. 74-84.

24. Benjamin Walter, *Illuminations*, 1973.
25. Upendra Baxi, *Marx, Law and Justice, Some Indian Perspectives,* 1991.
26. B.R. Ambedkar, *Mr. Gandhi and Emancipation of the Untouchables*, Jalandhar, 1943, pp. 30-1.
27. Ibid., p. 34.

4
The Ambedkarian Ideology: A Perspective

Raosaheb Kasbe

It is difficult to draw coherent principles of political philosophy from the published literature of Dr. Ambedkar, mainly due to the diversity of his scattered writings. They range from classic works like *Caste in India: Their Mechanism, Genesis and Development* (1916) and *The Buddha and his Dhamma* (1956), to memoranda submitted to the British Government and his lectures. Occasionally one finds contradictions in these writings that impede systematization of his work. However, in the sphere of political jargon a new 'ism', Ambedkarism, has been engaging the attention of the scholars. In this paper, an attempt is made to analyse the validity of this term. Naturally, it is essential to consider Ambedkar's thinking in the light of its philosophical basis.

II

In Indian philosophy, as far as the issue of caste is concerned, two distinct schools of thought, one upholding the institution as a boon and the other rejecting it as a bane, have emerged. Dr Ambedkar was of course avowedly an advocate of the latter view. This was in evidence by his declaring Buddha, Kabir and Mahatma Phule as his 'Gurus', revered teachers. So his main source of philosophical inspiration can be traced to the teachings of Buddha. In fact, Ambedkar used Buddha's doctrine as the foundation of his political ideas, as testified by *The Buddha and his Dhamma*. However, in using Buddhism as a base, Ambedkar encountered certain irksome difficulties, concerning the manifest contradictions found in it. Buddha's teaching, as preserved in the scriptures, has to some measure become obsolete, yet some of it still holds true. Dr Ambedkar seems to surmount this difficulty by accepting what is rational, logical, humane and definite as authentically Buddha's:

> If there is anything which can be said with confidence it is: He was nothing if not rational, if not logical. Anything therefore rational and logical, other things being equal, may be taken to be the word of Buddha. The second thing is that Buddha never cared to enter into a discussion which was not profitable for man's welfare. Therefore anything attributed to Buddha which did not relate to man's welfare cannot be accepted as the word of Buddha. There is a third test. It is that Buddha divided all matters into two classes. Those about which he was certain form Class I. On matters which fell into Class I, he has stated his views definitely and conclusively. On matters which fell into Class II he has expressed his views. But they are only tentative views. In discussing questions about which there is doubt and difference, it is necessary to bear these three tests in mind before deciding what the view of Buddha was thereon.[1]

THE ORDER OF THE WORLD

The human being, despite his enormous capabilities, only partially understands and controls the world and has a compulsion to guess beyond known facts, as Arnold Toynbee wrote: 'Religion includes both guesswork about unknown facts and action in accordance with these guesses'.[2]

Now, Buddha never tried to engage in such kinds of discussion and speculation, dubbing them futile. The main concern of Buddha's thinking was to delve into the causes of suffering and prevent them. The founders of Buddhism had no time for either ontology or epistemology. Buddha refused to discuss them himself. What interested him instead were moral questions, though inevitably in the form in which to him they appeared to be relevant.

According to Buddha, birth, old-age, sickness, death, to be unloved, to be separated from the loved and not to obtain what one desires, is suffering. In short the fivefold clinging (to the world) is suffering.[3] Therefore, the only questions finally considered valid by Buddha were those concerning this enormous mass of suffering. What was its cause? Could it be extinguished? If so, how was this extinction to be effected?[4] Ambedkar's thinking was based on the same premises and so he called it the Discovery of the New Dhamma.[5]

Now, the further question that arises is whether suffering is totally caused by God, or are there any other reasons behind it. This controversy in Indian philosophy centred around theism and atheism, the former subjecting human actions to the ultimate governance of God and the latter treating human actions as independent of any supernatural power. Buddha's arguments about the evolution of the world ('Buddha did not believe that the world was created. He believed that the world has evolved'[6]); his refutation of the existence of God (he argued that 'the doctrine of existence of God is not based on truth'[7]), appealed to Ambedkar.

From these ideas of evolution and non-existence of God arises the conception of the impermanence that pervades all composite things, individual beings and the selfnature of conditional states of events. Living bodies are composed of earth, water, fire and air and are heading towards decomposition: 'To believe that all compound things are impermanent is Dhamma.'[8] This leads to accepting the principle of 'Being is Becoming'.[9] Ambedkar's explanation does not imply out and out nihilism, but that the phenomena of the world are dynamic, revealing perpetual changes.

The scientific outlook manifested in the theory of *Pratitya Samupada* and the eternal continuity flowing from it offers a first basis to the argument for 'becoming'. According to Radhakrishnan:

> To account for the continuity of the world in the absence of a permanent substratum, Buddha announces the law of causation and makes it the basis of continuity. The law of eternal causation, with its corollary of the eternal continuity of becoming, is the chief contribution of Buddhism to Indian thought.[10]

Ambedkar looked at Buddha's basic theory of *Anita* from a moral angle and insists on being free from all sorts of impermanent things, like property, friends, etc.[11]

Thus, the underlying principle of emancipation of mankind is found in Buddhism and that, too, from a moral approach. Buddha was primarily interested in working out a practical programme for the emancipation of mankind from suffering.[12] The Buddhist approach was so broad that it pulled down all social barriers and was rightly called *Saddhamma* [authentic truth] by Ambedkar.[13]

THE CONCEPT OF RELIGION

Dr Ambedkar accepted Edmund Burke's notion that religion serves as the foundation for society and government: 'True religion is the foundation of society, the basis on which all true civil government rests and of both their sanction'.[14]

The mid-twentieth century exposed the spate of irrelevance in religion. Though India entered the era of independence, the Indian psyche was too weak to break the shackles of social taboos and blind beliefs. The Indian constitution was in the making. The lion's share in preparing the constitution went to Dr Ambedkar, but he was not happy about the result. In fact, because of the pressure of the majority of Constituent Assembly members, he did not mould it strictly according to his own vision.

In this desperate state of mind Ambedkar embraced Buddhism. His classic work *The Buddha and his Dhamma* clearly supports this contention. The chronological order of events as recorded in the traditional literature, was departed from in *The Buddha and his Dhamma* (barring the initial section of it). Emphasis has been shifted to a discussion of issues. A renowned authority of Buddhist literature, Bhadant Anand Kausalayan, concedes that Ambedkar inserted his own thinking into the Buddhist doctrine. However, this could never be said to constitute a distortion of the doctrine. He dealt with certain issues demonstrating an independent insight, without doing any harm to Buddhism.[15]

The meaning of Buddhism as interpreted by Ambedkar is relevant to contemporary social and political problems. For remedying social ills, he found the traditional philosophy inadequate. As we have seen, Buddha was the first Indian thinker who made dialectics, the law of eternal change, the central core of his philosophy.[16]

Buddhist philosophy arose in the context of the ideological struggle against the prevailing Upanishadic philosophy, which by that time had become completely rigid and metaphysical. With great vigour it shattered the obstacles to further philosophical thinking. Buddhism shook the conceptual foundations of both material and idealist thinking.

Dr Ambedkar realised that contemporary ideologies would not suffice, if unchanged, to solve the social and political issues of the day. In the complexity of the contradictions between spiritual nationalism and economic determinism, bourgeois democracy and a dictatorship of the proletariat based on a socialist economy having a total disregard for the caste hierarchy, Ambedkar, as if on behalf of Buddha, asked: 'How far do the established philosophies offer a solution to this problem ?'[17]

Dr Ambedkar never discussed the concept of religion as such. The main thrust of his analysis was directed towards indicating the drawbacks in Hinduism. Only a few stray thoughts on the concept of religion as such can be found in his thinking, such as the following one:

> Religion must mainly be a matter of principles only. It cannot be a matter of rules. The moment it degenerates into rules, it ceases to be a Religion, as it kills responsibility which is an essence of the true religious act.[18]

Considering his views on the subject, it is clear that Dr Ambedkar was looking at the concept of religion as a means to 'maintain' society and to provide salvation for the individual from the slavery of all worldly bondage. Thus, he denounced Hinduism as a religion because the Hindu religion had degenerated into law or into legalized class ethics.[19]

In his earlier life, he made efforts to locate the source of the caste system in material conditions; in his maturity, however, he had to modify his thinking because of the ill-treatment still meted out to the untouchables. He attributed the suffering of the untouchables to the basic philosophy of Hinduism.

HISTORICAL APPROACH

Ambedkar approached history in his own way.[20] On the occasion of the 101st anniversary of Justice Ranade he gave a crucial lecture, which was, later, published under the title *Ranade, Gandhi and Jinnah*. Here not only Ambedkar's historical approach is reflected but role of great personalities in shaping history is also discussed. Here he dealt with Augustine's theory, according to which:

> History is only an unfolding of a divine plan in which mankind is to continue through war and suffering until that divine plan is completed at the Day of Judgment.

Referring to Buckle, 'who held that history was made by geography and physics', Ambedkar also considers the Marxian theory that history is the result of economic forces. However, all these three theories ignore or deny the role of great men in making history. Augustine's theory is acceptable to none except theologians. 'As to Buckle and Marx, while there is truth in what they say, their views do not represent the whole truth'.[21] They are quite wrong in holding that impersonal forces are everything and that man does not constitute a factor in the making of history. That impersonal forces are determining factors cannot be denied. But that the effect of impersonal forces also depends on man must also be admitted:

> Flint may not exist everywhere. But where it does exist, it needs man to strike flint against flint to make fire. There are many areas devoid of metals. But where they do exist it needs a man to make instruments and machines which are the basis of civilization and culture.[22]

Ambedkar gave more weight to 'man'. Hence man's share in the creation of history is as much as that of material conditions. In fact, Marx did not entirely repudiate man's role in the process of shaping history. He said: 'History does nothing, it possesses no immense wealth, fights no battles. It is rather *man*, real living man who does everything, who possesses and fights.'[23]

Ambedkar stated that when a society is caught in a predicament, new ways are to be sought to get out of it, otherwise the entire society sinks deep into the mire. He wrote:

> Time may suggest possible new ways. But to step on the right one is not the work of the time. It is the work of man. Man therefore is a factor in the making of history and environmental forces, whether impersonal or social, if they are the first, and not the last things.[24]

The foregoing discussion accords with his principal objective of enhancing the status of the individual in the political system. The same theme is spelt out at length in his thoughts on the structure of the constitution. He endeavours to aid individuals with concrete safeguards against domination and exploitation which are the formidable by-products of capitalist democracy.

THE CONSTITUTION AND STATE SOCIALISM

Ambedkar's political thought is reflected in the memorandum submitted to the Constituent Assembly on behalf of the Scheduled Castes Federation. The background of the writing of the Constitution had called forth a vast literature. In the present context, I intend to consider Ambedkar's thought on the nature of the Indian Constitution.

Indian freedom was gradually appearing within reach and the Indian National Congress seemed resolved to put parliametary democracy into practice. Leaders like Pandit Jawaharlal Nehru, influenced by Socialism, attempted to prepare the Constitution with left of the centre leaning. Several members in the Constituent Assembly shared the views of Dr Ambedkar. Most of the democratic countries in the world mapped out only their political structure. The proposal offered by Dr Ambedkar distinguished itself from all the other constitutions, then in effect in the world.

> The Proposal marks a departure from the existing constitutions, whose aim is merely to prescribe the form of political structure of society, leaving the economic structure untouched. The result is that the political structure is completely set at naught by the forces which emerge from the economic structure which is at variance with the political structure.[25]

Dr Ambedkar urged that the state should take a bold step and carve out the economic structure. New states should take a lesson from the experiences gained by others. Said he:

> Time has come to take a bold step and define both the economic structure as well as the political structure of society by the law of constitution. All countries like India which are latecomers in the field of constitution-making should not copy the faults of other countries. They should profit by the experience of their predecessors.[26]

He depicted a clear picture of the economic structure to be included in the Constitution. He planned to place key and basic industries under state control. Article II, Section II, Clause IV of the proposal of Dr Ambedkar says that 'The United States of India shall declare as part of the law of its Constitution:

(1) The industries which are key industries or which may be declared to be key industries shall be owned and run by the state;
(2) That industries which are not the key industries but which are basic industries shall be owned by the state and shall be run by the state or by corporations established by the state;
(3) That Insurance shall be a monopoly of the state and that the state shall compel every adult citizen to take out a life insurance policy commensurate with his wages as may be prescribed by the legislature;
(4) That Agriculture shall be a state industry;
(5) That the state shall acquire the subsisting rights in such industries, insurance and agricultural land held by private individuals, whether as owners, tenants or mortgagees and pay them compensation in the form of debenture equal to the value of his or her right in the land. Provided that in reckoning the value of land, plant or security no account shall be taken of any rise therein, due to the emergence of any potential or unearned value or any value for compulsory acquisition;
(6) The debenture shall be transferable and inheritable property but neither the debenture holder nor the transferee from the original holder nor his heir shall be entitled to claim the return of the land or interest in any industrial concern acquired by the state or be entitled to deal with it in any way;

(7) The debenture holder shall be entitled to interest on his debenture at such rate as may be defined by law, to be paid by the state in cash or in kind as the state may see fit;

(8) Agriculture industry shall be organized on the following basis:
   (i) The state shall divide the land acquired into farms of standard size and let out the farms for cultivation to residents of the village as tenants (made up of group of families) to cultivate on the following conditions:
      (a) The farm shall be cultivated as a collective farm;
      (b) The farm shall be cultivated in accordance with rules and directions issued by the Government;
      (c) The tenants shall share among themselves, in the manner prescribed, the produce of the farm left after the payment of the charges properly leviable on the farm;
   (ii) the land shall be let out to villagers without distinction of caste or creed and in such a manner that there will be no landlord, no tenant and no landless labourer;
   (iii) It shall be the obligation of the state to finance the cultivation of the collective farms by the supply of water, draught animals, implements, manure, seeds, etc.
   (iv) The state shall be entitled:
      (a) to levy the following charges on the produce of the farm: (i) a portion for land revenue; (ii) a portion to pay the debenture-holders; and (iii) a portion to pay for the use of capital goods supplied; and
      (b) to prescribe penalties against tenants who break the conditions of tenancy or wilfully neglect to make the best use of means of cultivation offered by the state or otherwise act prejudicially to the scheme of collective farming;

(9) The scheme shall be brought into operation as early as possible but in no case shall the period extend beyond the tenth year from the date of the constitution coming into operation.[27]

Dr Ambedkar had the twin objectives of prescribing economic equity and ensuring its existence by constitutional means without leaving it to the caprice of the legislature. The plan, he said, has two special features. One is that it proposes State Socialism in important fields of economic life. The second special feature is that it does not leave the establishment of state socialism to the will of the law of constitution and thus makes it unalterable by any act of the legislature and executive.[28] He aimed at achieving high economic productivity with the appropriate adjustments to actualize equitable solution. To quote him:

> .... The main purpose behind the clause is to put an obligation on the state to plan the economic life of the people on lines which would lead to the highest point of productivity without closing every avenue to private enterprise and also provide for the equitable distribution of wealth.[29]

Ambedkar's political ideology stemmed from his experience in launching political movements. He fought on two fronts, those of the Indian National Congress and British imperialism. Realizing that the class of untouchables was not to become a majority and in the parliamentary system political decisions were reached by majority, he saw the political future of the untouchables sealed. He talked of the communal not the political, majority. The communal majority would continue in the future, the minorities would be designed to lead the life of subjects. This majority would be free to choose what is thought fit for the minorities, irrespective of their will.[30]

This indicates his distrust of the intentions of the majority. To ensure the minorities of their rights to freedom, equality and welfare, these rights should be embodied in the Constitution itself. Ambedkar was familiar with the necessary preliminaries for effecting political revolution. However, he knew that such revolution was not possible in the near future. He wanted to bring it about by legal measures; he hoped that the progressive group in the Congress Party would support him. As we have seen he wanted collectivization of land and rapid industrialization through State Socialism.[31]

Dr Ambedkar thought that the ordinary law would fall short of the fundamental objective of bringing economic justice to the exploited classes. The possible changes in majority rule might not have a similar approach to the ordinary provisions of law but the constitutional law would remain sacrosanct:

> Those who want the economic structure of society to be modelled on state socialism must realize that they cannot leave the fulfilment of so fundamental a purpose to the exigencies of ordinary law which simple majorities—whose political fortunes are never determined by rational causes—have a right to make and unmake. For these reasons political democracy seems to be unsuited for the purpose.[32]

DEMOCRACY

Dr Ambedkar attempted to establish a relationship between individual and society. In a conference which he convened for discussion on conversion, he spoke on this issue. What maintains society, is religion—this definition according to him was exposed to severe limitations, one of them relating to the restrictions to be imposed on society. In order to maintain society restrictions were essential and to understand the true nature of religion these restrictions, if prescribed, were to be reckoned with.

Of course, for him the well-being of the individual was the main point of concern. Sociologists describe the need of society for achieving the good of individuals, for developing the individual's personality and for the building of society itself, the last being contrary to the first. Hinduism places no emphasis on the individual but attends to inter-group interaction. Hinduism, according to Dr Ambedkar, was not individually-oriented and therefore he rejected it. The end of the individual lies in his upliftment and not in serving others. Hinduism did not extend sympathy, freedom and equality to all its followers. It left no way open to Ambedkar but that of taking recourse to conversion.[33]

The untouchables were deprived of their right to fetch water from the public wells and to enter temples. They were an object of abhorrence to the *savarnas*. The misunderstanding between *sawarna* and untouchable was deepening. The *Upanishads* declared that the spirit of God pervades the entire world. However, theory and practice were different. The followers of Hinduism pretend to honour human values but they have neither sympathy nor a feeling of equality with their untouchable brothers.

The untouchables need basic social freedom; in its absence other freedoms are meaningless. In addition, they must be psychologically freed. Dr Ambedkar stated that he whose conscience keeps him equally alive to freedoms and duties is really free. Such an emancipated individual is never enslaved by circumstances, rather he attempts to control them.

Hinduism deprives untouchables of their freedom of expression. The Hindus at the apex of the varna hierarchy have structured Hinduism so as to safeguard only their own interests. In these conditions, untouchables are no better than slaves. Dr Ambedkar did not agree with the view that the individuality of the individual vanishes only because he lives in society.[34] That is why he was intent upon connecting individual liberty with the economic structure. It was to prevent encroachment by one individual on the rights of others.

Dr Ambedkar pointed out that there are four premises upon which democracy rests:

(1) The individual is an end in himself.
(2) The individual has certain inalienable rights which must be guaranteed to him by the constitution.
(3) The individual shall not be required to relinquish any of his constitutional rights as a condition precedent to the receipt of a privilege.
(4) The state shall not delegate power to private persons to govern others.[36]

It is obvious that premises 3 and 4 are jeopardised when private enterprise has a free hand. Fundamental rights are sold for a paltry amount in order to gain the basic means to live. E.H. Carr wrote:

The moral precepts which we apply in history are in everyday life cheques on a bank. They have printed and written parts: the printed part consists of abstract words like liberty and equality, justice and democracy. These are essential categories. But the cheque is valueless until we fill in the other part, which states how much liberty we propose to allocate to whom, whom we recognize as our equals and up to what amount. The way in which we fill in the cheque from time to time is a matter of history.[37]

In effect, no one except the exploiters were to be benefited by the freedom granted by the Indian Constitution. Dr Ambedkar posed one fundamental question about liberty as a fundamental right enshrined in the democratic Constitution—'to whom and for whom is this liberty?' His answer to this question was: 'Obviously this liberty is liberty to the landlords to increase rents, for capitalists to increase hours of work and reduce rate of wages.' Ambedkar said: 'In other words what is called liberty must be liberty from the control of the private employer.'[38]

Ambedkar wanted to restrict not only the abuses of power of the government but to protect the less powerful from the more powerful. His plan seeks to limit not only the power of government to impose arbitrary restraints but also to restrict the more powerful individuals or the power to control the economic life of less powerful people.

The constitutional plan drawn up by Ambedkar fell on deaf ears. Other members of the Constituent Assembly flawed it. The reason for such connivance and indifference was the dominance of the rights lobby. According to the resolution moved by Pandit Govind Vallabh Pant, an advisory committee was formed, which further formed five sub-committees. The sub-committee of fundamental rights was presided over by Acharya Kripalani—Dr Ambedkar, Masani, Munshi and Azad being its membes. The first meeting of this sub-committee was held on 27 February 1947. Dr Ambedkar submitted his note, the same which he presented in *States and Minorities* (Art II, Section II, Clause IV). He requested that it should be considered in determining the third part of the constitution, that on fundamental rights.[40] However, Kripalini declined to accept it on the score that economic planning did not come within the scope of fundamental rights. Dr Ambedkar then requested Vallabhbhai Patel, the Chairman of the Advisory Committee to consider the proposal at some other relevant place, such as in the sub-committee on minorities or the special committee on economic planning. He urged that his suggestions should not be disposed of undiscussed on technical grounds. With Sardar Patel also the proposal met with the same fate. On 25 April 1947 Dr Ambedkar wrote a letter to Dr Rajendra Prasad and then on 14 May 1947 to Jawaharlal Nehru reiterating the proposal. Rajendra Prasad toed the line of Sardar Patel—but a letter of 22 May 1947 is very telling. In this letter Nehru expressed his agreement with Dr Ambedkar's plan and promised to consider it in a separate committee on economic planning. But he added that this should not be related to the Constitution and should not delay Constitution-making.

> ... I agree with your general approach to this problem, more especially in regard to industries, insurance and about agriculture also I agree, but it is not ... easily possible for us to take the step you suggest immediately. In theory there is nothing to prevent our introuducing such clauses into a constitution, though they are not in line with the old idea of fundamental rights. You are perfectly right in saying that the old conception must be widened and must include economic democracy. In a sense we have aimed at this, though rather vaguely, in the objective resolution of the Constituent Assembly. We are faced today in India with all manners of disruptive tendencies and forces. If we take at this stage very fundamental economic issues, in the process of constitution-making, we might add to the strength of the disruptive tendencies and achieve nothing at all.[41]

Thus Dr Ambedkar left no stone unturned for the preparation of the Indian Constitution. On 26 January 1950 India was declared a republic and on 15 March the Planning Commission was formed. Dr Ambedkar's name did not figure in the list of members. In September 1951, the Department of Economic Planning was created. Gulzarilal Nanda headed it, though Ambedkar was there in the council of ministers. Feeling suffocated, he quit the post in December 1952. On walking out of the ministry, however, he got an opportunity to express his thoughts frankly. In July 1954, he said that he was 'only a hack in the preparation of the Constitution' (*Times of India*, 3 July 1954). A little later, he told the Rajya Sabha: 'The Constitution was wonderful temple we built for the gods but before they could be installed, the devils have taken possession' (*P.T.I. News Service*, 20 March 1954).[42]

III

In sum, Ambedkar's thinking, as revealed in his writings, ostensibly shows that scores of issues have not been independently dealt with and he followed the line of some western and oriental predecessors; however, other features are exclusively original.

NOTES

1. B.R. Ambedkar, *The Buddha and his Dhamma*, Bombay, 1974, pp. 254-5.
2. Arnold Toynbee, *A Study of History*, 1976, p. 344.
3. Tr. H Oldenberg, *Mahavagga*, 6, 19, Calcutta, 1927, p. 28.
4. D.P. Chatopadhyay, *Indian Atheism*, Calcutta, 1969, pp. 96-7.
5. B.R. Ambedkar, op. cit, p. 55.
6. Ibid., p. 192.
7. Ibid., p. 176.
8. Ibid., p. 169.
9. Ibid., p. 170.
10. Radhakrishnan, *Indian Philosophy*, London, 1962, p. 370.
11. B.R. Ambedkar, op. cit, p. 170.
12. D.P. Chatopadhyay, op. cit, p. 99.
13. B.R. Ambedkar, op. cit, p. 215.
14. B.R. Ambedkar, *Annihilation of Caste*, Jalandhar, p. 89.
15. See the Preface written by Dr Anand Kausalayan to the Hindi translation of *Buddha and his Dhamma* entitled *Buddha aur Unaka Dhamma*, Bombay, 1979, pp 18-19.
16. Balaram Moorthy (ed), *Buddhism: A Marxist Approach*, Delhi, 1971, p. 37.
17. *Buddha and his Dhamma*, p. 17.
18. B.R. Ambedkar, *Annihilation of Caste*, p. 87.
19. Ibid., p. 88.
20. Cf Ambedkar's *Ranade, Gandhi and Jinnah*, Jalandhur, pp. 11-14.
21. Ibid., p. 12.
22. Ibid.
23. Marx-Engels, *Gesamtausgable*, vol. III, p. 625.

24. *Ranade, Gandhi and Jinnah*, p. 14.
25. B.R. Ambedkar, *State and Minorities*, Bombay, p. 35.
26. Ibid., p. 35.
27. Ibid., pp. 14-16.
28. Ibid., p. 31.
29. Ibid., pp. 30-1.
30. Ibid., p. 36.
31. Ibid., p. 31.
32. Ibid., p. 31.
33. M.F. Gangrare, *Babasaheb Ambedkaranchi Bhasane*, Nagpur, 1968, vol. 1, pp. 20-53.
34. Ibid., p. 53.
35. *States and Minorities*, p. 31.
36. Ibid., p. 53.
37. E.H. Carr, *What is History*, 1964, p. 82.
38. *States and Minorities*, p. 33.
39. Ibid, p. 33.
40. Nilakantha Khadikar, *Practical Socialism*, Bombay, 1985, pp. 14-77.
41. *Selected Works of Jawaharlal Nehru*, Series II, vol. II, Delhi, 1984, pp. 196-8.
42. Quotes taken from Eleanor Zelliot's unpublished thesis 'Dr Ambedkar and the Mahar Movement', p. 269.

5

The Man who Thought Differently: An Inquiry into the Political Thinking of Dr Ambedkar

Gopal Guru

Dr Bhimrao Ramji Ambedkar was undoubtedly the foremost leader of the toiling masses and thinker of the twentieth-century India. He was, in Pandit Nehru's words, a symbol of revolt against all the oppressive features of Indian society. His political life and thought spans forty years from 1916 to 1956. During this time, he wrote and spoke extensively on the socio-economic and political problems of not only the Dalit masses but the country as a whole. He tried to organize and politicize the deprived sections of society in the light of the ideas he developed throughout his active life.

After Ambedkar, his followers have been claiming that they are furthering the emancipatory struggle of the Dalit masses in this country in accordance with his philosophy. But despite this claim on the part of the Dalit leaders, the Dalits themselves are still socially backward, economically deprived and politically fragmented. In this totally frustrating state of affairs, some Dalits are demanding separate state to be called *Dalitsthan*. At the same time, the *Hindutva* forces are appropriating Ambedkar into their project of Hindu nationalism.

It seems that Ambedkar's followers never tried to criticially assess his ideas within the context of the changing socio-economic and political situation in India. Most of them seem to assume that Ambedkar's ideas are enough for the liberation of Dalits for centuries to come and hence require no critical reappraisal. Even Ambedkar scholars,[1] with the notable exception of Dr Gail Omvedt, Sharad Patil and Dr Raosaheb Kasbe, are much more liberal than Ambedkar himself in analysing his ideas. However, this lack of a critical approach towards an understanding of Ambedkar has done such harm, that it did not allow the strengths and, indeed, the weaknesses of Ambedkar's ideas to come to light.

In fact, Ambedkar himself never considered his ideas to be absolute or infallible. Therefore, the present paper attempts a critical scrutiny of his political ideas on nationalism, democracy, the state and bureaucracy. To do this is to make Ambedkar more relevant in understanding contemporary problems: it may also help us in liberating him from narrow theoretical confines. This would be an appropriate tribute, I think, to the great man.

II

ON NATIONALISM

Ambedkar's theory of the nation and nationalism in India constitutes a major aspect of his political thinking. According to Ambedkar:

> Nationality is a social feeling. It is a corporate sentiment of oneness which makes those who are charged with it feel that they are kith and kin. This national feeling is a double-edged feeling. It is at once a feeling of fellowship for one's own kith and kin and an anti-fellowship for those who are not one's own kith and kin. It is a feeling of 'consciousness of kind' which on the one hand binds together those that have it so strongly that it overrides all differences arising out of social conflicts on social gradation and on the other, severs them from those who are not of their kind.[2]

Ambedkar agrees with the French thinker Renana, saying:

> A nation is a living soul, a spirtiual principle. There are two things. One is the common possession of a rich heritage of memories, the other is the actual consent, the desire to live together, the will to preserve together, the will to preserve worthily, the undivided heritage which has been handed down.[3]

For Ambedkar, then, nationalism in relation to a nation as such should be based on the fundamentally strong feeling of social unity. However, nationalism in relation to internationalism should be founded on human brotherhood. He emphasized that nationalism should not be tyranny and a menace to any other community and country Ambedkar's idea of Nationality is related to consciousness of a kind mentioned previously, and awareness of the existence of that tie of kinship and nationalism is connected with the desire for a separate national existence of those who are bound by that tie.

He maintains the view that there cannot be nationalism without the existence of this feeling of nationality. He states that nationality per se did not in all cases produce nationalism. Moreover, he saw Nationality as a dynamic expression of the desire to live as a nation. He further suggests that there must be territory which nationalism could occupy and make into a state, as well as the cultural home of the nation. A community has a right to safeguards, but as a nation it also had a right to separation.[4]

Ambedkar's idea of nationalism and nationality leads to three questions. Firstly, did the Muslims form a separate nation? Secondly, was it possible for the untouchables to demand a separate nation: could they at all form such nationality? Were the Hindus, therefore, a separate nation? And finally, do kinship ties alone form the basis of nationalism as Ambedkar seems to be suggesting?

In regard to Muslims, Ambedkar's answer was in the affirmative. He believed that Muslims constituted a nation, as they possessed the feeling of nationality as well as nationalism. Ambedkar held the view that the Hindus wanted to use their Hindu majority to treat Muslims as though they were second-class citizens in an alien state.[5]

Ambedkar said that the anti-fellowship of Hindus towards Muslims led Muslims to demand a separate nation. The Indian Muslims, being afraid of Hindu domination, always made more and more political demands,[6] steadily exploited the weakness of the Hindus[7] and adopted pressure tactics in politics.[8] Ambedkar, therefore, suggested that there should be partition of India as an integral India was incompatible with independent India.[9] He argued that the creation of Pakistan was inevitable because even if India remained as one integral whole in political terms, it would never be an organic whole.[10] It was exceedingly difficult to find a basis for Hindu-Muslim settlement. Moreover, a forced political union would not eliminate the pressure of the Hindu party.[11]

Ambedkar's idea of nationalism seems to involve religion and culture as two distinct factors which constitute a political community. Here the notion of the British thinker Edmund Burke is clearly evident. Ambedkar said:

> I agree with Burke when he says that religion is the foundation of the society, the basis on which all governments rest and earn their sanction. ... The nineteenth century European thought about nationality and nationalism centred around the concept of religion and culture. Mill and Mazzini

developed a theory of nationalism on the basis of religion and culture.[12]

On the basis of this idea of nationalism, some scholars seem to argue that Ambedkar viewed nationality and nationalism in terms of religion and culture. Thus, he not only linked Indian nationalism with Hindu culture but regarded Islam and Christianity as dangerous to the Indian nation. These scholars find a similarity between Tilak, Shriram Munge and V.D. Savarkar's idea of Hindu nationalism and Ambedkar's idea of nationalism.[13] But, what is missing from this assumption is the question whether Ambedkar in fact believed that the Hindus formed a nation. He categorically did not believe this. He believed that the Hindus could not become a nation or even form a stable society. His arguments for this were:[14]

(i) Hindus did not possess the consciousness of kind, only consciousness of caste.
(ii) Similarity in habit and custom, beliefs and thought was not sufficient for being a nation. Otherwise, according to Ambedkar, the tribes would have to be called nations.[15]
(iii) To have similar things was totally different from possessing things in common.[16] There might be certain similarities on the surface, but this was not enough. What was needed was a sense of deep spiritual sharing, and the possession of certain vital properties in common.
(iv) The caste system prevented communication and activity in common in Hindu society.

In this regard, it is worth noting that even after the emergence of Pakistan, Ambedkar felt that Indians should be described as people of the land called India, not as a nation as such.

Similarly, the comparison between Ambedkar and Savarkar is wrong. There can be a comparison made between Savarkar and Jinnah because they both advocated two-nations theory: Savarkar for a Hindu nation and Jinnah for Pakistan. In fact, Ambedkar brought out the contradiction in the premises of Savarkar. He said that Savarkar admitted that the Muslims were a separate nation, but refused the claim of the Muslims for a national home.[17]

Ambedkar thought that if the Hindu raj did become a fact, it would without doubt be the greatest calamity for this country. He further argued that, no matter what the Hindus said, Hinduism was a menace to liberty, equality and fraternity. Becuase of this, it was incompatible with democracy. He said that the Hindu raj must be prevented at every cost. The lower castes of the Hindu society would be more ready to make common cause with Muslims for achieving common ends than they would with the high-caste Hindus, who have denied and deprived them of ordinary human rights for centuries. To him, partition as a remedy against Hindu raj was worse than useless.

However, Ambedkar saw that both the Hindu and Muslim communities were not qualitatively different from each other. He pointed out the social evils in both communities.

Ambedkar's political ideas about the imperialist rule in this country also require some attention at this juncture. When analysing Ambedkar's attitude to British rule in India, an attempt is always made by nationalist historians to situate him in a dichotomy between the Indian National Congress as anti-imperialist and Ambedkar as pro-imperialist.[21] It is true that Ambedkar did not make any common cause with the Indian National Congress in the freedom movement. There are two reasons Ambedkar offered for this. First, he believed that the Congress was controlled by the Brahmins and the Banias.[22] Consequently, he further argued that the national movement led by the Congress was not prepared to build an India in which Dalits would find a place. In the same way, there was a strong feeling among Dalits which made them believe that because of the internal caste/class conflict, no caste Hindu could speak in their interest.[23] The second and related reason for Ambedkar's refusal of association with the Congress lies in the nature of politics of nationalism. He observed:

> ... During the freedom struggle the Congress platform under the garb of national integration has done a great job for the governing classes. The governing class is aware of the fact that the political campaign based on class ideology or class conflict will toll its death knell. It knows that the most effective way of sidetracking the servile classes and fooling them is to play upon the sentiments of nationalism and national unity. It clings to the Congress because it realises that the Congress is the only platform that can effectively safeguard the interests of the governing class. For if there is any platform which despite all talk of conflict between rich and poor, Brahmin and non-Brahmin, landlords and tenants, creditor and debtor can still talk of and preach nationalism and national unity, this is what the governing class wants, as it is on this the safety of this class depends, but it prevents any other ideology inconsistent with this nationalism being preached from its platform. [24]

This dissociation from Congress did not, however, make him pro-

British. He had a clear understanding of the British role in India. He firmly believed that to remove the grievances of the untouchables and to bring about their salvation, Independence was necessary. He believed that the British had no intention of helping the untouchables; they had only one intention, that of retarding the political progress of India.

Ambedkar sought to solve the problem of the untouchables within the framework of India as a nation. As part of the strategy of Dalit emancipation, he only demanded separate village settlements. It would be a mistake to think of this as being in any way equivalent to 'Pakistan', as a Dalit nation or a separate Dalit state. No idea of separate political territory was implied, it was simply a rearrangement of villages.

It was historically untenable for Dalits to develop either an aspiration towards nationhood or press for a separate homeland. Dalits did not form a nationality because they had neither a common language, tradition and culture, nor a geographical location that amounted to such a nationality. Rather the distinctiveness of the Dalit group was to be found in its separate caste identity, which again was not a homogenous whole. What the Dalits did have in common as an ethnic group was the economic discrimination carried out against them. This alone could not articulate itself into the consciousness of self-determination.

III

ON LIBERAL DEMOCRACY

Ambedkar considered democracy as a historical movement. He maintained the view that the government of human society underwent some very significant changes. There was a time, he said, when the government of human society had taken the form of rule by the despotic sovereigns. This was replaced after a long, bloody struggle by a system of government known as parliamentary democracy. This democracy was believed to bring about the millennium, in which every human being will have the right to liberty, equality and fraternity.[25] Ambedkar defined democracy as a form and method of government whereby revolutionary changes in the economic and social life of the people are brought about without bloodshed.[26]

For Ambedkar, democracy was not merely a form of government

but a form of social organization and a mode of associated life.[27] He regarded a favourable social setting as a pre-requisite for the success of democracy: without this democracy would not last long. The formal framework of democracy was of no value in itself and would not be appropriate if there was no social democracy. To him social democracy involved two things: an attitude of mind, that is, an attitude of respect and equality towards one's fellows and social organization free from rigid social barriers. The roots of democracy were to be found in social relationship, in terms of the associated life between the people who formed the society. Thus, he considered caste distinctions as a positive danger to democracy.[28] However, while visualizing high political objectives, he said that democracy must be in harmony with social aims. He regarded democracy as both a social way of life and political method.

Ambedkar thought that democracy rested on four premises. The first is that the individual is an end in himself; the second that an individual has certain inalienable rights which must be guaranteed to him by the constitution. The third is that the individual shall not be required to relinquish any of his constitutional rights as a condition precedent to the receipt of privileges; finally, the state shall not delegate power to private persons to govern others.

In this way, we can see that the keynote of Ambedkar's concept of democracy as a way of life, was the necessity for the participation of every human being in the formation of the social, economic and political values that regulated men's lives and bound them together. The fundamental elements of his concept of democracy were, in short, liberty, equality, fraternity and natural rights. This framework of Ambedkar was influenced by the values of liberty, equality and fraternity which first came to the foreground in the French Revolution.

Now, a very important question that can be raised here is: can a human being actually realize his rights as visualized by Ambedkar? This modern concept of rights is basically a form of the ideology and a rationalization of capitalist society. Marx postulated that capitalist society has two conflicting tendencies. In the economic sphere, there is a distinction between the sphere of exchange (where all are free to buy and sell and are treated formally as equals) and the sphere of production (controlled by the capitalists). Citizens in a capitalist society are free to buy and sell. Thus, this society of free citizens ignores the distinguishing class differences between capitalist and proletariat. The logic of capitalism requires the definition of man of both subject for skill and power and as object in a juridical sense. Bourgeois legal theory takes over this view of man and gives it a juristic expression in its theory of rights. Since this conception of man is an abstract and formal one, so are his rights. These rights belong to an individual not as a concrete and socially situated human being occupying a specific position in society, but as a socially transcendent abstraction, a mere juristic fiction. Equality in capitalist society is therefore an equality of abstract subjects, not of concrete human beings. As concrete and socially situated beings, men belong to different classes, possess unequal resources and are obviously unequal in their powers, capacities and opportunities. Although in theory they possess equal rights, in practice those rights they exercise or enjoy are necessarily unequal.[29] In his Constituent Assembly speech, Ambedkar said:

> On January 26, 1950 we will have equality in politics and inequality in social and economic life. I urge you to remove this contradiction at the earliest possible moment or else those who suffer from inequality will blow up the structure of political democracy.[30]

Ambedkar went on to give an eloquent account of the economic oppression that normally went on within the framework of political democracy, of how the unemployed were ready to relinquish their political rights out of the compulsion of starvation, in order to get a job and how the employed were powerless. He said:

> Anyone who studies the working of the system of social economy based on private enterprise and pursuit of personal gain will realize how it undermines, if it does not actually violate, the individual rights on which democracy rests. How many have to relinquish their constitutional rights in order to gain their living? How many have to subject themselves to be governed by the private employers?[31]

In order to highlight this contradiction in liberal democracy, he further said:

> Ask those who are unemployed whether what are called fundamental rights are of any value to them? If a person who is unemployed is offered a choice between a job of some sort, with some sort of wages, with no fixed hours of labour and with an interdict on joining a union and the exercise of his right to freedom of speech, association, religion, etc., can there be any doubt as to what his choice will be? How can it be otherwise?[32]

The unemployed are thus forced to relinquish their fundamental rights for the sake of securing the privilege to work and to subsist. Indeed, Ambedkar, with remarkable insight, had seen the theoretical implications of the equality of rights which according to him must be more than a device to veil and legitimize the stark reality of inequality.

Ambedkar's attempt to place individuals in their concrete social and economic situation can be found in his idea of state socialism, which was to be realized through capturing political power. To empower both the Dalit and non-Dalit economically, he proposed that the state should be given political power for the regulation and control of both key industries and agriculture; to this end he proposed that economic powers should be incorporated into the body of the constitution itself. He called this an attempt to establish state socialism without abrogating parliamentary democracy and without leaving its establishment to the will of democracy.[33] To him this was the way to combine political democracy with socialism and avoid dictatorship. While elaborating upon his theme of state socialism he wrote:

> The soul of democracy is the doctrine of one man, one value. Unfortunately, democracy has attempted to give effect to this doctrine only so far as the political structure was concerned. It has left the economic structure to take the shape given to it by those who are in a position to mould it. Time has come to take a bold step and define both the economic structure as well as the political structure by the law of constitution.[34]

Though Ambedkar was to become the chairman of the constitutional drafting committee and though this constitution has since been paraded in his name, the constitution of India did not institute state socialism with parliamentary democracy by adopting the programme he suggested. It was in fact the normal type of liberal constitution, with economic changes (including limited nationalism) remaining at the will of the legislature and the Congress party which controlled it.

Thus Ambedkar's constitutionalism and his failure to make a complete analysis of an exploitative and conflict bound society left this programme in the end as only an abstract ideal without a material foundation. How could Ambedkar expect that a committee chosen by such a parliament and based on a narrow franchise provided under the Act of 1935, controlled by Nehru, Patel, Prasad and Azad would write such a constitution? How was it possible for the exploited Dalit and non-Dalit toiling masses themselves to influence and write this constitution?[35]

It must be noted that Ambedkar himself had realized the limitations of acquiring political power within this liberal constitutional framework, which he saw would fail to combine individualism and socialism. This assumption of Ambedkar's was based on his own experience within parliament and the political subordination of those Dalit Congress MPs that he witnessed during his time in parliament. For example, Ambedkar could not get the Hindu Code Bill passed in its entirety, though it contained legal provisions concerning the liberation of women in general. He had to streamline the Bill, thus making it innocuous as desired by the Congress members who held conservative views towards social reform. On one occasion he said:

> In the parliament there are 30 MPs belonging to the Congress Party. I ask them, have they done anything for our people? They never asked any question, they never moved any resolution and they never submitted a bill in the parliament because their voice is suppressed by the Congress leaders.[36]

Ambedkar attributes this political servitude of the Dalit leaders to the power nexus between different vested interests.[37] However, we certainly find a positive note in Ambedkar's discourse when he gives an alternative to Dalits of all castes, both at the theoretical and practical levels. At the theoretical level, Ambedkar sees the Buddhist *Dhamma* as a philosophical justification for a state in which it would be possible to establish socialism without abrogating individualism. And to redeem this project, Ambedkar visualized the formation of the Republican Party of India. But, unfortunately, many years of experience of the Buddhist Movement, particularly in Maharashtra and the frustrating politics of various Dalit groups in the country makes it imperative on our part to take a more critical view of Buddhism and Dalit politics in India.

NOTES

* Also published in *Dr Ambedkar Birth Centenary Souvenir*, vol. 1, London, 1992.

1. A.M. Rajashekhariah, *B.R. Ambedkar: The Politics of Emancipation*, Bombay, 1971; Eleanor Zelliot, 'Dr Ambedkar and the Mahar Movement', An unpublished Ph.D thesis, submitted to the Department of South East Asian Studies, Pennsylvania University, 1969; Lelah Dushkin, 'SC Politics in India', in *Untouchable Contemporary India*, ed. Michael Mahar, Tuscon, 1973; D.R. Jatav, *Critique of Ambedkar*, Delhi, 1975.

2. B.R. Ambedkar, *Pakistan or Partition of India*, Bombay, 1949, p. 13.
3. Ibid., p. 17.
4. *Thus Spoke Ambedkar*, ed. Bhagwan Das, Jalandhar, vol. I, p. 21.
5. Ambedkar, op. cit., p.1.
6. Ibid., p.17.
7. Ibid., p. 259.
8. Ibid., p. 260.
9. Ibid., p. 334.
10. Ibid., p. 335.
11. Ibid., pp. 185, 324-5.
12. F.H. Bennur, 'Ambedkar and Religion', *Mainstream*, vol. XXVI, no. 26, 23 April 1988, p. 23.
13. Ibid.
14. Ambedkar, *Annihilation of Caste*, Bangalore, 1987, p. 49.
15. Ibid., p. 60.
16. Ibid., p. 61.
17. Ibid.
18. *Constituent Assembly Debates* vol. VII, p. 980.
19. Ambedkar, op. cit., 1949, p. 187.
20. Ibid.
21. Gopal Guru, *Dalit Conversion*, Pune, 1984, p. 42.
22. Bipin Chandra and others, 'The Communist, the Congress and the Anti-Colonial Movements', *Economic and Political Weekly*, 28 April 1984, vol. X, no. 17, p. 73.
23. *Speeches of Dr B.R. Ambedkar* (Marathi), vol. III, ed. Dr F. Gangrare, Nagpur, 1975, p. 112.
24. B.R. Ambedkar, *What Congress and Gandhi have done to the Untouchables*, Bombay, 1945, p. 112.
25. B.R. Ambedkar, *States and Minorities*, Lucknow, 1978, p. 38.
26. Bhagwan Das, op. cit., p. 61.
27. Ibid., p. 61.
28. Ibid., p. 32.
29. Dhananjay Keer, *Dr Ambedkar, Life and Mission*, Bombay, 1954, p. 488.
30. Ibid.
31. Parekh, *Marx and the Theory of Rights*, ed. Upendra Baxi, co-editors Geeti Sen and Jeanette Fernandes, New Delhi, 1987, p. 16.
32. *Constituent Assembly Debates*, vol. XI, p. 979.
33. B.R. Ambedkar, op. cit., 1978, p. 44.
34. Ibid.
35. C.B. Khairmode, *Bhimrao Ramji Ambedkar* (Marathi), vol. 10, Bombay, 1989, p. 179.
36. Ibid., p. 176.
37. B.R. Ambedkar, *What Congress and Gandhi have done to the Untouchables*, p. 215.

6
Dr Ambedkar's Perception of the Indian Society and his Egalitarian Vision

S.K. Gupta

It is intended to study here Dr Ambedkar's critique of the Hindu social order and his counter-hegemonic discourse based on egalitarian ideas. The discussion is divided into three parts. Besides referring to his early life and bitter and unpalatable experiences, the first part discusses the wide variety of influences that moulded his thinking. The second part focuses on his critical appraisal of the Hindu socio-religious system. Through metaphysical and philosophical manipulations, the vested interests had laden the original system with many complexes sanctioning inequalities. Their hegemony was so complete that these complexes got internalized by the depressed classes. The third part discusses the counter-mechanism by which the great egalitarian thinker sought to create a society based on justice, equality, liberty and fraternity.

II

Dr Ambedkar, a versatile genius, was an erudite scholar, an impassioned advocate of the dumb and the downtrodden, and a national leader of great foresight and stature. He strove very hard to transform an apolitical, ostracized and indigent mass into a crucial factor in the political power structure. He was not born with a silver spoon in his mouth. Nor did he appear on the Indian firmament all of a sudden. He had to pass through a rigorous caste-ridden, social set-up, which breathed contempt for the untouchables. It kept them at its lowest rung through subtle strands of inequalitarian thought which had evolved over centuries and acquired a metaphysical, philosophical and religious ring.

Ambedkar's childhood and early youth were full of bitter and unpalatable experiences. None the less, he blossomed because of the care and kindness shown him by some philanthropic personalities such as K.A. Keluskar, S.K. Bole, the Arya Samajist Pandit Atma Ram, Shambaji Waghmare, Naval Bathena, Maharaja Sayajirao of Baroda, and Shahu Maharaj of Kolhapur. They appeared as a 'silver lining' on Bhima's otherwise obscure world. Some of them also provided the wherewithals for his education and training. Impressed by his intelligence, self-determination and dedication, they assisted and encouraged Bhimrao in his efforts and achievements. Thus they paved the way for his rise to higher and higher echelons.

The West too played a significant role in shaping the personality of Ambedkar. It was in America and England that he dived deep into knowledge, both Western and Indian, which added a new dimension to his personality and gave him a new vision. Under the stimulating influence of John Dewey, Charles Beard, Edwin R.A. Seligman, Edwin Cannan and a host of others, he studied ancient and modern history, anthropology, sociology, psychology, economics, and law. Of all the professors, Dewey and Seligman influenced him most. He took down every word that John Dewey uttered and could reproduce his lectures verbatim. Keer says,

> Ambedkar took to Seligman as a duck takes to water and ran after the Professor from class to class with special permission to attend his classes.

Apart from these academics, he was also inspired by the life and mission of Booker T. Washington, the founder of Tuskegee Institute which

> disseminated among the Negroes the doctrine of education of head, heart and hand, and thus broke the shackles of bondage which had crushed the Negroes for ages physically, mentally and spiritually.

Another two figures who left an indelible mark on his life and thought were: one of them was his beloved father, Subedar-Major Maloji Sakpal. He was a teacher in the army. He infused in his son an iron-will to resist worldly temptations, a rare and irresistible zeal for learning, and a keen sense of discipline, industry and social responsibility. His other source of inspiration was Lord Buddha. He learnt about his life and teachings at an impressionable age from a book gifted by Keluskar in 1907. Lord Buddha influenced him so much that Buddhism became the touchstone of his analysis of Hinduism. Besides, it also became Ambedkar's *prajan* (understanding against superstition and supernaturalism), *karuna* (love), and *samanta* (equality). It became the basis of his philosophy of universal love, equality and human brotherhood. Finally, Buddhism gave him all that he could take from Marxism. In short, it was *moksha* to him.

All these influences got well-knit in his personality and became an integral part of his perspective, his consciousness, his plan of action, his scheme of constitutional reforms and egalitarian social reconstruction. However, to visualize their impact in any tangible form, one would have to examine his critique of the Hindu socio-religious system, as also the egalitarian alternative for which he launched a lifelong struggle.

III

Dr Ambedkar's critique of Hinduism was neither socialistic nor sophomoric. It was based on a serious study of the Hindu religious literature. He also drew on his sociological and anthropological knowledge and a comparative perspective of other social orders. Undoubtedly, Ambedkar was also influenced by his bitter personal experiences, and by the pitiable plight of the depressed classes. He, therefore, often wrote with a caustic pen. Yet Ambedkar's analysis of Hindu philosophy was intended 'as a definite approach to the strengthening of the Hindu society on the basis of the human values of equality, liberty and fraternity'.

To Dr Ambedkar, philosophy of religion is a science, not descriptive and normative. It has three dimensions. The first revolves round the definition of religion but many arguments are often directed at cross purposes. Ambedkar regards religion as theology and distinguishes between its mythical, civil, natural and revelational forms; the last two being close to each other. He says: 'A genuine natural theology and a genuine revelational theology might stand in contradiction, may be safely excluded as not being possible.' As traditionally understood, the natural theology propounds three theses: (a) God exists and is the author of what we call nature or universe; (b) God controls all the events which make nature; and (c) God exercises a government over mankind in accordance with his sovereign moral law.

The second dimension of the philosophy of religion relates to the knowledge of the ideal scheme for which a religion stands. It defines the fixed, permanent and dominant part in the religion of any society. To separate the chaff from the grain is always difficult. In the case of religion the difficulty is greater because of the fact that its traditional usages grew only gradually over centuries. They reflected habits of thoughts during man's intellectual and moral development. In other words, religion grew from stage to stage, from the simplest childish prayers to the highest metaphysical abstractions. Quoting Max Mueller, Ambedkar says that

> in the majority of the hymns of Veda we might recognize the childhood; in the Brahmanas and their sacrificial, domestic and moral ordinances the busy manhood; in the Upanishads the old age of the Vedic religion.

As regards the Hindu scheme of divine governance, it is enshrined in the *Manusmriti*, a divine code. It lays down the rules which govern the religious, ritualistic and social life of the Hindus in minute detail and which must be regarded as 'the Bible of the Hindus and containing the philosophy of Hinduism'.

The third dimension of philosophy of religion focuses on the criterion to be adopted for judging the value of the ideal scheme of divine governance, for which a given religion stands. Religion must be put on trial, but by what criterion shall it be judged? The answer required the definition of the norm.

Dr Ambedkar contends that of the three dimensions, the third one is the most difficult one to be ascertained and defined. While evolving his own parameters, he lays emphasis on the study of revolutions which different religions have undergone. These revolutions pertain to the relation between God and man, society and man, and man and man. He divides these revolutions into two categories: external and internal. External revolution denotes the revolt of science against the extra-territorial jurisdiction assumed by religion over a field which did not belong to it. Internal revolution marks a true revolution. It might be compared to any other political revolution such as the French Revolution or the Russian Revolution. It involved a constitutional change and led to an alteration and re-constitution of the scheme of divine governance. Again Ambedkar distinguishes between (i) savage and civilized societies; and (ii) antique and modern societies, and reckons the march from one to the other as two different stages in the internal revolution. He says that in both savage and civilized societies the central interest of relgion was 'in the processes by which individuals are preserved and the race maintained'. However, the two societies differed in two important respects. In the religion of savage society, there is no trace of the idea of God, and morality is independent of religion. Ambedkar links the origin of the idea of God with the worship of the Great Man in society, the Hero—giving rise to theism. The idea of God might also have emerged from purely philosophical speculations about who created life—giving rise to Deism—with its belief in God as the architect of the universe. In any case, the idea of God was not integral to religion. Though it is difficult to say when and how the idea of God got fused into religion, God did become part of the scheme of religion in civilized society. Morality too became sanctified by religion. The second stage of the revolution was marked by a radical change. Instead of society, the individual became the end. Instead of utility, justice became the criterion for judging right or wrong. It was a revolution at the level of norms.

Dr Ambedkar, however, applied both the test of justice and the test of utility to judge the philosophy of Hinduism. He regarded the principle of justice as a compendious which included most of the principles of what has become the foundation of a moral order. Justice has always evoked ideas of equality, of proportion, of 'compensation'. Equity signifies equality. If all men are equal, then they are of the same essence and their common essence entitles them to the same fundamental rights and equal liberty. In a nutshell, justice is simply another name for liberty, equality and fraternity as far as Ambedkar was concerned Lamently, he finds Hinduism wanting in these tenets since the Hindu social organization is based on caste system. Varna is the parent of caste and both uphold the principle of gradation and rank, in other words inequality. He says that this inequality in status' is not merely the inequality that one sees in the warrant of precedence prescribed for a ceremonial gathering at a King's court. It is a permanent social relationship among the classes to be observed—to be enforced—at all times and in all places. In order to further elaborate the absence of equality and liberty in the Hindu social system, he refers to the rules evolved with regard to slavery, marriage, rule of law, occupation and education. Quoting Manu and Narada, he says slavery was recognized by Hinduism. Manu confined it to Shudras. As the practice differed from the law of Manu, a new rule was enacted by Narada which obtained that slavery would not be recognized by Hinduism. The same kind of asymmetry would underlie intermarriages, if at all such marriages were to take place. Rule of Law also did not mean equality before law; its guiding principle was discrimination based on varna. Inequality was writ large in the Hindu criminal jurisprudence. Punishment has to be in proportion to the gravity of the offence; instead Manu's penal code was based on inequality of punishment; the higher the caste, the less rigorous the punishment. In other words, social and religious inequality was embedded in the philosophy of Hinduism. It upheld privileges and caste-based immunities. All this, coupled with lack of economic independence and denial of access to knowledge, created an environment where liberty was conspicuous by its absence. Whatever liberty did exist, its praxis domain did not go beyond the contours well demarcated for each ascriptive group. Elaborating the case of Shudras vis-a-vis the savarnas, Ambedkar says that the rules not only put an interdict on the economic independence of a Shudra but also enjoined that he must serve others. Caste system was not a division of labour only but also a division of labourers. Manu's law of wages is

> not the minimum wage law. It is the maximum wage law. It was also an iron law fixed so low that there was no fear of Shudra accumulating wealth and obtaining economic security.

The position with regard to access to education was still worse. Ambedkar contends that the ancient world might have been guilty of refusing to shoulder the responsibility for the education of the masses. But never has any society been guilty of closing to generality of its people, the study of the books of its religion. Never has any society been guilty of prohibiting the mass of its people from acquiring knowledge. Never has any society declared that any attempt made by the common man to acquire knowledge would be punishable as a crime. As such education came to be primarily restricted to the Brahmins who, being inalienably vested with the authority of learning, teaching and interpreting the shastras, became the repository of knowledge. No wonder many distortions crept into Hinduism. Even other dvija castes were marginalized in the field of education. In their case, education was mainly domestic; it was practical. It only increased the skill to do a particular thing.

> It did not lead to new perception. It did not widen horizon, with the result that the practical education taught him only an isolated and uniform way of

acting so that in changing environment the skill turned out to be gross ineptitude. Illiteracy became an integral part of Hinduism by a process which is indirect but integral to Hinduism.

Fraternity, which is another name for fellow-feeling, was also chained within the caste contours and religiously ordained rules regarding the performance of religious rites and ceremonies. Ambedkar points out that religion as a basis of rules of precedence

manifests itself in three ways. Firstly, through religious ceremonies, secondly, through incantations that accompany the religious ceremonies and thirdly, through the position of the priest.

Some castes are allowed to perform certain ceremonies, whereas others are prohibited, e.g. upanayana, wearing of the sacred thread, can be performed only by the people belonging to upper three varnas. Precedence flows from this distinction: a caste which can perform all the ceremonies is higher in status than the caste which has a right to perform only a few. Turning to mantras, it is another source for rules of precedence. According to Hindu religion, the same ceremony can be performed in two different ways: (i) Vedokta and (ii) Puranokta. A caste which is entitled to use Vedokta form is superior to that entitled to use only Puranokta form.

Not only this, Hinduism requires the instrumentality of a priest for the derivation of full benefits from the performance of a religious ceremony. The priest appointed by the scriptures is a Brahmin. A Brahmin, therefore, is indispensable. But the scriptures do not require that a Brahmin shall accept the invitation of any and every Hindu irrespective of his caste to officiate at a religious ceremony. By long and well established custom it is now settled at the invitation of which caste he will officiate and at which caste he will not. This fact has become the basis of precedence between castes.

Another source for rules of precedence is commensality, viz., intermixing, inter-dining, inter-marriage. The rules in the case of intermarriages are quite strict, whereas in the case of food these are somewhat relaxed but none the less rooted in the rules of precedence. One might take 'kachcha' food from a caste above but should not accept such food from those below. Ambedkar regarded endogamy as the essence of the caste system. As already mentioned, rules regarding inter-marriages were required to be observed strictly. Purity and pollution syndrome that governed the Hindu system has added a very oppressive dimension to the whole philosophy of Hinduism.

The mass of the people called untouchables, unapproachables, unshadowables or even unseeables are the bane of this syndrome.

To sum up, it may be said that Ambedkar's appraisal of Hindu social order highlighted its inequalitarian strands and nodal points from which these originated. He belonged to the reformist school of thought and drew significantly from the nineteenth-century academics and thinkers. The prominent of these have already been mentioned. Others included: Robertson Smith, Max Mueller, Herbert Spencer, J.S. Mill, Burke, etc. If at all, there was any filament which vibrated in him the revivalist thought, it were the Buddhist tenets. These emphasized the law of causality and rational thinking, challenged the Vedic dogma of divine creation of social order, and past karma theory. He might have also been influenced by some protest and dissent movements of the medieval period but this is not certain. However, his family belonged to the Kabir cult, and Maharashtra was a land blessed by saints like Chakaradhar, Ramananda, Kabir, Chaitanay, Eknath, Tukaram, Raidas and Chokhamela. Of course, as regards the nineteenth-century Indian reformists, he is indebted to M.G. Ranade and Jotiba Phule.

Dr Ambedkar had a very sharp and analytical mind and made the best use of the sources he read during the course of his academic pursuits in India and abroad. He was a voracious reader and regarded books as his best companions. The knowledge which he acquired, he utilized for the amelioration, upliftment and service of the downtrodden. Moreover, he had the courage of conviction and a sense of purpose which never faltered even under insurmountable difficulties and strong pressures. Nothing could tempt him; nothing could make him compromise or betray the cause of his fellow brethren. He revelled in their service and made it a mission of his life.

Dr Ambedkar questioned each and every kind of theorization which denigrated or ostracized the depressed classes, or heaped contempt or humiliation on them. He also endeavoured to discover alternative theories from within the vaults of his rich and vast knowledge and the realm of his analytical acumen. *Who were the Shudras?*; *Untouchables*; *Caste in India*; *Annihilation of Caste*; and his unpublished writings, now printed by the Maharashtra government such as *Riddles in Hinduism*; *Revolution and Counter-Revolution in Ancient India*; *Buddha or Karl Marx*; *Untouchables or the Children of India's Ghetto and other Essays on Untouchables and Untouchability*, etc. —all were written to subserve the same end. His theoretical exercises were, in fact, exercises in the domain of praxis.

IV

Dr Ambedkar did not write any separate treatise on egalitarianism. Nor was he a theoretician or a philosopher in the formal/conventional sense of the term. His egalitarian ideas are not systematically enumerated in any of his works. These are spread out as 'jewels of thought' in his various writings and speeches; the best of them can be gathered from works which focus on the genesis and mechanism of the exploitation of the depressed classes. Some of these (see section II) works are of the nature of critique of the Hindu social order, whereas others centre around purely economic problems and the constitutional machinery he sought to create to usher in an egalitarian set-up. The latter category also includes his memoranda, which he submitted to the British government, and his speeches in the Constituent Assembly. Even during the course ,of his academic pursuits, his writings and ideas reflect his concern for the indigent masses. Unlike many moderates, he was not swayed by the beneficent character of the British Raj. His acute mind could weigh dispassionately the consequences of the British colonial intervention. In his work: *Administration and Finance of the East India Company*, regarded to be the balance sheet of British India, Ambedkar stated:

> Apparently the immenseness of India's contribution to England is as much astounding as the nothingness of England's contribution to India. Both are, however, true statements if looked at from economic point of view. ... England has added nothing to the stock of gold and silver in India: on the contrary, she has depleted India—'the sink of the world'. England's contribution lay in the uneconomic realm. The British had conferred on the people of India what was the greatest human blessing—peace. They introduced Western education and brought India in touch with modern institutions and life. Ambedkar posed a big question: 'Whether mere animal peace is to be preferred to economic destitution, let everyone decide for himself.'

He knew well that the destitution of the country would affect most the 'destitutes', the depressed classes.

Dr Ambedkar's concept of equality was neither rooted in Fabian, nor Marxist nor Commintern, nor Socialist, nor Gandhian ideological moorings or shibboleths. It hinged on those remedial measures which he thought were *sine qua non* for social reconstruction and vitalization of the Hindu society as also for the upliftment of the untouchables. As such Ambedkar's idea of equality has a conception and stamp of its own making, though the slogan of equality, liberty and fraternity resounds vocally in every strand of his equalitarian thought. He, in fact, drew copiously from different sources such as the French Revolution, Declaration of Rights of Man, Fourteenth Amendment of American Constitution, Government of Ireland Act, 1920, U.S. Civil Rights Protection Acts of 1866 and 1875, Marxist and Buddhist egalitarian thought. However, he did not subscribe to any particular ideology.

Dr Ambedkar did not approve wholly of the philosophy of Marx. In his work *Buddha or Karl Marx,* he rejected the Marxian philosophy as deficient. He says that society had been aiming to lay a new foundation based on fraternity, equality and liberty. The French Revolution was welcomed because of this slogan. It, however, failed to produce equality. The people welcomed the Russian Revolution because it aimed to produce equality.

> But it cannot be too much emphasized that in producing equality, society cannot afford to sacrifice fraternity or liberty. Equality will be of no value without fraternity or liberty. It seems that the three can co-exist only if one follows the way of Buddha. Communism can give one but not all.

Violence and dictatorship of the proletariat are the only two means outlined by Commintern to establish Communism and both violate the principles of liberty and fraternity. Man cannot live by bread alone. He must grow materially as well as spiritually. Ambedkar advocated state socialism tempered by a democratic base and also state ownership of land and other means of production. But he said that in

> an ideal society there should be many interests consciously communicated and shared. There should be varied and free points of contact with other modes of association. In other words, there must be social end-osmosis. This is fraternity which is only another name for democracy. Democracy is not merely form of government. It is primarily a mode of associated living, of conjoint communicated experience.

Dr Ambedkar was also critical of the Socialists. In his address prepared for the *Jat-pat Todak Mandal,* Lahore, he stated that the Socialists of India following their fellow brethren in Europe were applying the economic interpretation of history to the facts of India.

But could the Socialists ignore the problem arising out of the social order? He maintained that exploitation and inequality in India were not only due to economic exploitation but also due to social exploitation and degradation. Therefore to preach that 'political social reforms are but gigantic illusions and that economic reform by equalization of property must have precedence over any other kind of reform would be putting the cart before the horse'. If the Socialists wished

> to make socialism a definite reality then they must recognize that the problem of social reform is fundamental and that for them there is no escape from it. That, the social order prevalent in India is a matter which a Socialist must deal with, that unless he does so he cannot achieve his revolution and that if he does achieve it as a result of good fortune he will have to grapple with it if he wishes to realize his ideal, is a proposition which in my opinion is incontrovertible.

Gandhi and Ambedkar were close to each other in their concern for the *daridranarayana*, the destitute, but differed in their perception and solution of the problem. The former regarded varnashrama of the Veda as based on absolute equality of status. 'Arrogation of a superior status by and of the varna over another is a denial of the law. There is nothing in the law of varna to warrant a belief in untouchability.' He further pointed out that varna and asharam were institutions which had nothing to do with castes. The law of varna only taught that everyone had to earn his bread by following the ancestral calling. Most probably following the lines of Ruskin, Gandhi emphasized that there was no calling so low and none too high. All were good, lawful and absolutely equal. So caste and untouchability must go but not the varna system. Many, however, regarded Gandhi's philosophical differences between caste and varna as too subtle to be grasped by people becuase over the years for all practical purposes the function of both of them was one and the same. Ambedkar too challenged the stand of Gandhi and called him a hypocrite and conservative. He stated that varna was the parent of caste. Moreover, to a social revolutionary like Ambedkar, social change through exegesis could hardly appeal. Gandhi wanted to bring about social reconstruction in the Hindu society through his theory of change of heart, i.e. on the lines of least resistance and least social discord. He did not believe in coercion nor in legislation to usher in a new equalitarian social set-up. Ambedkar believed in the efficacy of legislation and struggled to evolve a constitutional mechanism for protecting the fundamental rights of the depressed classes as also their economic and political interests. This would be sufficiently evident from the various memoranda he submitted to the government from time to time as also from the book, *States and Minorities*, which itself is a memorandum submitted to the Constituent Assembly on behalf of the All-India Scheduled Castes Federation. While highlighting certain developments in the post independent India, Eleanor Zelliot stated in this context that the Constituent Assembly of independent India 'passed a provision legally abolishing untouchability on 29 November 1949, about ten months after the death of Mahatma Gandhi'. As the measure was approved, the house resounded with cries of "Mahatma Gandhi ki jai"—victory to Mahatma Gandhi—a tribute to Gandhi's thirty-years effort to remove the practice of untouchability from the Indian scene.' However, the irony is that a 'legalistic measure was taken in the name of Gandhi who had no use for legalism', whereas Ambedkar fought Gandhi to secure legalistic solutions to resolve the varied problems of the depressed classes. Irrespective of the merit of Dr Ambedkar's criticism of Gandhi, constitutional and legalistic, Ambedkarite solutions did have their fall out.

REFERENCES

Dr Babasaheb Ambedkar: Writings and Speeches, 15 vols., Bombay, d.d.

D.C. Ahir, *Buddhism and Ambedkar*, New Delhi, 1968.

Marc Galanter, *Competing Equalities: Law and the Backward Classes in India*, New Delhi, 1991.

V.R. Krishna Iyer, *Dr Ambedkar and the Dalit Future*, Delhi, 1990.

———, *Social Justice and the Undone Vast*, Delhi, 1991.

Dhananjay Keer, *Dr Ambedkar: Life and Mission*, Bombay, 1962.

A.S. Lokhande, *Bhimrao Ramji Ambedkar*, Delhi, 1982.

7
Undoing the Bondage: Dr Ambedkar's Theory of Dalit Liberation

Gail Omvedt

'Ambedkarism' is today a living force in India. It defines the ideology of the Dalit movement and, to a large extent, an even broader anti-caste movement. Yet, just as 'Marxism' as a trend in the working class movement has to be distinguished from the actual theorizing of Karl Marx similarly, the urge to abolish the social and economic exploitation involved in caste and capitalism must be distinguished from the complex grappling of an individual activist-theoretician with the interpretation of Indian reality.

In many ways, Ambedkar's thought was not always consistent and it did not (and the same of course can be said for Marx) fully resolve the problems he grappled with. But some themes stand out: First, an uncompromising dedication to the needs of his people, the Dalits (as he said once in response to a legislative council claim that he should think as 'part of a whole'—'I am not a part of a whole; I am a part apart') which required the total annihilation of the caste system and the Brahmanic superiority it embodied. Second, an almost equally strong dedication to the reality of India—but an India whose historical-cultural interpretation he sought to wrest from the imposition of a 'Hindu' identity to understand it in its massive, popular reality. Third, a conviction that the eradication of caste required a repudiation of 'Hinduism' as a religion, and adoption of an alternative religion, which he found in Buddhism, a choice which he saw as not only necessary for the mass of Dalits who followed him but for the masses in India generally. Fourth, a broad economic radicalism interpreted as 'socialism' ('state socialism' in some versions;

'democratic socialism' in others) mixed with and growing out of his democratic liberalism and liberal dedication to individual rights. Fifth, a fierce rationalism which burned through his attack on Hindu superstitions to interpret even Buddhism. And finally, a political orientation which linked a firmly autonomous Dalit movement with a constantly attempted alliance of the socially and economically exploited (Dalits and Shudras, 'workers' and 'peasants' in class terms), projected as an alternative political front to the Congress party he saw as the unique platform of 'Brahmanism' and 'capitalism'.

However, Ambedkar, like Marx, did not spend the major part of his active life in research and writing, with political activism as a sideline. Rather, the demands of leadership absorbed the major part of his time. Almost all of his writings came in the 1940s and 1950s, when he was spending most of his time in Delhi, as Labour Minister and the general political spokesman for the untouchables. During the 1930s he not only adopted but sought to give a political embodiment to a general left ideology combined with the theme of caste annihilation. Yet the decade came to an end with the failure of a left alternative to the bourgeois-Brahman Congress, and the 1940s were very different. An era of Congress hegemony was firmly established in the national movement at the same time as the traumatic transition to independence in a period of global upheavals overshadowed everything else. The particular characteristics of this latter epoch have to be understood as a background to Ambedkar's strategy and analysis.

II

A word about the context of strategy and theory. The 1940s were a period of brutal confrontation with the most reactionary social power known in the world up to that time, fascism. And they ended with the unleashing of atomic energies in the burning of two Japanese cities, forecasting the technological furies that would overshadow human development for decades. For many throughout the world, the peace that followed was a period of hope, with the emergence of newly liberated nations throughout Asia and Africa, and the achievement of socialism by many people of the world. That Stalin represented not only 'socialist' development but a brutal tyranny; that socialism came to vast areas not by working class revolt but with the march of the Red Army; that traditional (and sometimes new) elites remained firmly in control of independent Third World nations, all were debatable points that bothered very few in countries like India at the time. The final phases of the independence struggle represented for many an upsurge of hope and a direction towards a popular, socialistic independence.

Yet within India itself the period held a great deal of internal malaise. Several major characteristics defined it, and represented the context in which Ambedkar sought to win some share in liberation for the untouchable masses of India.

1. The hegemony of Marxism on the left: In India as in most of the world the liberation of exploited and oppressed groups was to be seen as being realized through socialism, defined in terms of collective ownership of the means of production and working class share in power as exercised through a party acting in its name. Yet this hegemony contrasted with an extreme immaturity and weakness of the communist movement in India, which could not exert any decisive influence on events. As in most other Third World countries, therefore, the hegemony of 'Marxism' evoked a situation in which 'collective ownership' was defined in terms of state ownership; the dominant nationalist party replaced the working class party with claims to represent the oppressed masses; and 'socialism' came to mean public control and planning of an industrialization conceived on the model of western capitalism.

2. Hindu-Muslism communalism was the overriding political reality by the 1940s. The constitution of the 'Muslim Community' and the 'Hindu Community' as dominant social realities was correlated with the explicit or implict acceptance of 'Hinduism' as the central religious cultural identity of India. The ideological approach of the Congress progressiveness was either to argue with Gandhi, for a reformed Hinduism in which the two communities lived in harmony, (i.e. interpreting the 'nation' as a federation of religious communities) or, with Nehru, for a secularism that exalted modernity and defined the 'nation', along with 'class', as transcending what were really feudal and backward, religious and cultural identities. The communists essentially followed the Nehru line, with an even stronger emphasis on class. Both accepted scope for Hindu nationalism because they did not confront the very basis of the 'Hindu' and 'Muslim' identities, of course, thereby eclipsing issues of caste and linguistic/tribal nationalities.

3. The events of independence and partition brought a near-

complete marginalization of Gandhi and Gandhism. With all the rhetoric of 'panchayat raj' and khadi, it was 'Nehruism' that gained hegemony ideologically. This approach advocated a broad Third World alliance and made 'socialism' and a heavy-industry oriented development—dominated by planning and controlled by the public sector—the themes of power. But with all its reasonableness and 'secular' focus in contrast to Gandhi's 'peasant backwardness', Nehruism, whose main tendency was to override, or at best to ignore, issues of caste and local identities, allowed even more for Brahman dominance. To a large degree, even while representation in the political sphere broadened, the 'public sector' was to be a high-caste preserve.

Contextually, the Dalit movement under Ambedkar's leadership could only be a passive observer of most major events, at best exerting its minor influence to achieve some gains and concessions. The failure of Marxism in India to open itself to fertilization of theory and practice by the anti-caste movements and failure of Gandhism to go beyond a spiritualistic and Hinduistic interpretation of a decentralized and village-based development, left the anti-caste movement in a vacuum. By the 1940s, it could effectively operate only as a pressure group.

III

In his 1938 speech to the peasants marching to Bombay, Ambedkar is reported to have siad that he felt the 'communist philosophy' to be 'closer than any other' (though significantly qualifying this 'in regard to the class struggle of toilers'). It is undeniable that his 'class-caste' paradigm was basically formed during the 1930s in the course of his confrontation with Marxism, as it was presented to him in India. This exerted an important and continuing influence not only over his economic theory but also over his interpretation of caste in society.

We have noted that during the 1920s Ambedkar had dismissed communism by saying that he agreed with the 'ends' of socialism but disagreed with the 'means' of violence. This theme was resurrected towards the end of his life as a major point of defense of Buddhism against Marxism. During the radical years of the 1930s, however, there was no such rejection of Marxism on the grounds of violence. The thrust of Ambedkar's attack was against the religiously inspired 'non-violence' of Gandhism. In fact the main point of his critique of violence was always that communist-led strikes and actions were often 'adventurous', and they needlessly harmed the weakest sections of the working class (Dalits) and sacrificed people's lives in campaigns that tried to be militant. In other words, it upheld non-violence more as a strategy than as a principle, and it specially rejected Gandhian non-violence as a religious principle. The critique as such, then, is not a major point separating Ambedkar from 'the communist philosophy', though when it was linked to the denial of the leading role of the proletariat it did become so.

In fact, aside from adding 'caste' to 'class' and 'Brahmanism' to 'capitalism' there were surprising similarities between the basic assumptions of Ambedkar and the leftists. In a situation in which communists and socialists alike took no official note of caste in the pre-independence period and simply assumed that radicalism required an explanation of all social problems in terms of their class content, Ambedkar of course strongly insisted on the addition of caste and Brahmanism as crucial social realities. Yet in doing so; he like most of his later followers, accepted some crucial assumptions of the class framework.

A serious critical article on Marxism appeared in a 1936 issue of *Janata* and was reprinted in 1938 as a front page article entitled 'The Illusion of the Communists and the Duty of the Untouchable Class'. In taking the relations of production as the basis of the 'economic interpretation of history', the article made a clever twist or reversal in the often used architectural analogy of 'base and superstructure':

> But the base is not the building. On the basis of the economic relations a building is erected of religious, social and political institutions. This building has just as much truth (reality) as the base. If we want to change the base, then first the building that has been constructed on it has to be knocked down. In the same way, if we want to change the economic relations of society, then first the existing social, political and other institutions will have to be destroyed.[1]

The article went on to make other important reversals. To build the strength of the working class, the mental hold of religious slavery would have to be destroyed; the precondition of a united working class struggle was the eradication of caste and untouchability. Similiarly, destruction of casteism could be taken as the main task of the democratic stage of a two-stage revolution: it would not be fully anti-capitalist because capitalism would not be opposed to the eradication of caste as such (freeing potential workers from caste restrictions would increase the reserve army of labour) and, at the same time, socialists should welcome the effort at uniting the working class. (Thus there was some unity of interests between workers and the radical bourgeoisie in the 'democratic' stage.) The removal of untouchability and caste discrimination is thus the first stage in the struggle for the Indian revolution, and it is impossible for socialists to bypass it. However, expressing great disillusionment with the Congress socialists and Nehru, the article concluded that untouchables, would have to pool all their strength into the fight against untouchability, without expecting much socialist help.

The positions taken here represented a reaction to and a sharing of the assumptions of a mechanical, economistic form of Marxism. Only class exploitation was seen as having a material base and as being part of the relations or production; caste and all other 'non-class' types of oppression (women's oppression, national oppression, etc.) were seen as primarily socio-religious, in the realm of consciousness and not material life. Ambedkar accepted this framework and simply reversed it to assert the causal importance of social-religious-political factors; he took a mechanical architectural analogy and turned it around to give primacy to the 'superstructure'. The logic of the process exemplifies the way in which a mechanical materialism fosters idealism. If caste oppression/exploitation was central (and Ambedkar and all Dalits and low caste activists could not but help understanding it as central) then the basic logic led them to argue that social-religious factors and factors of 'consciousness', were important and even primary. In other words, there was no theoretical trend that sought to analyze a material base for caste as Phule had done at a primary level half a century before.

Thus we can see clearly in the argument the results of the often heard cliche that an anti-caste struggle is a part of the democratic revolution, not of socialist revolution. For communists this could not mean (at some basic emotional level) that the issue was of secondary importance. Ambedkar of course saw it differently. In effect he was motivated to say: all right, if this is 'only' the democratic revolution, this is what *we* have to be concerned about here and now; you far-sighted revolutionary leaders go ahead and worry about the socialist revolution, we have to go on with the immediate task (which you are not helping with in any case); it's all the more urgent to concentrate on this since no one else is around to do it. We will fight for the democratic revolution. This logic was what undoubtedly moved Ambedkar, to put his efforts during the 1940s into building the Scheduled Caste Federation as a strong pressure group within a democratic framework, with an indefinite postponement of a broad revolutionary struggle.

Ambedkar's acceptance of many of the basic assumptions of a mechanical Marxism remained throughout his life and can be seen in his final writings on Buddha and Marx. Its most important aspect is the identification of economic exploitation with private property. Ambedkar's note took it as established that a great many errors in Marx's original analysis (including the concept of the inevitability of socialism, the vanguardship of the working class) made it invalid, but concluded,

> What remains of Karl Marx is a residue of fire, small but very important. ...
> (i) the function of philosophy is to reconstruct the world and not to waste its time in explaining the origins of the world,
> (ii) there is a conflict of interest between class and class,
> (iii) private ownership of property brings power to one class and sorrow to another through exploitation,
> (iv) it is necessary for the good of society that the sorrow be removed by the abolition of private property.[2]

Ambedkar went on in this article to argue that Buddhism, in the Sangha, abolished private property more thoroughly and without bloodshed and was therefore superior to Marxism, but that is besides the point. The point here is that he accepted the definition of class and exploitation as being a result of private property. This was the common theme of the Marxism of his time. It led to defining 'socialism' in terms of 'nationalism' in which collective ownership of the means of production (or the abolition of private property) could be achieved through state control; and it continued to accept the idea that modern factory production, i.e. industrialization constituted the economic basis of socialism. Thus, Ambedkar could term his own version of socialism as 'state socialism' and call for 'nationalization of land', or public control of the 'commanding heights' of the economy. Just as the Nehru socialists did without much concern for the structures of domination and exploitation embodied in state-owned properties.

Taking standard left economic assumptions for granted had two consequences for Ambedkar and the Dalit movement. First, it led to attempts to formulate a historical theory of caste and social struggle in India. One that functioned primarily at the superstructural level, stressing factors of political conflict and ideology apart from those of economic development. Second, it effectively suppressed any dialogue with alternative economic models and ignored the degree to which a state-controlled heavy industry would be effectively a Brahman and high caste-controlled economy.

But was there any real alternative before Ambedkar at the time? His state socialism was, after all, part of a very broad consensus that saw development in terms of industrialization and nationhood in terms of a centralized, strong, unitary state. Liberal capitalists shared this as much as socialists, and though they disagreed about whether private or state control would be most effective, all developmental economists by the late 1940s and early 1950s accepted some major role for the state. Today this developmental model has come into question at many levels, from the environmental movement with its rejection of Nehru's big dams as 'modern temples' to the farmers' movement and women's movement, all putting forward calls for some kind of alternative development. But in Ambedkar's time decentralized socialism did not appear as a politically viable alternative. In India, a decentralized, village-based form of development was connected with the Gandhian tradition. However, to Ambedkar and militant Dalits or non-Brahmans this did not simply promote a village society and development along the lines of Indian tradition, it promoted *Rama-raj*. The belief in *chaturvarnya*, the moralistic acceptance of *brahmacharya* and a claimed principled belief in non-violence were not acceptable to Ambedkar. Nor could they meet the needs of low castes aspiring for liberation. The fact that no other tradition of an alternative decentralized socialism existed in India helped to push Ambedkar towards a bureaucratized state socialism, with all the dilemmas of Brahmanic statism that this involved.

III

Ambedkar's writings on economic issues bear the mark of a generally neo-classic economic theory, and show both his general identification with the working classes and a harsh critique of imperialism. 'The Problem of the Rupee', though dealing with the general history of the state and currency in British India, was published in 1923 in the very specific context of a struggle between nationalists and the British government over the exchange rate. Following the war, the government had maintained a high official exchange rate of 2 shillings (2s.) to the rupee, which was opposed fiercely by Indian businessmen with the backing of the Congress. They attacked it as overvalued, an 'enormous wrong and legalized plunder of Indian resources' which aided the British bureaucracy (whose salaries and pensions became more valuable in terms of the sterling) and British exporters to India at the expense of Indian producers and exporters. They agitated for a low exchange rate of 1s.4d. The government appointed a royal commission; Ambedkar testified before it, broadly supporting devaluation but at a compromise ratio (1s.6d.) which he argued would maintain the interests of the 'business classes' as well as the 'earning classes' who would suffer from the price rise brought about by devaluation.[3]

The book itself was a scathingly critical analysis of British currency policy over the years. Read in the context of current debates on economic policy,[4] it shows Ambedkar as a moderate supporter of devaluation and an economist who assumed that within an open economy India could well compete at the global level (he notes that Indian exports and manufactures gained at the expense of the British during the period of the low rupee).[5] Yet there are qualifications: the concern for balancing capitalist and labour interests, the argument that Indian growth and exports were actually at the cost of falling real wages of the working class, and a tone of hostility both to businessmen and commodity-producing peasants. His conclusion perhaps gives his perspective: with a high ratio, 'the burden ... imposed upon the active and working element of a society would be intolerable' but a too-low ratio would put the burden on wage earners.

> I myself would choose 1s.6d. as the ratio at which we should stabilize ... (1) it will conserve the position of the investing and earning classes; (2) it does not jeopardize our trade and prosperity by putting any extra burden on the business class; and (3) being the most recent in point of time it is likely to give greater justice to the greater number of monetary contracts most of which must be recent in time.[6]

And in fact it was the 1s.6d. ratio which the British government accepted.

The Evolution of Provincial Finance in British India, published in 1925, also condemns British imperialism in its description of the way in which British fiscal politics had impoverished India. Ambedkar attacked the irrationality of British taxation methods, charging that 'while the land tax prevented the prosperity of agricultural industry, the custom taxes hampered the manufactures of the country. There were internal customs and external customs, and both were equally injurious to trade and industry'[7] and that basic taxes like the salt tax and the form of the land tax itself lay most heavily on the poor. It was clear, he noted, that the British government was running Indian trade in the interest of British manufacturers.

Both this critique and the discussion in *The Problem of the Rupee* were well within the framework of standard economics: that is, Ambedkar did not see the 'development' of a backward ex-colony as a problem, once the artificial barriers imposed by the colonial state were removed. Many aspects of colonial rule were described as progressive (primarily those having to do with establishing the infrastructure for growth) and the primary barriers to progress were seen as more social than economic. The British government, Ambedkar noted, not only exploited economically but it could not act against social evils:

> It could not sympathize with the living forces, operating in the Indian society, was not charged with its wants, its pains, its cravings and its desires, was inimical to its aspirations, did not advance education, disfavoured swadeshi and snapped at anything that smacked of nationalism ... the Government of India dared not abolish the caste system, prescribe monogamy, alter the laws of succession, legalize intermarriage or venture to tax the tea planters. Progress involves interference with the existing code of social life and interference is likely to cause resistance. ...[8]

Ambedkar went on to aruge that it would be social, more than economic, causes that led to nationalist revolt:

> It is foolish to suppose that people will indefinitely favour a bureaucracy because it has improved their roads, constructed canals on more scientific principles, effected their transportation by rail, carried their letters by penny post, flashed their messages by lightning, improved their currency, regulated their weights and measures, corrected their notions of geography, astronomy and medicine and stopped their internal quarrels. Any people, howsoever patient, will sooner or later demand a government that will be more than mere engine of efficiency.[9]

This period, in other words, sees Ambedkar as a general supporter of a capitalist organization of the economy, assuming its inevitability and capability of providing growth and being amendable to a balancing of interests. In this model, the role of the state was to provide infrastructure and generally handle currency and exchange so as not to discriminate against any of the major business or agricultural classes of the country. Though he referred to Keynes, the period is clearly as much pre-Keynes and pre-'development' as pre-Marx. That capitalist economies could come into major crisis; that specific state-guided development and even state enterprise was necessary to lift Third World countries out of their poverty was not part of economic discourse at this time.

Then came the late 1920s and the 1930s, the depression, the new momentous force for change represented by the Russian Revolution, the upsurge of the working class in India itself and Ambedkar's own theoretical and practical confrontation with Marxism. Not only did socialism, defined in terms of state ownership of the means of production, begin to appear as a viable reality for working class emancipation; it also began to seem to be the best route to development for an economically backward ex-colony. Even standard 'developmental economics' by the post-war period began to assume the necessity of a major role of the state. In the context of all of these developments, Ambedkar became a socialist, but not a socialist who had time to work out his economic theory. There were, in fact, no economic writings after the 1920s.

By the middle of the 1930s, he swung into an economic radicalism that included the main themes of his time: the exploitation of capitalists and landlords, the need for state control. His economic thrust underwent a major change. This could be seen especially in regard to agriculture. His early writings had expressed support for small peasant property as the alternative to landlordism (in fact arguing that in terms of available capital equipment, farms were if anything too large); by the time of the Scheduled Caste Federation election manifestos he was arguing that for enhanced production agriculture had to be mechanised. This meant that large farms would replace small ones, and this could be most effectively done through cooperative or collective farms.[10] The notion of state-guided development, oriented to industrialization, was taking precedence.

The climactic statement of this economic radicalism came in *State and Minorities*, written as a submission to the Constituent Assembly in 1948, and expressed in the form of proposed constitutional clauses. As a statement of a general economic and social programme, this is a somewhat eccentric form. In fact, only two years before Ambedkar had rejected the idea of a Constituent Assembly, in language that made it clear he did not see the constitution as a means for either establishing socialism or liberating the scheduled castes. He had said,

I must state that I am wholly opposed to the proposals of a Constituent Assembly. It is absolutely superfluous ... there are hardly any big and purely constitutional questions about which there can be said to be much dispute among Indians. It is agreed that the future Indian Constitution should be federal. It is also more or less settled what subjects should go to the Centre and what to the Provinces. There is no quarrel over the division of Revenues between the Centre and the Provinces, none on Franchise, and none on the relation of the Judiciary to the Legislative and the Executive... The only function which could be left to a Constituent Assembly is to find a solution of the Communal Problem.[11]

Yet, two years later he was submitting a memorandum that sought to make the constitution a means for the establishment of socialism!

The economic section of *States and Minorities* calls for 'state socialism', including for the nationalization not only of basic industries but also of land and its working in collective farms, with peasants treated as tenants of the state. Arguing in terms of both developmental needs and protection of working class rights, Ambedkar wrote, 'State Socialism is essential for the rapid industrialization of India. Private enterprise cannot do it, and if it did it would produce those inequalities of wealth which private capitalism has produced in Europe.'[12] He described pithily the effects of poverty as making 'Fundamental Rights' meaningless, and talks of capitalist tyranny:

Constitutional Lawyers ... argue that where the State refrains from intervention in private affairs—economic and social—the residue is liberty. What is necessary is to make the residue as large as possible and State intervention as small as possible. ... [But] to whom and for whom is the liberty? Obviously this liberty is liberty to the landlords to increase rents, for capitalists to increase hours of work and reduce rates of wages. It must be so It cannot be otherwise. For in an economic system employing armies of workers, producing goods *en masse* at regular intervals some one must make rules so that workers will work and the wheels of industry run on. If the State does not do so the private employers will. ... In other words, what is called liberty from the control of the State is another name for the dictatorship of the private employer.[13]

Clearly Ambedkar, like all socialists and nationalists of his time, was conceiving 'socialism' as a regimented industrialized economy.

Thus the basic proposals of 'state socialism' called for state ownership and management of 'key' industries and state ownership of 'basic' industries; a monopoly of insurance; and agriculture declared as a state industry, with the state to acquire (with compensation) rights in land, divide the land into farms of 'standard size' and let them out for cultivation to the residents of the village 'as tenants' to cultivate as a collective farm, in accordance with rules and directives issued by government, with the produce to be distributed in shares among the tenants. It was added,

(i) The land shall be let out to villagers without distinction of caste or creed and in such manner that there will be no landlord, no tenant, and no landless labourer;

(ii) It shall be the obligation of the state to finance the cultivation of the collective farm by the supply of water, draft animals, implements, manure, seeds, etc.

The state would then levy charges for land revenue, to pay the compensation charges, and pay for the capital goods supplied.[14] Clause (*iii*) could be interpreted to argue that the state would provide the necessary inputs according to the wishes of the farming community, or simply provide financing for inputs that may be procured locally; but still there seems to be an assumption (as with private 'industrial-chemical agriculture') that inputs for state agriculture would come primarily from outside the village. Here is an assumption, not only that the state is benign but that agricultural production (like industrial production) can very well be managed and directed from above. The fervour to abolish the inequalities of social relations of ownership is clear (though even here, in allowing compensation, Ambedkar is not going as far as left radicals), but neither the problems of economic exploitation involved in state management nor those of the process of production in agriculture have been given any thought.

Following this, a completely separate section on the protection of scheduled castes as minorities describes their oppression by caste Hindus and argues strongly not only for a series of safeguards but also for separate electorates and separate village settlements, which the state is to set up by giving Dalits forest lands or waste lands. In regard to this, Ambedkar argues that the roots of discrimination lie in the village system itself:

So long as the present arrangement continues it is impossible for the Untouchables either to free themselves from the yoke of the Hindus or to get rid of their Untouchability. It is the close knit association of the Untouchables with the Hindus living in the same village which mark them out as Untouchables ... it is the system of the village plus the Ghetto which perpetuates Untouchability and the Untouchables therefore demand that the nexus should be broken and the Untouchables who are as a matter of fact socially separate should be made separate geographically and territorially also and be settled into separate villages exclusively of Untouchables.[15]

While this passage is followed by a description of the dependence of Dalit labourers on caste Hindu peasants for wages, it makes no reference to a solution in terms of giving Dalits a share in the land in the same village (in fact the first paragraph rules this out by describing untouchability as a reality even beyond economic oppression), while the section on the 'nationalization of land' makes no mention of whether the nationalized villages of untouchables are to be separate. It is as if these are two parallel solutions to the problems of Dalits, one economic, one social, lines which never meet.

States and Minorities is in many ways a puzzling, though remarkable book. At one level it shows the heights of radicalism Ambedkar reached in terms of both economic and caste issues, with his calls for 'state socialism' on the one hand and the path of protective measures, separate electorates and separate villages for Dalits on the other. Yet it also shows the disjuncture between these—as if the programme for liberation was itself paralleling the mechanical Marxist posture of 'class' and 'caste' as separate phenomena operating on different levels of social reality.

Not only is there no linkage between the economic section and the scheduled castes-as-minorities section of the book, there is also no linkage to strategy. Ambedkar discussed the fallacies of leaving the construction of socialism to 'the whims of a parliamentary majority', giving this as the justification for the necessity of writing the clauses into the constitution itself. But both in regard to state socialism and to the strong concessions to scheduled castes, was there any possible basis for thinking that the tremendous influence of landlords, capitalists and upper caste Hindus would admit such a constitution?

Ambedkar was after all a political realist. *States and Minorities* was, it must be concluded, not intended as a serious political document outlining a programme but as a manifesto designed to be extreme and provocative, not so much to achieve the implementation of the points it set forth as to draw attention to its author. Its focus was social equality, not a plan for organizing the economic production of a society. Whether or not he thought it was 'superfluous', a constituent assembly was being called; Ambedkar had not been included, though he wanted to be, if only to ensure the continued provision of safeguards for the Dalits. *States and Minorities* was designed to achieve this goal mainly, and secondly to throw some ideas for the future of India before the public. It was a radical, idealistic manifesto armed at some very partial but highly political goals.

In the end, what is striking about Ambedkar's economic radicalism is the extent to which it was interpreted in terms of the rationalistic 'modernism' of his time: it included a belief in the necessity of industrialization, and the guiding role of the state as inherently progressive if it could be shielded from the vagaries of often manipulated political majorities. By the time *States and Minorities* was written, Ambedkar was intensely pessimistic about these 'political majorities'; there was no organizing on general economic issues, and the non-Brahman or Shudra worker-peasant masses seemed ready to identify as 'Hindus' in opposition to the Muslims and sometimes to the Dalits. State protection for Dalits had always been seen as essential, even in his periods of greater faith in the majority; and how in an atmosphere in which India under Nehru appeared set to adopt planning and a 'socialist pattern of society' Ambedkar's main thrust was to look to this stage-guided development as a solution.[16]

On the whole, his socialism had grown out of his interpretation of democracy rather than, as with Marxism a belief in the revolutionary destiny and world-creating powers of the proletariat. Thus, while he shared the belief of both liberals and Marxists of his time in the progressive forces of industrialism, science and 'modernity', he distinguished his views from communism both in terms of the means necessary to achieve them and in terms of stressing democracy over the 'dictatorship of the proletariat'. In a sense, 'state socialism' was aptly named in contrast to 'proletarian socialism'; it retained the belief in the state as a necessary phenomenon in even a socialist society and sought a share in power of workers and Dalits without seeing this as creating any unique kind of state. From an orthodox Marxist point of view, this could justify a rejection of Ambedkar as essentially 'petty bourgeois', identifying the idealism (return to religion) and reformism presumed to be implicit in his theory with a kind of backward 'peasantist' consciousness; this has invariably been the response of even the most favourable left assessments.[17] But this is not a very helpful classification and implies assumptions about the meaning of 'proletarian', 'peasant', etc., which do not stand the test of time very well.

In fact, the development of 'Ambedkarism' in India can be seen as the particular expression of a worldwide 'democratic revolution',[18] indeed perhaps the most consistent one possible in Indian conditions (certainly more consistent than a 'proletarian socialism' which ignored cultural-caste issues and accepted identities such as 'Harijan' and 'Hindu'), one which had grown out of the experiences and situations of the most oppressed sections of the people. 'Democratic revolution' in this sense almost invariably leads towards some kind of socialism, and this in fact was how Ambedkar saw it. As he wrote towards the end of *States and Minorities*:

> The soul of Democracy is the doctrine of one man, one value. Unfortunately, Democracy has attempted to give effect to this doctrine only so far as the political structure is concerned by adopting the rule of one man, one vote. ... It has left the economic structure to take the shape given by those who are in a position to mould it. This has happened because Constitutional Lawyers ... never realized that it was equally essential to prescribe the shape and form of the economic structure of society, if Democracy is to live up to its principle of one man, one value. Time has come to take a bold step and define both the economic structure as well as political structure of society by the Law of the Constitution. ...[19]

Ambedkar's specific recommendations for 'prescribing the economic structure of society' was state ownership of basic industries and collective farms; this would be questioned by many today along with his faith in a centralized, industrial factory-based economy. But that the market by itself cannot guarantee equality, that the state must play a defining and guiding role—or rather that the members of society must act collectively through the state to regulate, limit and at points supersede the market—is a thesis that few (at least in the Third World) would question. This flexible 'socialism', coupled with political democracy and non-violent mass struggle, makes Ambedkar's economics still relevant today.

IV

Reinterpretation of India's culture and history occupied an important place in Ambedkar's scheme of things. The fact is that all through the 1940s, in the face of political-economic tumult and frustrations, Ambedkar focused his intellectual effort not into the economic problems of India's future but into the political questions of its present (such as Pakistan and partition) and into the cultural interpretation of its past. The great questions of identity concerned him, questions that arose immediately on the Dalits' assertion of autonomy from 'Hinduism' and the dominant cultural-national framework of his time. For the rejection of the Hindu nationalism, which was beginning to acquire a cultural hegemony in India, led to the necessity of answering the following questions:

Who were Dalits if they were not 'Hindus'?
What was their place in Indian society and history?
Who were the other caste groups, Shudras and Brahmans in particular?
What were the driving forces of Indian history?
What would be the driving forces to constitute a future Indian society in a democratic and equalitarian fashion?

These were the questions that drove Ambedkar to the reconstruction of India's caste and religious history. He was not doing this in a vacuum, for in his time, besides the incorporative Hinduistic tendency, there were existing answers within the Dalit movement itself, deriving partially from Phule and expressed most vociferously in the 1920s by E.V. Ramasami (Periyar) of Tamil Nadu.

Phule, during the nineteenth century, influenced on the one hand by the European-originated 'Aryan theory of race' and on the other by the theistic doctrines of the 'Rights of Man', had formulated some very strong answers: Dalits, along with the Shudras, were part of an original 'non-Aryan' community conquered by invading Aryans from whom were derived the Brahmans; their unique feature was that they had been the bravest warriors in defence of the subjugated peasant community and so were the ones most discriminated against by the arrogant conquerors. Violence and ideology were the driving forces of history; 'Hinduism' was nothing but the religious deception of Bhats to maintain their hold on the masses; peasants were exploited by Brahmans through the state machinery (consolidation of violence) and religious trickery. A future Indian society would be constructed not from the false 'nationalism' of a Brahmanic elite but from the energy of the Shudra-Atishudra masses, and its construction should begin from the villages (Phule's writings also included important sections on the development of agriculture and what environmentalists today would call 'watershed development').[20] A necessary feature was the replacement of Hindu superstition by a universalistic, equalitarian (including the important stress on women's rights) and rationalistic religion which Phule called the 'sarvajanik satya dharma' or 'true religion of the community'.

By Ambedkar's time, with the impact of socialism and the limitations of the new framework of class-caste, these themes were expressed mainly in the 'adi' ideologies which continued to stress Dalits as original inhabitants and Brahmans as Aryan conquerors, continued to insist on religious reform and a radical rejection of 'Hinduism', but left aside most of the economic element, the overall interweaving of violence/conquest and exploitation—and thus very often came down to general racial themes which either posed caste and class or simply left class issues aside. Ambedkar himself took up some of these themes, rejected others, and wove a new whole in his interpretation of Indian history, directed to a large degree to the association of Dalits with Buddhism.

But Ambedkar was also a man of his time, influenced by the general assumptions of liberalism, socialism and industrialism. In many ways, the assumptions of mechanical materialism handicapped his efforts at giving a historical interpretation of caste. In his early period he had dealt with economic theory only (though in his very rational way) in terms of issues of financial and monetary policy, leaving aside the analysis of exploitation, capital accumulation and changing forms of production. Later, though influenced by economic radicalism and the belief in the necessity of the state for development, the impact of mechanical Marxism meant that economic exploitation was interpreted in a way divorced from the social (caste) structure. For Ambedkar (as for Marx and for Phule) social processes involved contradiction, violence and exploitation; but he saw these almost entirely in terms of political and group conflict, without looking at changing economic structures that underlay or influenced these. This left his interpretation of ancient Indian history incomplete in crucial ways.

Above and beyond this was his overriding rationalism. This was clearly a crucial part of his very identity, ranging from the hopes he placed in industrialism to his insistence on wearing modern dress, with the greatest critique of Gandhi expressed in his condemnation of his backwardness: 'the Gandhian age is a dark age'. Here there were differences with Phule at many levels: where Phule had excoriated Hinduism primarily for its exploitation and oppressiveness (while also seeing it as irrational), Ambedkar attacked it even more strongly for its irrationality and superstition; where Phule (and other low caste reformers of the nineteenth and twentieth centuries, such as Narayana Guru of Kerala) had still felt the need to incorporate a god in his 'religion', Ambedkar could feel comfortable only with a religion that effectively sidelined god and was itself reinterpreted in a rationalized way. Both stressed the need for religion as a code of morality for an equalitarian society; both attacked Hinduism as a systematization of superstition, hierarchy and exploitation, but Ambedkar used, throughout his works, the discourse of 'reason', of rationality, irrationality, whereas Phule was likely to stress benevolence and compassion as the most important moral value.

In their historical interpretations, similarly, Phule was likely to stress the sheer violence and brutality of conquest, while Ambedkar wrote in terms of calculations and conspiracies. In a sense, their historical interpretations themselves worked at different levels: Phule's was more in the nature of a re-mythologizing, building on and creating new symbols important to the Shudra-peasant community and using the Brahmanic myths and historical figures, such as Shivaji from this point of view. Ambedkar, in contrast, was defining himself as a scholar, arguing history, contesting historical interpretations, concerned for the logic and proof of his arguments. In spite of obvious empirical gaps, for instance not dealing with the Indus Valley Civilization, his work remains a more enduring part of historical discourse in India, able to contest the Hindus' nationalist interpretation on the grounds of historical validity as well as ideological morality.

V

With Phule and then Ambedkar's writings on Indian history begins the construction of an 'Indian nation' or 'Indian people' not dominated by elite reinterpretations. One of the most recent influential analysis of nationalism Benedict Anderson's *The Imagined Community*[20] focuses on the degree to which in modern nationalism, the nation as community itself is a constructed phenomenon. In truth, throughout the nineteenth and twentieth centuries the high caste elites of India had been constructing or 'imagining' it as a Hindu community, incorporating some of the language of democracy but most often using a Romantic imagery stressing a community of blood and race. 'Hindus' as a 'people' inhabiting the subcontinent, assaulted by outside forces defined as 'Muslim', British or whatever, dominated their discourse.[21] While the Congress and left secularists wanted to assert another 'unity of India' inclusive of Muslim and other religious traditions, and Gandhians wanted to reinterpret 'Hinduism' to allow for a significant reformism, both accepted the elements of the framework. In particular they took for granted the identification of the majority of people as 'Hindus' and the identification of the ancient Indian tradition as basically a Hindu one. This was expressed in the common framework of both British and nationalist historical writing, which spoke of 'ancient, medieval, and modern' Indian essentially as 'Hindu, Muslim and British' (for the nationalists, then, modern) India.

The Phule/Ambedkar/Periyar tradition represents the effort to construct an alternative identity of the people, based on non-north Indian and low-caste perspectives, critical not only of the oppressiveness of the dominant Hindu caste society but also of its claims to antiquity and to being the major Indian tradition. Much more than the 'Hinduistic' perspective it took its stand from a firm rationalism and equalitarianism; the freedom from the needs of the elite to justify, in part if not *in toto*, the dominant caste framework of pre-capitalist society, allowed a much greater expression of democratic values. Thus the tradition appears—with its concern for abolition of caste, for the equality of women, for the economic welfare of peasants and workers, for a rational and scientific society—as the most consistent expression of its time of a broad democratic revolution. The fact that Ambedkar focused his intellectual energies on the task of developing this tradition rather than, say, on the problems of economic liberation of the Dalits might lead to charges of 'idealism'—were it not for the fact that the failure of any other major social—political force to really confront the underpinnings of Hindu nationalism (today expressed so forcefully in the rise of the Bharatiya Janata Party (BJP) and all its kin) made this an urgent need for Dalits and other oppressed.

Ambedkar's basic perspective begins with a firm rejection of the degenerate 'racial' form which Phule's 'non-Aryan theory' had taken by his time:

> As a matter of fact the Caste system came into being long after the different races of India had co-mingled in blood and culture. To hold that distinctions of Caste are really distinctions of race and to treat different Castes as though they were so many different races is a gross perversion of facts. What racial affinity is there between the Brahman of the Punjab and the Brahman of

Madras? What racial affinity is there between the untouchables of Bengal and the untouchables of Madras? What racial difference is there between the Brahman of the Punjab and the Chamar of the Punjab? ... The Brahman of the Punjab is racially the same stock as the Chamar of the Punjab, and the Brahman of Madras is the same race as the Pariah of Madras. Caste system does not demarcate racial division. Caste system is a social division of people of the same race.[22]

This statement in *The Annihilation of Caste* is as clear as could be made and should stand against all attempts today to use Ambedkar's name as a justification for a racial theory of caste differences.[23] With this, also, though less drastically, Ambedkar's emphasis shifted from Phule's emphasis on conquest, war and violence as factors in history to one in which the main historical development was interpreted in terms of conflict between social systems representing different religious-cultural values, a conflict carried on in terms of both force and violence as well as political manoeuvring and creations of systems of ideological deception.

Ambedkar's extensive writing was published only partially during his lifetime with *The Untouchables* (1948) and *Who were the Shudras?* (1955). Both books were with a fairly limited purpose, with a broader, comprehensive theory being formulated in the background, to be published only as incomplete manuscripts after his death. *Who were the Shudras?* is in part a refutation of a racial interpretation; it argues that the 'Shudras' were originally a section of Aryans in competition with Brahmans and downgraded in the course of intense factional and political struggle; only later (and it is added as almost an afterthought) were masses of non-Aryans absorbed into the now inferior 'Shudra' category. It is in the introduction that Ambedkar identifies himself as a 'non-Brahman scholar'. *The Untouchable* does not even bother to discuss the racial theory; it argues for a late origin of untouchability, after the major structures of the caste system were formed, when conquered tribals or 'Broken Men' were forced to settle in villages; it also, strikingly, associates the untouchables with Buddhism and their strong degradation with the competition of Brahmanism and Buddhism.

These books were tips of an iceberg that embodied a much more comprehensive theory that Ambedkar was working on up to the time of his death, which he outlined as 'Revolution and Counter-Revolution in Indian History'. In this work, the particular interpretations of the social origin of Shudras and the untouchables was put in a much broader, more fundamentally conceived historical context in which the conflict between Buddhism and Brahmanism is represented as a civilization clash in the process of social evolution in India.

Ambedkar's thesis is posed most sharply (though without identifying its proponents by name) to the 'nationalist' school which was in reality a Hindu nationalist school. His argument was essentially that no united ancient 'Hindu India' had ever existed; instead there were 'three Indians' preceding the Muslim period. These were:

(1) 'Brahmanism' describing the Aryan society of the Vedic period and in reality a barbarian phase;
(2) 'Buddhism', with the Magadha-Mauryan empires embodying in a 'Buddhist revolution', the rise of civilization and the assertion of basic forms of human equality;
(3) 'Hinduism', or a 'Hindu counter-revolution' marked with Pushyamitra Sunga's rise to power in north India and associated with Manu, the triumph of caste, and the subordination of women and Shudras.[24]

Ambedkar's phases represent vastly different social systems, with fundamentally different principles of organizing human life; their conflict was both at the level of a clash of values and of armies. As he argues, 'it is clear that the Muslim invasions are not only invasions. ... If Hindu India was invaded by the Muslim invaders, so was Buddhist India invaded by Brahmanic invaders.'[25] There was a racial-ethnic element in all of this in which Ambedkar identifies his heroes to some extent with non-Aryans, for instance arguing that the Mauryan empire was that of the Nagas,[26] but it is underplayed. As he was always concerned to argue, the clash was not a racial one but rather 'social', involving the efforts of a particularly defined social group, the Brahmans, to establish and maintain their superiority.

This is a fundamentally different perspective on ancient India not only from the theorizing of established 'nationalist' historians and political leaders but also from the rather mechanical arguments of leftists, all of which tended to see Indian civilization as a basically 'Hindu' one originating in the Vedic period and proceeding in an unfolding fashion after that. S.A. Dange's crude application of the 'five-stage theory of history' to India beigns with an idealization of Vedic Aryan society as 'primitive communism'; even the southern communist leader E.M.S. Namboodiripad treats caste and the village defined by it as a stable structure inherent in Indian society.[27] In contrast, Ambedkar's theory stresses the contradictions and exploitation inherent in caste and the revolutionary 'breaks' in the formation of the system. It denies, the ancient character of the Hindu religion and it also denied in effect, the inevitability of its hegemony, the irrevocable and essential character of its association with 'India'. In 'Revolution and Counter-Revolution', the victory of 'Hinduism' was not, in contrast to Phule and other 'non-Aryan interpretations', a once-and-for-all result of an Aryan conquest; it came after a period of social developments and group clashes and after an important 'break', even breakthrough into civilization, represented by Buddhism, culminating in the Mauryan empire. In spite of its incompleteness, this approach is methodologically for an ongoing analysis of the development of Indian society. It also strikes a theme radically different from his political writings of the 1940s which accepted a 'Hindu' identity.

In very many ways, the mass conversion to Buddhism in 1956 was the logical result of this historical-social interpretation: it was Ambedkar's effort to put into practice the assertion of a unique identity of Dalits, and to project it as a possibility for all of India. If his cultural interpretation had seemed at odds with his political writings which accepted the reality of the division of India into 'Hindu' and 'Muslim', now with the conversion to Buddhism he attempted to put his contestation of Hinduism on a material or real footing. Buddhism itself was given a 'liberation theology' interpretation, as *dhamma* or social morality and not dharma or religious ethics. Ambedkar's constant comparisons of Buddhism and communism were not simply ways of being 'anti-communist'; the assertion of a socialist content to Buddhism was a kind of insistence of the transformation of existing Buddhism also.

The conversion was the major, massive event of the last stage of Ambedkar's life, overshadowing the transformation of the Scheduled Caste Federation into the Republican Party, overshadowing the alliance of the Samyukta Maharashtra movement as part of a broad left anti-Congress front. These were political and economic thrusts due to which the Dalits were uniting in a broad left movement towards economic emancipation; but the conversion to Buddhism was seen, by Ambedkar and by large number of those who took part, as a social rebirth, a gaining of new identity, a way in which the Dalits were leading, not simply joining a movement for the recreation of India.

An editorial in his weekly announced its change of name to

Prabuddha Bharat and interpreted the process of development of the Dalit movement through the names of its organs; from *Mukanayak* ('Voice of the Silent') to *Bahishkrit Bharat* ('Boycotted India')—both stressing helplessness and suppression—to *Samata* ('Equality') to *Janata* ('The People'), the main journal throughout the 1930s and 1940s, finally to a name that in part identified it with Buddhism but on the other hand simply meant 'Enlightened India'.[28] Conversion was not an individual act; hundreds and thousands of Dalits joined him in massive open grounds at Nagpur, and as the conversion swept the Mahar community throughout Maharashtra it included the practical consequence of social rebellion, refusing to 'do the work of a Hindu', that is, to carry away dead cattle or perform any other of their ordained caste duties. Such refusals, in individual villages, had brought reprisals and atrocities from the 1930s onwards, and they were to be a continuing source of tension in villages throughout the state. Yet the implementation in practice of a non-Hindu identity, socially conceived, was a massive achievement and in many areas it did get the support of caste Hindu peasants, influenced by radical movements and the Satyashodhak tradition.

The inherent problems in simply a 'religious' solution remained; Dalits embracing Buddhism could get caught up in other forms of superstition; very often Ambedkar's very rationalism (in contrast to Phule, the disdain for the idea of reinterpreting existing mass religious traditions) seem simply to have left ground for re-entry of superstitions centred around Ambedkar himself, 'the king of Dalits'. Nevertheless it produced powerful and positive results. With the conversion to Buddhism Ambedkar achieved what Phule and Periyar, for all their resistance to Hinduism, had failed to achieve: making a conscious non-Hindu identity a collective material and radicalizing force in India.

VI

More than any of the other 'social movements' in India, arguably more even than the working class movement (to the extent we can distinguish that from its communist self-claimed vanguard), the Dalit movement has had a political thrust: insistence on a share in power as a precondition for Dalit liberation, interpretation of reservations in terms not simply of economic gain but of access to power, rejection of the politics of patronage all have been major themes up today and we can see their full expression in Ambedkar: 'we must become a ruling community', was only one of his never-to-be-forgotten slogans.

The political level is one of state power and of the parties that contest for state power; this, not scholarly research even of a radical type, was the milieu in which Ambedkar moved and lived. He was above all a man of strategy, of practical politics, even with his most radical public statements. Thus, even more than the economic goals he placed before the Dalit movement, taking precedence for much of the time over his long-term concerns with cultural-historical reinterpretation, the questions of the strategy and political forms in which Dalits might mobilize for change was central to him and to the legacy he left for the movement.

The core of Ambedkar's political strategy remained constant: 'Brahmanism' and 'capitalism' were the main enemies (and 'Brahmanism' was basically a synonym for 'Hinduism', as nearly all his writings made clear). Dalits, as the super-oppressed and exploited, must maintain their autonomy, but they also needed an alliance with Shudras or 'non-Brahmans' as a group, and a broad worker-peasant mobilization that would be the basis for a political alternative to the Congress, which Ambedkar—like Phule, Periyar, all the social revolutionaries of India—saw as inevitably dominated by upper castes and exploiting classes.

All of these points remain controversial today, of course, and we can only briefly deal with them here. The acceptance and analysis of 'Brahmanism' as linked with 'capitalism' in defining the nature of the Indian state and social system, for instance, is a question of the basic theorization of caste and economic exploitation. The assertion of the need for and possibility of an alliance between the Dalits and Shudras (and not simply as a Dalit-worker alliance, a concept which would assume that the working class had left its caste identities behind), also remains controversial. It is related to the analysis of caste and capitalism, since the possibility of the alliance rests in the identification of 'Shudras' as a caste-exploited toiling section. In spite of their controversial theoretical character, however, an increasingly large section of progressive forces in India have accepted, at least to some degree, these points—in part because a vigorous Dalit movement continues to insist on them.

Just as controversial, however, is the assessment of the Congress Party. In fact, while Ambedkar's characterization of it as 'bourgeois-

Brahman' was very close to that of the communists in their early period, it is at odds with the mainstream of left analysis (expressed most eloquently today in the writings of historians Bipan Chandra and Shashi Joshi[29]) which has depicted the Congress as an 'anti-imperialist united front'. This was, for example, the argument used by Swami Sahajanand in his meeting with Ambedkar in 1938.

Ambedkar's rejection of this position was not based on any 'proletarian essentialism' which felt that a non-communist or non-working class nationalism had to be inevitably 'bourgeois'. He argued in terms of the caste character and actions of the Congress leadership (asserting that if it were to be genuinely anti-imperialist he would join it), and there were certainly solid reasons in his time to seal its high-caste leadership as much too solidly entrenched and organized to be open to change by the forces he represented. Further, every 'radical' force working with this 'united front' appeared to get absorbed by its more reactionary, and 'Hinduistic' logic. Social reformers were enticed by the Gandhian setting of caste-reformism in the language of *Rama-raj*, communists adopted the expedient habit of leaving aside all discussion on the issue of caste/cultural change and simply accepting identities such as 'Harijan' and 'Hindu'. There was every reason to think that only within the framework of *an alternative political centre* could working class and anti-caste forces be unified into being a broad force for cultural as well as economic change.

There was also no reason to assume that the Congress itself as a party should monopolize the essence of an 'anti-imperialist united front': from the beginning the Congress had included very moderate and compromising 'anti-imperialists' while many militant and radical fighters against the British operated outside of it. By Ambedkar's day also, though the Congress was absorbing more of these political forces in practice, stigmatizing its opponents as 'pro-British' and borrowing the language of the left to characterize both itself and its opponents, there continued to be important political forces outside it which were by no means in the hands of the British. A genuine 'anti-imperialist united front' would have to comprise, through some form or another, as many of these forces as possible, and not just remain limited to one party. The problem with the most forceful argument today for the 'anti-imperialist united front' character of the Congress, that of the Chandra-Joshi school, is a logical inconsistency: its basic argument is that rather than building a separate and thus inherently sectarian/diversionary Communist Party fighting against the Congress, the communists should have worked as part of a 'left bloc' along with Nehru and others within the Congress itself. But if activists could be 'communists' without being identified with a particular party, surely they could also be 'anti-imperialists' without being part of the Congress or any other political party. They could also, from outside, have as crucial a chance to influence its politics as from inside. A 'left bloc' could operate to comprise both groups within and without the Congress fold, according to the needs of the time. This was the question not of the effect of having different political formations, but of the effect of their modes of relationship with one another.

Ambedkar rejected the 'left bloc' forming within Congress during the 1930s under Nehru's leadership just as strongly as he rejected Gandhism. He accused Indian socialists of being unfaithful of their ideals due to their upper caste base, and he warned that no socialist movement in India could ignore this issue. The fact was that the Nehruvite left was even more unwilling to give attention to caste than Gandhi was. The masses of youth who thronged Congress campaigns at the time were still very largely high caste, and the notion of Dalit or low caste empowerment, which was so central to their movements for liberation, did not even have a hearing. The neglect of caste issues for the overriding commitment to 'class' was the crucial point in which Ambedkar distinguished himself from the socialist political trend. In other respects, he saw the socialists, and particularly the Lohiaite socialists who took the issue of caste seriously as his firmest allies.

To characterize the Congress as 'Brahman' and 'bourgeois' did not mean that it was incapable of undergoing any change or admitting any low caste people to leadership positions; but its structures of dominance, both organizationally and ideologically, were such as to draw its members into a Brahmanic-Hindu framework of interpreting the 'Indian' nation and into incorporation within a capitalist system. It may be argued that Ambedkar's understanding of this—particularly of the 'bourgeois' character of the Congress, rather of the statist 'Nehru model' of development which it came to accept—was inadequate. The characterization itself, however, and Ambedkar's argument for an alternative political force can be said to have stood the test of time.

Thus Ambedkar's political career was devoted to finding forms through which Dalits could exert themselves in an autonomous fashion and at the same time build an enduring alliance with non-Brahmans, Shudras, workers and peasants. The problem was that by the 1940s and 1950s, this strategy was becoming more and more difficult to implement.

The alliance attempts went through major phases. The Independent Labour Party, his first political party, put this directly into practice during the radical 1930s, as a worker and peasant party with a red flag and Dalit leadership. But, while it won some major success (both electorally and in terms of leadership in mass movements) in the Marathi-speaking districts, it could not make an impact at the all-India level. And while different forms of 'peasant-worker' or peasant-based parties were coming up in parts of India, usually with specific ethnic identities, the failure of any national (left) political force to promote an alternative to the Congress, the fact that both socialist and communist trends were working within the Congress, left these attempts isolated.

Under the pressure of events, Ambedkar wound up the Independent Labour Party and formed the Scheduled Caste Federation in 1942. This sought to represent Dalits only but on an all-India scale, and had programmes which focused on Dalit autonomy in the absence of alliances, i.e. separate village settlements and separate electorates. It expressed a general disillusionment with the ability of even poor Shudra peasants to shake themselves out of the 'Hindu fold' and the discrimination against untouchables that this embodied. The long period during which even radical peasant organizing had not touched on caste issues, the failed dialogue with peasant leaders and the non-Brahman parties, was apparently having its effect. Ambedkar continued to see Shudras as oppressed by the caste system, but was discouraged by their apparent unwillingness to shake off Hindu illusion; as he wrote in one of his unpublished manuscripts:

> It is obvious that these three classes [untouchables, Shudras and tribals] are natural allies. There is every ground for them to combine for the destruction of the Hindu social order. But they have not ... the result is that there is nobody to join the untouchable in his struggle. He is completely isolated. Not only is he isolated, he is opposed by the very classes who ought to be his natural allies.[30]

Behind this was also the reality of the overriding political importance of the 'Hindu-Muslim' question, which meant seeing the large body of non-Brahmans as essentially 'Hindus'. Along with leaders and activists throughout the country, Ambedkar was being forced to take the major identities of 'Hindu Community' and the 'Muslim Community' as the overriding reality beyond either class or regional identities.

A pessimism about a 'peasant' alliance accompanied that about the 'Shudra' alliance. The turn to a traditional left type of economic radicalism, in fact, was also making the prospects of forming a peasant alliance more difficult. As we have seen, Ambedkar had never hesitated to support peasant movements (in spite of the tensions and contradictions between mainly labourer Dalits and caste Hindu peasants) and in his early days he had argued for an economy of peasant with small property, expressing fears about the upper caste control that large centralized properties would bring. Thus he supported not only anti rent campaigns against landlords, but also anti revenue, i.e. anti state campaigns. So did the early communist movement. In fact the earliest statements of programmes saw anti-revenue as the central form of peasant struggles in ryotwari areas, comparable to anti rent struggles in zamindari areas.

After this, however, the communists switched to discussing only anti moneylender struggles, leaving out the question of the state as a direct exploiter, an extractor of economic surplus; and Ambedkar more or less followed them. Collective farms, i.e. state management, which he proposed as 'nationalization of land', came to be the main radical programme for agriculture. The earlier support for small peasant holdings was gone. Both proposals for collective farms and 'separate village settlements' assumed that within a primarily small holding of inequalitarian peasant community it would be impossible for the Dalits and other sections of the landless to fight for and win access to land and other resources. In effect they assumed that there was no overriding common interest that could unite the Dalits (primarily labourers but also small peasants) with a large section of Shudra caste peasants.

But collectives could not be a solution that laid a basis for such an alliance. Peasants with small holdings tend to resist collectivization and top-down cooperative farms; whether one sees this as a 'petty-bourgeois' holding on to small property or as a toiling people's resistance to an oppressive statism. Today, decades of experience of collectivization, as well as some of the oppressive aspects of even 'cooperatives' when they are accompanied by pressures on peasants, the promotion of mechanized and high-energy using chemical agriculture, and the forced purchases of peasant products at low prices, are all leading to a search for different kinds of rural restructuring. Decentralization and community control of natural resources, the combination of small individual holdings and collectively-managed 'common property resources', the balance of needs for equity within the village and that of a strengthening of village autonomy and access to resources against the central state, are all becoming major themes of 'alternative development' models. But none of this thinking and experience was available during Ambedkar's time. It was quite natural for him, representing the most 'proletarianized' section of the villages, to place his hopes in collective (or statist) forms in agriculture as well as industry. But, in a long transition in which traditional feudal landlords were gradually being overridden and peasant farmers were coming to confront the 'developmentalist' state, in which landlords extracting rent were being replaced by state agencies as the main source of peasant debt, meant that it was increasingly difficult to have an alliance with the peasantry.

A 'Dalit-Muslim' alliance has been another theme of movements claiming to fight Brahmanism and capitalism. As we know, it was strongly supported by sections of the Indian Dalits, particularly in Hyderabad and Bengal. In contrast to the issues of 'Shudras' and 'peasant', however, it has to be stressed that Ambedkar never took this up as a *strategic* alliance. He had his periods of discussion with Jinnah, and even joined him in 1939 in celebrating Congress resignations from the provincial ministries. He wrote in detail on the question of Pakistan as well as on linguistic states, setting out the justifications first for forms of federal autonomy that would have given Muslims sufficiently controlled territories to maintain a broadly united India, like some Dalit spokesmen today, that he had any great personal attraction for Islam and its presumed militancy, or that he saw a Dalit-Muslim alliance as a core of his strategy.

Nor did he see 'oppressed nationalities' as potential allies; the concept was not even within his framework of thinking. His writings on the issue of linguistic states and on Maharashtra as a linguistic state reveal a strong emotional resistance to 'linguistic nationalism'. They endorse the often expressed fears that linguistic states would generally mean an increased dominance of large 'peasant jatis', and they argue for the formation of smaller states. But this is done more on grounds of administrative rationalism, calling for the break-up of large states into smaller common language states, i.e. four Maharashtras, three states in each Madhya Pradesh and Uttar Pradesh and so on. Ambedkar's conviction of the overriding caste reality of India was so strong that he did not see separate linguistically-based cultures as a major reality, and he (perhaps understandably) lacked the particular Marxist linkage of language and nationality.

Thus, in a period during which the major social and political forces that might have made a broad liberatory movement possible were becoming separated from one another, with some of their dynamic elements simply absorbed into the Congress. When Gandhians and the leftists alike were being marginalized, when neither 'Shudras' nor 'peasants' nor 'minorities' nor 'oppressed nationalities' appeared as viable allies for building a united movement or coalition with the Dalits, much of the Scheduled Caste Federation organizing was on a pressure group thesis. The significant period of the 1940s and 1950s thus appears as a basic defeat of Ambedkar's major project, that of creating a revolutionary and equalitarian mass political platform.

However, both Ambedkar's practical political enthusiasm and the enduring character of his efforts for a non-Congress Dalit worker-peasant alliance went into another phase at the end of his life, a rebirth that came with the movement for a united Maharashtra state (the Samyukta Maharashtra Movement). Strikingly here the issues of nationality or 'sub-nationality' (linguistic nationality), caste and economic exploitation were combined.

Ambedkar had been, as noted, extremely ambivalent on the issue of states reorganization, generally opposing language as a basis for state formation, calling for smaller states. His theorizing on 'nation-formation' did not give scope for seeing language as uniquely a national feature; he generally shared the centralizing tendencies of industrially-oriented modernists and with the majority of India's political elite he accepted partition as a necessity for disengaging from a Muslim minority whose demands for autonomy would have made a strong central state impossible.[31]

Once the call of politics came, though, he was unambiguous: the demand for a united Maharashtra was to be supported, in spite of fears of Maratha caste domination. Part of this was perhaps a strong Marathi identity; his criticisms of the Maharashtrian Brahman Congress leaders that they wanted a '*rajya of bhats*' was accompanied by the charge that a bilingual Bombay state would mean a subordination of Marathi-speakers:

Just as *bhatjis* built Maharwadas to provide village workers for free in India, so our Gujarati *shetjis* have in an aggressive way established a bilingual state that would be useful for them and turned all of Maharashtra into a Maharwada for Gujarat.[32]

Even more, he was enthusiastic about the movement because of its potential for a powerful anti-Congress front. Spokesmen of the Scheduled Castes Federation took the lead in arguing for a massive oppositional unity, this time including the communists, and for militant struggle to achieve a united Maharashtra.[33] It was the period during which the Federation was being transformed into a new party, the Republican Party of India, which was now aimed at becoming a party of all the exploited and oppressed and not merely of Dalits. The Federation's executive resolution to establish the party was put in the specific context that the time had now come to establish one united front to oppose the Congress in the forthcoming general elections.[34] Y.D. Phadke's study of the Samyukta Maharashtra Movement also argues that Ambedkar made three conditions for the Republican Party's alliance with the Samyukta Maharashtra Samiti, that the Samiti would take up the issues of the rural poor and that it would not just be a one-time ad hoc alliance but would be made permanent as a broad, left movement.[35]

In fact this very brief period saw a return to the radical politics of the 1930s. The Samyukta Maharashtra Samiti represented a coming together of socialists, communists, Dalits, a new upsurge of a left-Dalit struggle and the first united left political front in Maharashtra after independence. It brought forward leaders and themes, including those rooted in satyashodhak traditons, that had been part of the broad democratic movement throughout the colonial period in Maharashtra. At the popular level the upsurge of 'communist tamashas' such as the one led by the Dalit communist poet Annabhau Sathe could unite themes of caste and class oppression.

Furthermore, it was relatively successful. What could not be achieved prior to independence, a decisive defeat of the Congress in Maharashtra, was done by the Samiti, with many Dalits elected on its tickets. The Samiti itself disappeared and Congress dominance returned, but some alliance campaigns remained focused on the rural poor. Most notably Dadasaheb Gaikwad of the Republican Party and radical left peasant leaders such as Nana Patil (hero of the 'parallel government' in Satara and a new member of the Communist Party) joined to lead large satyagrahas for Dalit, tribal and other landless to get forest land for cultivation, first in 1956 and then in 1965, the most massive struggles in India on land and peasant issues before the re-emergence of radicalism during the 1960s. Thus, the information of a party in which Dalits would lead all exploited sections, and the formation of a united left front were, along with conversion to Buddhism, major events just before Ambedkar's death.

NOTES

* Also published in Gail Omvedt, *Dalits and the Democratic Revolution: Dr Ambedkar and the Dalit Movement in Colonial India*, Sage, New Delhi: 1994.

1. *Janata*, 25 June, 1938. This may have been written by Ambedkar himself or by A.V. Chitre (information from Y.D. Phadke); at any rate it can be taken as representing Ambedkar's views.
2. *Dr Babasaheb Ambedkar: Writings and Speeches*, Bombay, 1987, vol. III, p. 444.
3. B.R. Ambedkar, 'The Problem of the Rupee', in *Writings and Speeches*, Bombay, 1989, vol. III, pp. 680-1; see also Rajat K.Ray, *Industrialization in India*, Delhi, 1979, pp. 245-7 for a description of the controversy.
4. See Narendra Jadhav, *Dr Ambedkar: Economic Thought and Philosophy*, Pune, 1993.
5. See B.R. Ambedkar, 'The Evolution of Provincial Finance in British India', in *Writings and Speeches*, vol. VI, pp. 425-30.
6. B.R. Ambedkar, 'The Problem of the Rupee', op. cit., p. 681.
7. B.R. Ambedkar, 'The Evolution of Provincial Finance', in *Writings and Speeches*, vol. I, p. 75.
8. Ibid., p. 233.
9. Ibid., p. 234.
10. Election Manifesto of the Scheduled Caste Federation (n.d., probably 1951), Vasant Moon's Collection.
11. B.R. Ambedkar, 'The Communal Deadlock', in *Writings and Speeches*, vol. I, pp. 355-80.
12. B.R. Ambedkar, *States and Minorities: What are their Rights and How to Secure them in the Constitution of Free India* (1st published, 1947) in *Writings and Speeches*, vol. I, p. 408.
13. Ibid., p. 410.
14. Ibid., pp. 396-7.
15. Ibid., p. 425.
16. For the most recent leftist interpretation see Thomas Mathew, *Ambedkar: Reform or Revolution* (New Delhi, 1991), esp. pp. 134-43. Mathew very cautiously refrains from making his critique of Ambedkar directly.
17. For the main contemporary analysis, see Ernesto Laclau and Chantal

Moufee, *Hegemony and Socialist Strategy*, London, 1989; for a discussion that is used for analysis of India see the writings of Thomas Blum Hansen, especially *Politics and Ideology in Developing Societies: An Exploratory Essay*, Copenhagen, 1991.

18. Ambedkar, 'States and Minorities', p. 412.
19. See Bharat Patankar, *Jotiba Phule ani Sanskrutik Sangarsh* (in Marathi), Bombay, 1991.
20. Benedict Anderson, *The Imagined Community: Reflections on the Origins and Spread of Nationalism*, London, 1983.
21. See Hansen, *Politics and Ideology*.
22. 'Annihilation of Caste', in *Writings and Speeches*, vol. I, p. 49.
23. For example, *Dalit Voice*.
24. *Writings and Speeches*, vol. III, pp. 419-20.
25. Ibid., Buddhists today, in response to Ayodhya claims, are seeking the Buddhist stupas and caves underlying 'Hindu' ones in India. The 'Pandava caves' near Nasik in Maharashtra could be cited as an example: their main figures are Buddhist ones from the Satavahana period. The current struggle (1992) over 'liberating' the Bodh Gaya centre from Hindu control also examplifies the issue.
26. Ibid., p. 273.
27. S.A. Dange, *India: From Primitive Communism to Slavery*, New Delhi, 1972. This is savagely critiqued by D.D. Kosambi, 'Marxism and Ancient Indian Culture', in A.J. Syed (ed.), *D.D. Kosambi on History and Society*, Bombay, 1985; and E.M.S. Namboodiripad, *Kerala: Yesterday, Today and Tomorrow*, Calcutta, 1968.
28. *Prabuddha Bharat*, 4 February 1956.
29. Shashi Joshi, *The Struggle for Hegemony in India, 1920-1948: The Colonial State, the Left and the National Movement*, vol. I, *1920-34* (New Delhi, 1992). Bipan Chandra, Mridula Mukherjee, Aditya Mukherjee, and Sucheta Mahajan, *India's Struggle for Independence, 1857-1947* (New Delhi, 1989).
30. 'The Untouchables: Children of India's Ghetto', in *Writings and Speeches*, vol. V, pp. 115-16.
31. See *Pakistan or the Problem of Partition*.
32. *Janata*, 15 October 1956; also 5 November 1956.
33. Ibid., 17 December 1955.
34. Ibid., 6 October 1956.
35. Y.D. Phadke, *Politics and Language*, Bombay, 1979, pp. 60-1, 241-2.

8

Empowering the Powerless: Dr Ambedkar's Contribution to the Ideology of Dalit Protest

K.C. Yadav

Of late, there has been a sort of proliferation of writings on Babasaheb Ambedkar, Dalits and their problems.[1] A serious perusal of this voluminous literature shows, however, that although much has been said about these subjects, still a great deal remains to be said. The present study is a case in point.

It is intended here to supply a part of the desideratum, that is, Dr Ambedkar's contribution to the Ideology of Dalit Protest to effect their empowerment. The orientation of the study is historical. I have in the first instance tried to see what was Dr Ambedkar's perception of the problems of the Dalits? What precisely were the factors and forces, social, economic, political and so forth, that went into the making of this perception? How far was this perception different from those of his predecessors and contemporaries? I have then tried to see as to how on the basis of his 'new' perception the Dalits were empowered with a new ideology of protest to fight the vested interest and to have their rights? What in brief was this ideology like? Why did this particular ideology attract the Dalits and how far did it serve them? And finally, how much of this ideology is dead and how much of it is alive today, and what use can it be put to now?

II

Before we take up the above questions, it seem pertinent to define the technical terms, like Dalit, empowerment, and the ideology of protest which are being used here in the study, for a knowledge of the meaning, scope and limitations of these terms is essential for understanding the discourses involving them.

Let us begin with the term Dalit. The Indian society is divided into hundreds of castes, neatly placed upon one another in a three-layered hierarchy: (i) high castes; (ii) low castes (touchables); and (iii) low castes (untouchables), based on '(a) power, or ability to control people's lives, including their own; (b) economic position, i.e. income, wealth, and access to means to produce it; and (c) privileges, like education, security, leisure, luxury, etc.'[2] In other words, in this peculiar division, people who have power, property, and privileges have usurped the top position in the society; those who have a part of the three things have occupied the second rung; and those who have absolutely nothing with them are accorded the third or the lowest position. They are Dalits that we are concerned here with.

Dalit is a Sanskrit word which means 'oppressed', 'downtrodden', 'broken'.[3] It is difficult to say with any modicum of certainty as to who coined this word and when. In the present state of our knowledge we can say only this that it was the great social activist Jotiba Phule from Maharashtra who gave it wide currency through his writings and speeches sometime in the later part of the nineteenth century.[4] The term was, it seems, not an 'instant click' with the people who continued to use various terms, like the *avaranas, panchamas, achhutas, ati-shudras, bahiskritas,* etc., instead. The British officials liked to address the neglected people first as 'depressed classes'[5] (although some among them had liking for terms like the 'broken men' or 'outcasts') and later (in 1930s), as 'the scheduled castes'.[6] Indians had no attraction for the official usage until the advent of freedom (1947) when they fell· for the latter Gandhiji coined a high-sounding, big word—Harijan (children of God)—and popularized it through his writings and speeches on a grand scale. Dr Ambedkar, however, opposed the usage tooth and nail, for it was derogatory, he said. His own preference was for 'untouchable' or 'protestant Hindus' or 'Non-conformists'.[7] The Constitution of India, as indicated above, uses the old official term—'the Scheduled Castes'. The concerned people, however, like to be addressed as Dalits.[8] And that actuates us to use this term for them in the present paper.

Now a word on 'Empowerment'. Ordinarily, it means giving power to some one who is weak, marginalized, unprivileged and oppressed so that he is able to maximize his capacities, resources and opportunities and thereby makes himself capable of full participation, as the recent World Summit for Social Development held at Copenhagen[9] (March 1995) suggests, in the formulation, implementation and evaluation of decision determining the functioning and well-being of our societies. Superficially, the process appears to be very simple. But actually it is not so, for those who have power ordinarily do not wish to relinquish or share even a small part of it with others. A good example to bring home this truth can be the so-called 'Mandal agitation' of 1990.[10]

How can, one may ask here, the social underdogs go about it then? Unfortunately, there is no answer to the question with us, for our languages which have *shaktikarana* for *empowerment* are as ambiguous if not more on the point as the English language is. The Chinese has a clear answer to the question: the process (of empowerment) has two different words for it there: (i) *shou* (give) *chuanli* (power) and (ii) *zhua* (seize) *chuanli*[11] (power). If the state or those who possess power do not give it to the social underdogs, they are left with no alternative but to go for *zhua chuanli*, i.e. to *seize* it per force. Thus, in present context, empowerment means 'to seize power'.

Finally, we come to the last term, the ideology of protest. This is a modern phenomenon. Earlier religion was the only 'formal system of ideas' that had any hold on the common men, and a protest ideology then invariably meant either the thinking of a sectarian/religious leader or the common men's interpretation of the social message of their religion/faith. Political ideas had hardly any place in the sporadic protests of the common men in those days. And this explains why the protests against the oppression and deprivation that the Dalits suffered at the hands of the caste system were either non-existent or feeble. For religion, like the Christianity in Europe (including its major protestant sects) 'with its focus on heavenly rewards, lulled discontent more often than it inflamed it'. However, from the Enlightenment on, the situation changed, first in Europe, and then elsewhere. Soon Liberalism, Radicalism, Socialism, Anarchism, Syndicalism and several other socio-political movements, though differing in crucial respects, strengthened the protest ideology a great deal by making it vigorously political, avowedly progressive, largely popular and forthrightly direct.

Though they have different designations or lables, these modern protest ideologies have many common characteristics. All of them, for instance, inspire a leadership that is willing to make sacrifices for them. They have organizations through the instrumentality of which they try to reach the masses directly. They vigorously condemn the existing order and suggest strategies and tactics to replace it by a better one. They carry in the main a social message outweighing political demands, and pay considerable attention to the methods and organizations of protest.[12]

Dr Ambedkar was highly impressed by the modern protest ideologies and went to create one like them in form, but different in content and nature, to suit his followers, the poor , helpless Dalits, as we shall see later.

III

Dalits are a numerous community found in almost every state and union territory throughout the country, as Table 1 shows. They are, however, not a socially homogenous class/group, as some people erroneously think. They are divided into over 400 castes, some of which are, like the Chamars (including Chambars), for instance, as big as to be having millions of people in their ranks, while others, like Jalkeots, Irikas, etc., do not count even more than a few hundred.[14] These castes differ from each other, as other Hindu castes do, and there is nothing common among them, except for poverty, deprivation, dispossession and social degradation.

During the period under study, the Dalits were broadly speaking of three types: (i) untouchables, i.e. those who caused pollution by physical touch; (ii) unapproachables, i.e. those who caused pollution if they came within a certain distance (e.g. Puvada Vannas of Tamil Nadu); and (iii) unseeables, i.e. those who caused pollution if they came within sight (e.g. the Nayadis of Karnataka). The pitiable conditions that these people had been living in for thousands of years and the atrocities perpetrated on these hapless mortals by their countrymen are beyond description. Even a sensitively expressive person like Dr Ambedkar could only say this much on the subject:

> What must be the hardships of the unapproachables and unseeables? How must they be passing their lives? If their sight or their approach even is not tolerated, what work can they obtain? What else can they do except to beg and live on dog's meat? Surely, no civilization can be guilty of greater cruelty! It is indeed a great mercy that the population of the unapproachables and of the unseeables is so small. But are millions of Untouchables entitled to any civilization?[15]

TABLE 1: STATE-WISE POPULATION OF DALITS, 1991

Sl. No.	India/State or Union Territory	Total Population ('000)	Dalits Population ('000)	Percentage of total Population
	INDIA*	838,584	138,223	16.48
	STATES			
1.	Andhra Pradesh	66,508	10,592	15.93
2.	Arunachal Pradesh	865	4	0.47
3.	Assam	22,414	1,659	7.40
4.	Bihar	86,374	12,572	14.55
5.	Goa	1,170	24	2.08
6.	Gujarat	41,310	3,060	7.41
7.	Haryana	16,464	3,251	19.75
8.	Himachal Pradesh	5,171	1,310	25.34
9.	Karnataka	44,977	7,369	16.38
10.	Kerala	29,099	2,887	9.92
11.	Madhya Pradesh	66,181	9,627	14.55
12.	Maharashtra	78,937	8,758	11.09
13.	Manipur	1,837	37	2.02
14.	Meghalaya	1,775	9	0.51
15.	Mizoram	690	1	0.10
16.	Nagaland	1,210	—	—
17.	Orissa	31,660	5,129	16.20
18.	Punjab	20,282	5,743	28.31
19.	Rajasthan	44,006	7,608	17.29
20.	Sikkim	406	24	5.93
21.	Tamil Nadu	55,859	10,712	19.18
22.	Tripura	2,757	451	16.36
23.	Uttar Pradesh	139,112	29,276	21.05
24.	West Bengal	68,078	16,081	23.62
	UNION TERRITORIES			
1.	Andaman & Nicobar Islands	281	—	—
2.	Chandigarh	642	106	16.51
3.	Dadar & Nagar Haveli	138	3	1.97
4.	Daman and Diu	102	4	3.83
5.	Delhi	9,421	1,795	19.05
6.	Lakshadweep	52	—	—
7.	Pondicherry	808	131	16.25

*Excludes figures of Jammu & Kashmir where 1991 census was not taken.

Source: *Census of India, 1991, Series 1, Paper 1 of 1993*, Delhi, 1993, p. 11.

Precisely, not. During the period under study, these poor fellows mostly living in India's half a million villages were not touched even indirectly by what is called civilization. They lived, unlike their touchable counterparts, as 'a poor and a dependent community'. They were 'a subject race of hereditary bondsmen'.[16]

Worse, these unfortunate mortals were forced to follow an oppressively exploitative code the like of which might not have been in vogue anywhere—not even in the so-called 'uncivilized societies'. Substantiation: the following catalogue of the contents of the code documented by Dr Ambedkar:

1. The untouchables must live in separate quarters away from the habitation of the Hindus. It is an offence for the untouchables to break or evade the rule of segregation.
2. The quarters of the untouchables must be located towards the South, since the South is the most inauspicious of the four directions. A breach of this rule shall be deemed to be an offence.
3. The untouchables must observe the rule of distance, of pollution or shadow of pollution as the case may be. It is an offence to break the rule.
4. It is an offence for a member of the untouchable community to acquire wealth, such as land or cattle.
5. It is an offence for a member of the untouchable community to build a house with tiled roof.
6. It is an offence for a member of an untouchable community to put on a clean dress, wear shoes, put on a watch or gold ornaments.
7. It is an offence for a member of the untouchable community to give high sounding names to their children. Their names be such as to indicate contempt.
8. It is an offence for a member of the untouchable community to sit on a chair in the presence of a Hindu.
9. It is an offence for a member of the untouchable community to ride on a horse or a palanquin through the village.
10. It is an offence for a member of the untouchable community to take a procession of untouchables through the village.
11. It is an offence for a member of the untouchable community not to salute a Hindu.
12. It is an offence for a member of the untouchable community to speak a cultured language.
13. It is an offence for a member of the untouchable community, if he happens to come into the village on a sacred day which the Hindus treat as the day of fast and at or about the time of the breaking of fast, to go about speaking, on the ground that their breath is held to foul the air and the food of the Hindus.

14. It is an offence for an untouchable to wear the outward marks of a touchable and pass himself as a touchable.
15. An untouchable must conform to the status of an inferior and he must wear the marks of his inferiority for the public to know and identify him, such as:
    (a) having a contemptible name;
    (b) not wearing clean clothes;
    (c) not having tiled roof;
    (d) not wearing silver and gold ornaments.[17]

A contravention of any of these rules was an offence.[18] And as if this was not enough to dehumanize Dalits, they were assigned a large number of what they called 'duties' also, which briefly speaking, were as follows:

1. A member of an untouchable community must carry a message of any event in the house of a Hindu such as death or marriage to his relatives living in other villages no matter how distant these villages may be.
2. An untouchable must work at the house of a Hindu when a marriage is taking place, such as breaking fuel, and going on errands.
3. An untouchable must accompany a Hindu girl when she is going from her parent's house to her husband's village no matter how distant it is.
4. When the whole village community is engaged in celebrating a general festivity such as Holi or Dashera, the untouchable must perform all menial acts which are preliminary to the main observance.
5. On certain festivities, the untouchables must submit their women to members of the village community to be made the subject of indecent fun.[19]

To add insult to injury, the *savarna* Hindus forced Dalits to do these mean 'duties' without remuneration. The reason? To appear taller to the poor mortals. For, as rightly observed by Dr Ambedkar:

Every Hindu in the village regards himself as a superior person above the untouchables. As an overlord, he feels it absolutely essential to maintain this prestige. This prestige he cannot maintain unless he has at his command a retinue to dance attendance on him. It is in the untouchable that he finds a ready retinue which is at his command and for which he does not have to pay the untouchables who by reason of their helplessness cannot refuse to perform these duties and the Hindu villager does not hesitate to exact them since they are so essential to the maintenance of his prestige.

These offences are not to be found in the Penal Code, enacted by the Government. Nonetheless, so far as the untouchables are concerned, they are real. A breach of any of them involves sure punishment for the untouchables.[20]

The sceptics may argue here that how such a vast number of diligent and vivacious people like Dalits could be condemned to live such a horrible life for such a long time? Happily, history comes to our help here. Such arrangements, it says, which offer institutional inequality, poverty and oppression have been all through history, no matter whether made by caste, class, race or ethnicity, invariably 'endured the world over not because people agreed on their legitimacy but because they were enforced by those who benefited by them.[21] India was no exception. Clearly, the vested interest employed force,[22] fraud and feint on the Dalits[23] to deprive them of property, wealth[24] and learning,[25] ostensibly to create their 'labour pool',[26] as also to sustain it for countless years.[27]

Was there no protest one might ask, against this suffering, and painfully unjust and shockingly inhuman arrangement by the sufferers? Surely, it was there, and it had to be there, for every grievance hurts and every hurt brings forth protest. But, as noted above, the protest was not modern in its nature or form, and it lacked the back-up of an ideology—modern ideology, to be precise. As a result, though the vested interests were opposed and even fought at various levels, in many ways, the protests were mostly ineffective. At least this was, in brief, the position when Dr Ambedkar came on the scene as a Dalit leader determined to empower his powerless people through an appropriate ideology of protest.

IV

How did Ambedkar set out to do his work? Precisely, very slowly, but steadily and strenuously. His was a very delicate work, he knew, and, therefore, he handled it with great care and caution. First of all he prepared a blueprint for the purpose which comprised the following processes: (i) to study the existing conditions; (ii) to supply correct information to his people; (iii) to educate them; (iv) to motivate them; (v) to mobilize them; and (vi) to take action in the matter.

In the second place, he dealt with each of these processes at length, beginning with the stocktaking of all the available protest ideologies—viz., the *Bhakta* and *Sant* ideologies, *Phulevada,* Ranade, Agarkar, Shinde ideologies, foreign idelogies—like those of the liberal constitutionalist democrats, Marxists, and current Indian social and political ideologies like those of Gandhiji, M.A. Jinnah, et al.[28] in a cool, calculating manner, so that he could choose a correct ideology for himself and his followers. Unfortunately, however, none of these ideologies was found fit enough to serve his purpose in entirety. Therefore, he developed his own ideology on the basis of the reinterpretation of Hindu religion, culture, tradition, history, and social and political processes and institutions. For it was their misinterpretation and misuse by the vested interest which had made Dalits disinherited, deprived, and demoralized, living almost at the subhuman level, if not worse. In other words, he supplied correct information to these poor, hapless souls on all these things so that none could befool them to meet one's selfish ends.

He started with religion, for he regarded it as the foremost thing in life, not only of an individual but of the entire society. It was the magic touch of a religion, he said, which transformed one into a human being in the real sense of the term and unlocked the treasure of love, understanding, brotherhood and security which helped in building a better society and a better world to live in. But not all the religions were like this: some religions, he lamented, did just the opposite of it. He cited the example of Hinduism to prove the point and exposed its irreligiousity and injustice, its weaknesses and vulgarities. And having done that, he launched an attack with every conceivable weapon in his armoury of scholarship, logic and scientific reasoning on almost all its social structures (like caste), its social institutions (like untouchability) and its economic diktats (like compulsory hereditary occupation for each caste) which it not only consecrated but also made sacred, eternal and inviolate.[29]

A demolisher of oppressive institutions, Ambedkar challenged the obnoxious authority of Hinduism and its instruments of exploitation, systematically, logically, but forcefully, by challenging what legitimized it—*vedas, shastras* and *smritis.*[30] He specially came very heavily on the *Manusmriti* and went even to the extent of burning it (1927).[31] One may ask a pertinent question here, however: Why was Ambedkar so harsh on this particular book? Why did he single it out for burning? Why did he not burn the *vedas* which were the real source of the Hindu *dharma*? I cannot think of better words than those of Dr Ambedkar himself to give a suitable answer to these questions:

The word *Dharma* means the privileges, duties and obligations of a man, his standard of conduct as a member of the Hindu community, as a member of one of the castes, and as a person in a particular stage of life. ... The Vedas do not profess to be formal treatises on *Dharma*. They do not contain positive precepts (*vidhis*) on matters of *Dharma* in a connected form. They contain only disconnected statements on certain topics concerned with *Dharma*. On the other hand, *Smritis* are formal treatises on *Dharma*. ... They form the law of the *Dharma* in the real sense of the term. Disputes as to what is *Dharma* and what is not *Dharma* (*Adharma*) can be decided only by reference to the text of the law as given in the *Smritis*. The Smritis form, therefore, the real source of what the Hindu calls *Dharma*, and, as they are the authority for deciding which is *Dharma* and which is not, the *Smritis* are called *Dharma-shastras* (Scriptures) which prescribe the rules of *Dharma*.

The number of *Smritis* which have come down from ancient times have been variously estimated. But the *Smritis* which can be called standard and authoritative will be the *Manusmriti*, *Yajnavalkyasmriti* and the *Narad-smriti*. Of these *smritis* the *Manusmriti* stands supreme. It is pre-eminently the source of all *Dharma*.[32]

It were the rules of *Dharma* which this supreme *Smriti* propounded were responsible for the degradation of the Dalits. Hence Ambedkar burnt the *Manusmriti* and advised his people to challenge the false rules of *Dharma* with all the power at their command.

Dr Ambedkar's next concern was Hindu tradition. For he believed that most of the practices forbidding Dalits to wear good cloths, to live decently, to make pucca houses, to dig wells and to go for what are called 'finer' things in life, which deprived his people of their legitimate rights of a human being and destroyed their self-respect and self-confidence, were created, strengthened and perpetuated by tradition. He made a powerful onslaught on these vulgar practices and questioned their perniciousness as to why should these not go away lock, stock and barrel:

Why should an untouchable be tyrannized, he asked, if he wears clean clothes? How can it hurt a Hindu? Why should an untouchable be molested because he wants to put a tiled roof on his house? How can it injure a Hindu? Why should an untouchable be persecuted because he is keen to send his children to school? How does a Hindu suffer thereby? Why should an untouchable be compelled to carry dead animals, eat carrion, and beg his food from door to door? Where is the loss to the Hindu if he gives these things up? Why should a Hindu feel outraged if an untouchable calls himself by a decent, respectable name? How can a good name taken by an untouchable adversely affect the Hindu? Why should the Hindu object if an untouchable builds his house facing the main road? How can he suffer thereby? Why should the Hindu object if the sound made by an untouchable falls upon his ears on certain days? It cannot deafen him. Why should a Hindu feel resentment if an untouchable enters a profession, obtains a position of authority, buys land, enters commerce, becomes economically independent and is counted among the well-to-do?[33]

By his profound scholarship, clarity of thought and forceful logic, Dr Ambedkar showed the inhuman face of Hindu tradition to his people, and to those who had not seen it before in its real form.

Next, he took up history which he regarded as an immensely important thing in life, for without it, he said, no individual or collectivity could function properly. It was a sort of beacon-light, he believed, which helped one to reach one's destination. But as in religion and tradition, so here the vested interest, he pointed out, had done great mischief by making it its hand-maid to subserve its interest. At its command, the high caste historians, he observed, did not record inconvenient facts; or if they did, they misrepresented them in a way that the opposites looked the realities: *black was white and yes was no, and down was up and stop was go.*

He discredited such effort and prepared his own version of history (following Mahatma Jotiba Phule) and proved on .the basis of his researches that history had been misused to demoralize and dehumanize his people so that they could serve the vested interest 'loyally' and 'effectively'. To make the record straight, he corrected the distortion: the Shudras were not the low people—they were once rulers, he said, for instance. The purpose of this was to replace the feeling of inferiority in his people with an air of superiority by equating Shudras with the ruling races.[34] Similarly, he showed a hundred and one misrepresentations, interpolations and distortions in the religious texts and other works with the help of which the vested interest had made the life of his people miserable by robbing them not only of things like wealth and resources but also of self-respect, self-confidence, and so on.[35]

Next, he took up culture. Dalits were as low here, if not more, as they were in other aspects of life. They were usually told in the good old days—and they continue to be told even today—that they themselves were to be blamed for their poverty of culture. Ambedkar, however, exploded this myth once for all: it were not the Dalits, he emphatically declared, but the high caste masters of India's destiny through the ages who were responsible for making them the wretched of the earth by denying education, wealth, property and all that which contributed to cultural well-being and advancement of a collectivity.[36]

Next, he moved to the socio-economic field. As elsewhere, here, too, the position of Dalits was pretty bad. Ambedkar was furiously incensed. And for one, he came very heavily on 'Hindus' whom he held a great deal responsible for perpetrating this crime on the poor, helpless Dalits. For another, he reprimanded the British Government for doing next to nothing to correct this position during the course of about 150 years of what they called their 'just and caring rule'. Said he in his forthright and inimitable style in London itself, in a Round Table Conference presided over by none else but the Prime Minister of England:

> When we compare our present position with the one which it was our lot to bear in Indian society of the pre-British days, we find that, instead of marching on, we are only marking time. Before the British, we were in the loathsome condition due to our untouchability. Has the British Government done anything to remove it? Before the British, we could not enter the temples. Can we enter now? Before the British, we were denied entry into the Police Force. Does the British Government admit us in the Force? Before the British, we were not allowed to serve in the Military. Is that career now open to us? To none of these questions can we give an affirmative answer. That the British, who have held so large a sway over us for such a long time, have done some good, we cheerfully acknowledge. But there is certainly no fundamental change in our position. Indeed, so far as we were concerned, the British Government has accepted the social arrangements as it found them, and has preserved them faithfully in the manner of the Chinese tailor who, when given an old coat as a pattern, produced with pride an exact replica, rents, patches and all. Our wrongs have remained as open sores and they have not been righted, although 150 years of British rule have rolled away.[37]

Why was it so? Was it owing to 'indifference' or want of sympathy for the Dalits? he asked, and went on to answer the complex question himself:

> We do not accuse the British of indifference or want of sympathy. What we do find is that they are quite incompetent to tackle our problems. If the case was one of indifference only it would have been a matter of small moment, and it would not have made such a profound change in our attitude. But what we have come to realize on a deeper analysis of the situation is that it is a case of sheer incompetence to undertake the task.[38]

Detailing the causes which had rendered the British government incompetent to handle the Dalit problems, the Dalit Messiah gave a profound explanation:

The depressed classes, he said, find that the British Government in India suffers from two very serious limitations. There is first of all an internal limitation which arises from the character, motives and interests of those who are in power. It is not because they cannot help us in these things but because it is against their character, motives and interests to do so. The second consideration that limits its authority is the mortal fear it has of external resistance. The Government of India does realize the necessity of removing the social evils which are eating into the vitals of Indian society and which have blighted the lives of the downtrodden classes for so many years. The Government of India does realize that the landlords are squeezing the masses dry, and the capitalists are not giving the labourers a living wage and decent conditions of work. Yet it is most painful thing that it has not dared to touch any of these evils. Why? Is it because it has no legal powers to remove them? No, the reason why it does not intervene is because it is afraid that its intervention to amend the existing code of social and economic life will give rise to resistance. Of what good is such a Government to anybody? Under a Government, paralysed between two such limitations, much that goes to make life good must remain held on.[39]

The remedy? Precisely this, he suggested:

> We must have a Government in which the men in power will give their undivided allegiance to the best interests of the country. We must have a Government in which men in power, knowing where obedience will end and resistance will begin, will not be afraid to amend the social and economic code of life which the dictates of justice and expediency so urgently call for. This role the British Government will never be able to play. It is only a Government which is of the people, for the people and by the people that will make this possible.[40]

That was not all, Dr Ambedkar continued, the problems of the Dalits would not be solved even after India became free. These would be solved only after Dalits got freedom, power and authority or in other words when they got *swaraj*—their due share in the governance of the country. For

> we feel that nobody can remove our grievances as well as we can, and we cannot remove them unless we get political power in our own hands. No share of this political power can evidently come to us so long as the British Government remains as it is. It is only in a swaraj constitution that we stand any chance of getting the political power into our own hands, without which we cannot bring salvation to our people[41].

But how could political power, one may ask, be the answer of a problem which was social in every sense of the word? Let us go to Ambedkar again for an answer to this complex question also, for I do not think anybody can improve upon him:

We are often reminded, he said, that the problem of the Depressed Classes is a social problem and that its solution lies elsewhere than in politics. We take strong exception of this view. We hold that the problem of the Depressed Classes will never be solved unless they get political power in their own hands. If this is true, and I do not think that the contrary can be maintained, then problem of Depressed Classes is, I submit, eminently a political problem and must be treated as such. We know that political power is passing from the British into the hands of those who wield such tremendous economic, social and religious sway over our existence. We are willing that it may happen, though the idea of swaraj recalls to the mind of many of us the tyrannies, oppressions and injustices practised upon us in the past and fear of their recurrence under swaraj. We are prepared to take the inevitable risk of the situation in the hope that we shall be installed, in adequate proportion, as the political sovereigns of the country along with our fellow countrymen. But we will consent to that on one condition and that is that the settlement of our problems is not left to time. I am afraid the Depressed Classes have waited too long for time to work its miracle.[42]

V

To propagate his views and convince his men and others of the correctness of these, Ambedkar followed every conceivable means and measures. He organized meetings, *melas*, conferences, seminars, symposia, round tables, lectures, table talks, and so on to express their needs and problems and to suggest ways and means to meet them properly.[43] He contributed to newspapers, magazines and journals, touching the issues connected with them.[44] He wrote books, monographs, treatises, pamphlets, tracts, leaflets, handbills and so forth;[45] used radio and television, to serve his cause. In so doing, he did not hesitate to appear before any committee, commission or forum, no matter how controversial it was. Sometimes, he had to taste very bitter criticism at the hands of his countrymen for doing so. But he would care a dime for this, for he believed that it was in the interest of his people who had, unlike his critics, no means to trumpet their grievances to the world.

Indeed, these were great endeavours. But these could hardly satisfy Ambedkar. For he knew that no matter how hard he struggled thus individually, he would not be able to achieve much without a well structured, well geared and well oiled party organization. But he knew this, too, and a little too well of course, that it was a pretty difficult job. For

> there are agents of other political organizations which decoy our people by false blandishments, by false promises and by false propaganda. There is the ignorance of our own people, who do not know the critical nature of the times we are living in and who do not know the value of organizations for achieving our political objects. There is a lamentable lack of resources at our command. ... We have no funds to maintain our machinery, to render help to our people and to educate, agitate and organize them.[47]

The task was difficult, no doubt, but to be successful in his mission, Ambedkar had to accomplish it somehow. And he did it—in three stages. First, he formed a workers' political alliance—Independent Labour Party (1938). To his bad luck, however, the upper caste Hindu workers did not join hands with him there. Therefore, he went for another outfit—the Scheduled Caste Federation (SCF) in order to draw together the Scheduled Castes all over India in a united attempt to win recognition as a political minority. The Party did some real good job (like obtaining separate electorate, for instance) for sometime but it failed to deliver after the advent of freedom (1947). In the new milieu, Dalits needed a broad-based party through the instrumentality of which they could reach the mainstream by joining hands with their natural allies—the STs, OBCs, etc. Hence the Republican Party of India (RPI), formed in 1956. This was indeed a right step in the right direction at right moment. But before he could give even the so-called finishing touches to the organization, the great man reached his earthly extremity on 6 December 1956.

Unfortunately, none of the organizations formed by Dr Ambedkar was a success in the real sense of the term. We have already indicated the reasons which were responsible for this. Nevertheless, Ambedkar did his very best to change the situation. But unpropitious circumstances and uncontrollable factors and forces so conspired against him that he was hardly left with any elbow room to move about. However, a genius who knew how to make the best of a bad bargain, he made even these small weak outfits to yield results which, in most of the cases, even their most successful counterparts, with far greater power and resources, could not secure.[48]

VI

Having prepared the ground thus, Ambedkar set out in 1920s to effect a change in the conditions obtaining then by putting his newly acquired ideology of protest to use. As a result, his people, weak and powerless though, came out in the open, gave up their old approach to their problems and took to 'direct action to redress their wrongs'. However, for a proper comprehension of this seemingly incredible phenomenon, let us try to understand, briefly of course, this ideology, its make-up, its functioning, its direction, pace, et al.

We have indicated above that every grievance hurts, and every hurt brings forth protest. In such a case, should the Indian history not be an unending chronicle of protests—risings, revolts, fights and feuds between the oppressers and the oppressed, torturers and the tortured, exploiters and the exploited, Dalits and *savarnas*? It should have been like that. But actually, it has not been so, for the simple reason that there was always a conspiracy of silence about such happenings in our histories. The high caste people did not talk about these protests, and if they had to do it for some unavoidable reason, then they invariably mispresented them in a totally different manner.[49] Let me cite an example to bring home the truth clearly. Some backward class people, protesting against forcing them not to wear *yajnopavita* (sacred thread), battled with the high castemen in Uttar Pradesh before independence on the scale that the government had 'to call army to quell the disturbance'. The chroniclers—high castemen—would, however, call the incident not a protest, but *sanskritization*—a gentle effort on the part of the lowly to go up in the hierarchy by 'elite emulation', through general consensus.[50]

Factually, protests against their oppression, suppression and exploitation has always been there on the part of the Dalits throughout history. But these were, as indicated above, not very effective in the pre-modern times. For devoid of any appropriate ideology, these had a great deal of religious content in them. Things changed for the better, however, in the recent times when the old brand of the protest ideology was replaced by a modern political phenomenon,[51] the main features of which were, in brief terms, as follows: (i) correct perception of the grievance/problem; (ii) correct understanding of its solution; and (iii) correct use of adequate strategies and tactics through well organized, controlled effort of the masses guided by a dynamic and resourceful leader/leaders enjoying the support of a modern party outfit.

VII

The new, modern ideology of Dalit protest was put to an effective use for the first time in 1924 when Dalits protested against the denial of the right to use the public roads which skirted a temple at Vaikom (Travancore state). The aggrieved people offered *satyagraha*. It was a powerful move. In consequence, the government and the *savarna* Hindus yielded. They permitted the Dalits to use the roads but only after enlarging the temple compound and realigning the roads in such a way that even if the Dalits used them these were 'no longer within the polluting distance of the temple'.[52]

Three years later, a still bigger thing came the 'Dalits' way. It was the so-called Chawdar Municipal Tank Movement at Mahad (district Kolaba—Maharashtra). The Government had passed a piece of legislation in 1927 to the effect that the Dalits be allowed to use all public watering places, wells, etc., built and maintained out of public funds.[53] On receiving the happy tiding, Dalits of Mahad approached their Municipal Committee for permission to use the tank water. The Committee obliged them but not the *savarna* Hindus, who would not allow the pollution of their tank by Dalits.

Dalits protested against this blatant injustice. On 20 May 1927, about 2,500 of them marched in a procession to the tank to challenge the unchallengeable. What followed can be adequately described in the words of the leader of the procession only:

> The Hindu inhabitants of the town saw the scene. They were taken by storm. They stood aghast witnessing this scene which they had never seen before. For the moment they seemed to be stunned and paralysed. The procession in form of fours marched past and went to the Chawdar tank, and the untouchables for the first time drank the water. Soon the Hindus, realizing what had happened, went into frenzy and committed all sorts of atrocities upon the Untouchables who had dared to pollute the water.[54]

These developments did not dishearten the Dalits; however, they accepted the challenge of their adversaries. They gave a call for launching a civil disobedience movement in December 1927. Fortunately for them, however, the occasion for the action never came because the court gave a verdict in support of their claim to use the tank.[55] A great victory indeed!

Although the Mahad agitation was aimed at redressing 'a particular wrong', it, however, went a long way in helping the agitation to mature into a protest movement which had potential 'to demolish the Hindu social order by applying dynamite to its very foundation'.[56] Don't the following resolutions which are, to say in the words of their framer—Dr Ambedkar—'a landmark in the history of the movement of the untouchables', passed at the Mahad assemblage (20 December 1927) substantiate the point?

RESOLUTION 1
DECLARATION OF THE RIGHTS OF A HINDU

This Conference is firmly of opinion that the present deplorable condition of the Hindu Community is only an illustration of how a community becomes fallen by reason of its tolerating social injustice, following erroneous religious beliefs and supporting economic wrongs. The fall of the Hindu community is due entirely to the fact that the masses have not cared to know what are the birth-rights of a human being and much less have they cared to see that they are recognized and not set at naught the base acts and deeds of selfish people. To know what are these birth-rights of man and to endeavour to see that they are not trampled upon in the struggle between man and man and class and class, are the sacred duties of every person. In order that every Hindu may not know what are in the opinion of the conrerence the inalienable birth-rights of man, this Conference resolves to issue the following proclamation containing a list thereof:

(i) All Hindus have the same social status from birth. This equality of social status is an attribute which they retain till death. There may be distinctions and differences between them in point of their functions in society. But that must not cause differences in their social status. This conference is, therefore, opposed to any action—whether in the political, economic or social field of life—which would result in producing a difference in social status.
(ii) The ultimate aim of all political, economic or social changes should be to maintain intact the equal status of all Hindus. That being the view of the Conference, the Conference strongly disapproves of all literature of the Hindus, whether ancient or modern, which supports in any way the pernicious doctrine of inequality underlying the Hindu social system.
(iii) All power is derived from the people. The privileges claimed by any class or individual have no validity if they are not granted by the people. This Conference therefore repudiates the social and religious privileges enjoyed by some classes of Hindus in as much as they are

founded upon the Vedas, Smritis and Puranas and not upon the free consent of the people.

(iv) Every person is entitled as his birth-right to liberty of action and speech. This liberty could be limited only for the purpose of saving the right of another person to his liberty and for no other purposes. Further this limitation can be imposed only with the sanction of the people and not by any injunction of the Hindu shastras. This Conference, therefore, repudiates all restraints on religious, social and economic freedom imposed upon the thought and action of the Hindus in as much as they are imposed by the shastras and not by the people.

(v) Hindus can be deprived of their rights other than their birth-rights only by law. What is not prohibited by law, a Hindu must be free to do and what is not obligatory by law, a Hindu must not be forced to do For this reason there must be no obstruction to persons using public roads, public wells and tanks, public temples and all other public utilities. Persons causing obstruction in matters where law has laid down no prohibition, are in the opinion of this Conference, enemies of the public.

(vi) Law is not a command of an individual or a body of,individuals. Law is the people's prescription for change. That being so, law to be respected, must be made with the consent of all and must have equal application to all without any distinction. Social divisions if they are necessary for the ends of society can only be made on the basis of worth and not of birth. This Conference repudiates the Hindu caste-system, firstly as being detrimental to society, secondly as being based on birth and thirdly as being without any sanction from the people.

RESOLUTION 2

Taking into consideration the fact that the laws which are proclaimed in the name of Manu, the Hindu lawgiver, and which are contained in the *Manusmriti* and which are recognized as the code for the Hindus are insulting to persons of low caste, are calculated to deprive them of rights of a human being and crush their personality. Comparing them in the light of the rights of men recognized all over the civilized world, this Conference is of opinion that this *Manusmriti* is not entitled to any respect and is undeserving of being called a sacred book to show its deep and profound contempt for it, the Conference resolves to burn a copy thereof, at the end of the proceedings, as a protest against the system of social inequality it embodies in the guise of religion.[57]

The *Manusmriti* was burnt: openly, contemptuously and defiantly. Then two other resolutions were passed: (i) to give up skinning of the dead animals, and (ii) not to eat carrion. The object of these resolutions, in the words of their framer, was twofold.

> The one object was to foster among the untouchables self-respect and self-esteem. This was a minor object. The major object was to strike a blow at the Hindu Social Order which is based upon a division of labour which reserves for the Hindus clean and respectable jobs and assigns to the untouchables dirty and mean jobs and thereby clothes the Hindu with dignity and heaps ignominy upon the untouchables. The resolution was a revolt against this part of the Hindu Social Order. It aimed at making the Hindus do their dirty jobs themselves.[58]

In sum, the Mahad resolutions were, all said and done, 'an echo of Voltaire's denunciation of the Catholic Church of his time. For the first time in their long history, a cry was raised by the wretched of the earth against the Hindu dominated '*Ecraze la Infame*'. Clearly, it was an unprecedented thing, a revolution of a sort.[59]

VIII

The message from Mahad spread to other parts of India in no time. As a result, millions of Dalits, the lesser mortals bowed by the weight of centuries, with the emptiness of ages in their faces and burden of the world on their backs[60], gained, thanks to Babasaheb, and his ideology of protest which they imbibed forthwith, unshakable self-assurance, confidence and courage. With this new ideology they could dare challenge now, like Shankar Limbale, the unchallengeable thus:

> I do not ask
> for the sun and moon from your sky
> your farm, your land,
> your high houses or your mansions.
> I do not ask for gods or rituals,
> castes or sects.
> Or even for your mother, sisters, daughters.
> I ask for
> my rights as a man.

You give me my rights. Or else:

> I'll uproot the scriptures like railway tracks.
> Burn like a city bus your lawless laws.
> My friends !
> my rights are rising like the sun.
> Will you deny this sunrise?[61]

NOTES

1. A good introduction to this literature is found in Ghanshyam Shah's *Social Movements in India: A Review of Literature,* Delhi, 1990, pp. 107-20; Eleanor Zelliot, *From Untouchables to Dalits,* Delhi, 1992.
2. G.D. Berreman, *Caste and other Inequities,* Delhi, 1979, pp. 156-63.
3. V.S. Apte, *The Practical Sanskrit-English Dictionary,* Delhi, 1989, p. 493.
4. James Massey, *Dalits in India,* Delhi, 1995, p. 15.
5. *The Government of India Act, 1919* makes use of the term for the first time.
6. The Government of India Act, 1935 makes use of it as per the recommendations of the Simon Commission.
7. James Massey, op. cit., p. 15.
8. Besides this, another reason for my not using the official term—i.e. the Scheduled Castes—is that about 10 per cent of the castes listed as Scheduled Castes are not Dalits or Untouchables.
9. *Vide* Manoranjan Mohanty, 'On the concept of Empowerment', *E & PW,* 17 June 1995, pp. 1434-6.
10. For details see K.C. Yadav, *India's Unequal Citizens: A Study of OBCs,* Delhi, 1994.
11. Manoranjan Mohanty, op. cit., pp. 1434-6.
12. For details see P.N. Stearns, *'Protest Movements'* in *Dictionary of the History of Ideas,* New York, 1973, vol. III, pp. 670-7.
13. *Census of India, 1991, Series 1, Paper 1 of 1993,* Delhi, 1993.
14. For details see K.S. Singh (ed.), *The Scheduled Castes,* vol. II, Delhi, 1995.
15. *Dr Babasaheb Ambedkar. Writings and Speeches* (hereafter *BAWS*), Bombay, 1989, vol. V, pp. 139-40.
16. Ibid., pp. 20-3.
17. Ibid.
18. Ibid.
19. Ibid.
20. Ibid.
21. G.D. Berreman, op. cit., Delhi, 1979, p. 281.
22. It is unthinkable that millions of people could be reduced to sub-human level by the high castes to serve as their 'labour pool' without oppression. And who would not revolt against oppression? Even animals do. The high caste scholars would, however, tell us that the lower castes mostly enjoyed this position and hence there is no tradition of revolt against caste in India. Contrary to this, the lower castes revolted against the oppression in the villages, in the towns, somewhere or the other almost every day in the past. They do it today. The revolts are not documented or discussed, however, for the reasons which we have discussed in the text above.

23. The Brahmanas have, for instance, interpolated almost every religious text to tell the lower castes that it was in line with their *dharma* to serve them loyally. The *Manusmriti* is the best example of this interpolation. For example, it says at X.65 that a Shudra could become a Brahmana but forbids his teaching at IV. 78-81. How could he do that without education?
24. 'Nothing at all belongs to a Shudra as his own. He is one whose property may be taken by his master'. *Manusmriti*, VIII. 417.
25. 'And one may not teach him (Shudra) the law or enjoin upon him religious observances ...' (*Manusmriti*, IV. 78-81).

    'A Shudra is like a burial ground ... , therefore, *Veda* be never recited in his presence ...' (*Vashisthadharamsutra*, XVIII, 11-15).

    Interestingly, there is a remarkable universality about this problem the world over. For instance, the American white masters did exactly the same as our Brahmana masters did to their 'labour pool', the slaves, in the New World (USA): they made the biblical knowledge a taboo and learning a crime for them. For details, see W.E.B. Dubois, *Black Folk, Then and Now*, New York, 1918; C.L.R. James, *Black Jacobins*, New York, 1971; Richard Fruncht, *Black Society in the New World*, New York, 1972.

    This was however, not in line with vedic authority, which entitled all to education (including *vedic* education)—even Shudras were not barred from this. For substantiation, see *Yajurveda*, 26.2.
26. 'Shudra ... serves the higher *varnas*. From them he shall seek to obtain his livelihood (*Gautamadharamasutra*, X.50, 56-9, xii.1. 7).

    A Shudra desiring some means of subsistence may serve a Kashatriya; or (if) anxious to support life (may do so) by serving a wealthy Vaishya. But he should serve the Brahmana (free) for the sake of heaven ... (*Manusmriti*, X. 121-5)
27. For details see K.C. Yadav, op. cit., pp. 25-41.
28. For details see K.K. Kaulekar and A.S. Chauslkar, *Political Ideas and Leadership of Dr B.R. Ambedkar*, Pune, 1989, pp. 1-31; K. Raghvendra Rao, *Babasaheb Ambedkar*, Delhi, 1993, pp. 34-53.
29. See K. Raghvendra Rao, op.cit., pp. 66-80.
30. *BAWS*, vol. v, for details.
31. Ibid.
32. Ibid.
33. Ibid.
34. See his famous book entitled *Who were the Shudras?*
35. *BAWS*, vol. V, p. 149
36. Ibid.
37. Ibid., vol. II, p. 504.
38. Ibid., vol. II, pp. 404-5.

39. Ibid.
40. Ibid., vol. II, p. 505.
41. Ibid.
42. Ibid., vol. II, p. 506.
43. Dhananjay Keer's biography of Dr Ambedkar is by far a good source for this and other such details.
44. Ibid.
45. See the 'Further Readings' at the end.
46. The worst of such experiences came his way in 1928 when he cooperated with the Simon Commission. He faced opposition from not only his political opponents, then, but even his students boycotted his classes and harassed him.
47. *Writings and Speeches*, vol. I, p. 357
48. Ibid.
49. K.C. Yadav, op. cit., pp. 4-5.
50. Ibid.
51. *BAWS*, vol. V, p. 247.
52. Ibid.
53. Ibid., pp. 248-9.
54. Ibid., p. 250.
55. Ibid., pp. 251-2.
56. Ibid., p. 252.
57. Ibid., pp. 253-4.
58. Ibid., p. 258.
59. Ibid., p. 255.
60. Expression borrowed from the famous US black poet, Edwin Markham.
61. Shankar Kumar Limbale, 'White Paper', in *Poisoned Bread*, ed. Arjun Dangle, Bombay, 1992, pp. 64-5.

9

The Process of Securing Places of Power for Dalits: A Note on Dr Ambedkar's Contribution

Eleanor Zelliot

Let me begin with my American experience. The goal of anyone in America working with the poor, the homeless, the dispossessed, is *empowerment*—giving people the power to help themselves. The ways to empower a group are many: political organizing (which works only if a group is large enough); using legal means to enforce laws; conducting non-violent, direct action campaigns for rights; promoting education and especially the education of a group of *leaders* from the mass of dispossessed (or Dalits) themselves; and the forcing of shared power. It seems to me that Dr Ambedkar understood very early in his work that empowerment—not pity or sympathy or a simple kind of help for the needy—was the goal.

Dr Ambedkar's first actions from 1918 through the 1920s were all aimed at empowerment: a newsletter, *Mukanayak* (which might be translated 'The Leader of the Silent') and hostels for education; a plea to the British Franchise Commission for representation of 'Depressed Classes' in governmental bodies; efforts to get the Government to include Dalits in the police; and the formation of various local organizations to create a spirit of independence and pride. All of these early efforts are still being used to empower Dalits in India. Educational institutions begun by Dalits, starting with Ambedkar's People's Education Society in 1942 in Bombay, dot the landscape of Maharashtra and I know of colleges or universities in Karnataka and Andhra Pradesh. Here I want to call for more of these efforts, particularly in engineering and the fine arts, but I also want to urge that there be a Ph.D. dissertation on the educational institutions run by Scheduled Castes and Buddhists. A survey and evaluation would make a grand Ph.D. topic, and would help us understand what else must be done.

Representation in governing bodies for Scheduled Castes and Schedules Tribes continues, and although it is under continuous attack as being non-productive, the idea of a fixed percentage of seats in local and district governing bodies for women (actually thirty per cent) has taken hold in several states. This way of empowerment seems essential. Even if representatives of the Dalits are elected by non-Dalit majorities, each elected representative has access to at least some power, and every bit of that power can be shared with powerless groups. We have studies of Scheduled Castes and Scheduled Tribes elected representatives, but do they really see how far down into the mass of Dalits the shared power goes? And who will take on the task of seeing if thirty per cent of women in panchayats leads to better treatment of women? The United States has no such reservations, but the configuration of urban populations has resulted in the election of Blacks, and the political participation encouraged by the education has resulted in the election of extraordinary Blacks in majority White areas. My own nearby city of Minneapolis can boast the first Black woman mayor in the United States, and she won that post through many years of political participation in a liberal party, a way that is open to Dalits in India to some degree also.

Non-violent direct action was a method used by Dr Ambedkar in the Mahad (water) and temple satyagrahas in the 1927-35 period and again in 1946 in massive campaigns to express the need for separate electorates. None of these efforts led to much success, although the Mahad and temple efforts awakened many Dalits to the possibilities of a movement led by Dr Ambedkar. Interestingly enough, this kind of activity has ceased among Blacks in the United States. Enormous gains were made in the 1960s in campaigns led by Dr Martin Luther King Jr. Since then, no one can turn away a Black person from a restaurant or a university or the front seat of a bus! But this method has limits, and those limits may have been reached in India as well as the United States. There is, however, a campaign recently that achieved success in Maharashtra. A 'Long March', and a continuous campaign finally resulted in the naming of Marathwada University as 'Dr Babasaheb Ambedkar Marathwada University'. I hope this recognition of Dr Ambedkar's work for education in a neglected region of India works toward empowerment. It will if those involved turn to more efforts to secure economic power and to secure safety for those Dalits who challenge the status quo in villages.

Legal means of empowerment are used in both countries. Many of my students in America have become lawyers and are working for the rights of women not to be abused by their husbands, for the environment to be protected, for the rights of the mentally retarded to have a safe and kind environment, and for an end to discrimination against Blacks and the aged. India also, thanks to Dr Ambedkar, has laws allowing for the rights of Dalits to be protected by the courts. But the backlog of cases is huge, and where are the Dalit lawyers making every effort to help? Are there enough legal clinics in the slums run by young Dalits to make a difference in empowerment?

One of my friends, Janet Contursi, studied slum groups in Pune, and found that in the Dalit part of the slums, many young leaders were using their education not only to get concessions in education and job for their neighbours, but also were showing other Dalits how to get school entrance *themselves* for their children, how to apply for jobs *themselves*. This is true Ambedkarism.

In both America and India, the most effective and controversial method of empowerment is the reservation system. This method is called Affirmative Action in America, and although no one in the United States can use the word 'quota', and everyone pretends quotas do not exist, it is clear that both systems have changed the face of the Government and the educational systems, and in America, private business also. Those who say reservations or affirmative action affects only a few do not understand the nature of power and empowerment. Without channels to power, the dispossessed can never achieve their rights, or society achieve equality. Do Indians realize that India and America are the only countries that strive in this way for equality? Do they realize that Indo-Americans in the U.S. got themselves legally declared a majority so that they could take advantage of affirmative action? I do not criticize them; I only point out that intelligent people everywhere realize the necessity of forcing, or encouraging with every means, the inclusion of all people in all institutions.

But, again, I call for study. Where is the Dalit sociologist who will travel the face of India evaluating the fruit of the policy which places a Dalit (but only one!) in every department of an educational institution which receives government funds? What an opportunity to learn how change comes. Do students in India change attitudes as they do in the history department of my own college when they study with my articulate, intelligent Black colleague?

Dr Ambedkar began this process of securing places of power for Dalits. During the early 1940s he insisted that 'Scheduled Caste boys' be among the group of 'Began Boys' studying in England. He was disappointed in the subsequent career and commitment of some of those men, but he persisted in promoting programmes that shared power.

Sometimes I wonder if India or America will be the first to overcome prejudice, casteism or racism. Both countries have had magnificent leaders from within the dispossessed groups. Both countries have achieved much. Both countries have a long way to go.

10
On the Relevance of Dr Ambedkar's Ideology

Yogendra Yadav

What follows is a preliminary assessment of an aspect of Babasaheb Ambedkar's ideas. There are two major limitations to it. One, the assessment does not cover all or even all major aspects of Ambedkar's thought; it is limited to his 'ideology' as defined below in a somewhat narrow manner. And two, it is only a first sketch. The purpose is not to pass anything like a final judgement but to raise a few questions and to learn from the scholars who know much more about Dr Ambedkar than I do. Given the preliminary nature of this exercise, I have permitted myself a rather schematic presentation (incidentally, a style favoured by Ambedkar himself) and somewhat careless speculations.

Such an attempt must answer, first of all, two questions. Relevance of what? From which point of view? As suggested in the title, this note is limited to assessing the relevance of Dr Ambedkar's 'ideology', in the sense of the programmatic content of his ideas. Of the wide range of his idea from interpretation of history, analysis of the present society and its critique to his suggestions about the kind of change required and the way to bring it about, I am interested in the latter. More specifically, I am interested in his programme for the depressed classes, the ex-untouchables. Are Dr Ambedkar's views on what should be done for the depressed classes relevant today?

Fixing a point of view for the assessment is, however, far more difficult. For the only way to discover it, is to engage in the actual assessment; we come to know the right view-point after having viewed things from there and not before it. But a few negative decisions can be taken right away. His relevance must not be judged for any given doctorine. Dr Ambedkar had the courage—he thought he also had good reasons—to reject all the available ideological packages; it would be less than fair to evaluate him from a standpoint he knowingly rejected unless special reasons can be given for that. Nor would it be quite appropriate to use an artificially large category (e.g. the poor, the nation) as the measuring rod; Dr Ambedkar addressed himself largely to the question of the depressed classes and it is from the point of view of their interest and upliftment—howsoever defined—that the relevance of his ideas should be examined. In the context of today's India, the question, then, is: Does Dr Ambedkar's ideology show us the way for transforming the state of the scheduled castes or dalits? What can a dalit activist learn from Dr Ambedkar's idelogy?

II

Let me begin by summarizing the basic ideas of Dr Ambedkar's ideology in the sense defined above. His analysis and critique of the contemporary India led him to believe that:

(1) The goal should be the establishment of a social order which realizes the values of liberty, equality and fraternity; this would mean putting an end, first of all, to the gross inequality and oppression based on caste/varna. The goal cannot be realized by following the conventional methods.

(2) In particular, the nationalist movement for political independence, the socialist action for economic emancipation of all classes or other general programmes for socio-political development cannot be relied to achieve social emancipation: social reforms need an exclusive and prior attention.

(3) Nor can the usual social reform which seeks to work within the basics of Hinduism be depended upon, for the caste/varna inequality and oppression has in fact the sanction of Hindu scriptures.

(4) In positive terms, social emancipation would involve effective outside intervention with the help of three different (but not mutually exclusive) instruments:
   - (a) use of *state* power to protect the depressed classes and to launch a series of special measures to benefit them;
   - (b) progressive *legislation* aimed at the reform of the Hindu family and the reorganisation of Hindu society; and
   - (c) spread of *education* to raise consciousness and self-respect among the depressed classes.

(5) Constitutional and parliamentary activities (elections, petitions, protests, etc.) through a separate political organization of and for dalits so as to get them a share of state power.

(6) Either a complete reorganization of Hindu religion by destroying the belief in the sanctity of shastras or, more realistically, a rejection of Hinduism by the depressed classes in favour of a religion like Buddhism which gives them a place of dignity.

I believe this was the essence of Dr Ambedkar's scheme of social transformation, although he does not put it like this anywhere. The central idea underlying this scheme was that the traditional Hindu social order is completely static. It has no capacity to generate change from within it, change can come only from outside, with the help of modern ideas and institutions.

III

There is a lot in this scheme that is still relevant. Take his statement of the goal (point 1) to begin with. One could say that there is nothing remarkable about wishing to end caste/varna based inequality (who doesn't, at least in speeches?), that the ideal of 'liberty, equality and fraternity' is a borrowed ideal with little applicability in India and that the priority given to social emancipation is misplaced. But such criticisms are not difficult to meet. True, the talk of social emancipation is not novel today (even if much of it is empty rhetoric), but that does not render this ideal obsolete. In fact, faced with the contemporary rhetoric about social justice, it is even more important that we remember and go back to a concrete statement of these ideals given by Dr Ambedkar. Moreover it is important to remember that Ambedkar did not merely take over the slogan of the French Revolution; he used it as an analytical tool to throw critical light on the Hindu civilization.[1]

There could be another counter-argument, quite popular in contemporary urban India. Ambedkar was relevant to his time, so goes the argument, but now the conditions have changed, now the task of social emancipation has at least partially been accomplished. Is it so? An answer to this question would require taking into consideration a large number of facts—and this is not the place for that—but I think the answer would be fairly close to a 'no'. It is true that there is greater mobility for the depressed classes than before and some empowerment of their elite. But there has hardly been any inter-mixing of castes (that is, of dalits with others), nor have the attitudes of the caste Hindus changed much vis-a-vis the ex-untouchables. On the contrary, there is for the first time now quite an articulate resentment and protest against the limited benefits of reverse discrimination available to these sections. (This was seen during the students protests in early 1990 at the time of extention of reservations for another decade and even during Mandal agitation.) Dr Ambedkar's suspicion that the higher classes will not easily give up their entrenched privileges appears quite well placed in this context.

The question of autonomy of social reform from political independence or economic emancipation and its priority over these is related to it. As for autonomy, Dr Ambedkar's argument in his Annihilation of Caste is that the usual demands for political and economic reforms leave the fate of dalits unaffected, and to that extent cannot fulfil even their own objectives.[2] Particularly useful was his critique of the socialist/marxist economic reductionism :

> The fallacy of the socialist lies in supposing that because in the present stage of the European Society property as a source of power is predominant, that the same is true of India or that the same was true of Europe in the past. Religion, social status and property are all sources of power and authority, which one man has, to control the liberty of another. One is predominant at one stage, the other is predominant at another stage. ... If the source of power and domination is at any given time or in any given society social and religious then social reform and religious reform must be accepted as the necessary sort of reform.[3]

Needless to say, this argument remains valid even today as the communists have themselves come round to believe recently. Socialists, at least Lohia and his followers, had accepted it long back.

The question of priority is more problematic and in a sense itself somewhat irrelevant now. This was a major question during the national movement when the British presence resulted in a peculiar question of power which made it (state sponsored) social reforms *vs.* struggle for political independence. Dr Ambedkar had taken a clear position of social reform even if it meant going against the current of nationalism. Nationalist historians naturally find this position rather disagreeable and sectarian. But if this decision is to be judged from the point of view of the depressed classes and if we also keep in mind Congress' rather poor record on this question (despite Gandhiji's sincere efforts and wishes), I do not see how Dr Ambedkar can be faulted on this score. In any case all that is a matter of past. Social reform is no longer opposed to political nationalism. The question of relative priority of economic and social reform can still be raised but there is nothing, except ideological dogmas, which prevent their being taken up simultaneously.

There is another related question. Must the question of social emancipation be raised exclusively, that is, to the exclusion of other concern and by a separate organisation/party? No, it is true that Dr Ambedkar did not take the extreme position on this question which he is supposed to have taken. Two of the three political parties he sponsored, Independent Labour Party and Republican Party of India (formed after his death, but he had prepared the blueprint; see Keer 1987: 498) were open to everyone; only the All India Scheduled Castes Federation was 'exclusive' in this sense. But his general inclination was for a politics of, for and by the depressed classes. The problem here is not with the 'sectarianism' of such a position; if there is one sectarianism that should not be objected to, it is that of the ex-untouchables. The problem is that of effectiveness. Is it politically more prudent for the Dalits to fight their battle alone? Or is it wiser to be part of a broader alliance of various disadvantageous sections of the Indian society and fight the battle collectively? An exclusivist strategy was no doubt more effective vis-a-vis the colonial state, but the logic of electoral and parliamentary politics has altered the rules of the game which dalit activists need to take into account. (Dr Ambedkar himself entered into electoral understanding with the PSP, but it was confined to that.) While merging the Dalit cause completely in the larger struggle against injustice is still difficult to advocate, there does not seem to be a case for partial reconsideration of Dr Ambedkar's policy on this score.

IV

In this final section I wish to take up for examination the relevance of the remaining aspects of his ideology which revolve around the theme of modernity and tradition. Although he did not use this vocabulary of the dichotomy of modernity/tradition (this was to become fashionable in the 1960s, thanks to American social scientists), much of what he has to say on the programmatic aspects (points 3 to 6 in my summary) was determined by this awareness. To put it simply, he believed that the Indian traditions lacked the resources from which a movement for social emancipation could be built. The inspiration therefore has to come from outside. Modern ideas and institutions introduced by the colonial rulers provide the necessary material. Hence he completely rejected the Hindu religion, its social order and material base and relied on modern education, law, state and parliamentary politics.

But that is too neat and artificial a picture. It is necessary here to reconstruct Ambedkar's ideas more faithfully than the account above may suggest.

As early as in 1936 Dr Ambedkar had announced his complete lack of faith in Hindu religion and declared the prospects of achieving social emancipation within the Hindu religion 'well-nigh impossible'.[4] With the passage of time his rejection of Hinduism got more and more complete and bitter. These lines from the introduction to Riddles in Hinduism, a book he could not publish in his lifetime, bring it out:

> If the Hindu intellect has ceased to grow and if the Hindu civilization and culture has become a stagnant and stinking pool, this dogma must be destroyed root and branch if India is to progress. The Vedas are a worthless set of books. There is no reason either to call them sacred or infallible. ... But the time has come when the Hindu mind must be freed from the hold which the silly ideas propagated by the Brahmins have to them. Without this liberation India has no future.[5]

His vehement critique was not confined only to the scriptures of Hinduism or to Brahminism and the Varnashrama system. He was no less critical of the villages, the basic unit of Indian society. Speaking in the Constituent Assembly, he declared:

> I hold that these village republics have been the ruination of India. I am, therefore, surprised that those who condemn provincialism and communalism should come forward as the champions of the village. What is the village but a sink of localism, a den of ignorance, narrow-mindedness and communalism?[6]

In other words he opposed the entire traditional set-up of Indian society, its ideas, its institutions.

There are, of course, some exceptions. He is quite different towards the saints like Ramanuja and Kabir who tried to change the Hindu tradition from within, but says in the same breath that such attempts can have little effect.[7] He takes lot of interest in Brahmins which in his opinion could serve as an alternative to the dominant orthodoxy of Brahaminism and provide foundations for a true democracy.[8] The biggest exception was his attitude towards Buddhism and the decision to get converted to it. It is worth stressing that this conversion was neither abrupt nor surprising. His complete rejection of Hinduism did not lead him to reject religion as such. In fact he continued to believe that religion was a must in human life[9] and kept searching for another religion which fitted his idea of a true religion. He has a long standing attraction for Buddhism and it was not surprising when twenty years after declaring that he would not die a Hindu, he embraced Buddhism.[10] Although these exceptions enable us to separate Dr Ambedkar from the nineteenth century radicals, like Dorazio or their twentieth century counterparts. Like the Indian Communists who would have nothing to do with religion or other traditional form of ideas, these do not contradict the point made earlier that he showed a definite preference for modernity over the traditions. It is not accidental that he chose Buddhism, a religion that comes fairly close to modern atheist sensibilities and has therefore attracted many modern Indian intellectuals (Nehru and Narendra Deva, to name two). His expectation from a religion and the interpretation he puts on the basic tenents of Buddhism are so strikingly modern.[11] His critique of Hinduism also consistently employs modern European standards.[12]

This comes clearer when we turn to his attitude towards modern institutions themselves. These were to create both the subjective and the objective conditions for the rise of the hitherto depressed classes. Modern education and science was to alter the state of their consciousness, modern state and law were to provide the material environment and security necessary for that. Here is Ambedkar on higher education:

> Coming as I do from the lowest order of the Hindu society, I know what is the value of education. The problem of raising the lower orders is deemed to be econonuc. This is a great mistake. The problem ... is to remove from them the inferiority complex which has stunted their growth and made them slaves to others, to create in them the consciousness of the significance of their lives for themselves and for the country, of which they have been cruelly robbed by the existing social order. Nothing can achieve this purpose except the spread of higher education. This is in my opinion the panacea of our social troubles.[13]

If the education was long-term measure to alter the consciousness of the depressed classes, state and its laws were to be immediate guarantee of their freedom and dignity and also a vehicle for bringing far-reaching changes in their material conditions of life. Right in *Annihilation of Caste*, Ambedkar had visualized a major role for the state in the fundamental reorganization of Hinduism. He wanted hereditary priesthood to be abolished and converted into another governmental job open to everyone. In his own blueprint for the Constitution (different from the draft Constitution) he made provision for the state ownership of the entire agricultural land. His role in formulating the Constitutional safeguards for SCs and his initiatives for Hindu Code Bill to reform the Hindu family system are too well known to need a restatement. In the free India he wanted to lead and promote a political formation of the Scheduled Castes which would secure greater state intervention, more progressive legislation to serve the interest of the Scheduled Castes.[14]

NOTES

1. *Dr Babasaheb Ambedkar: Writings and Speeches* (hereafter *BAWS*), vols. I-XV, complied by Vasant Moon, Bombay, 1979-95, pp. 57-8.
2. Ibid., vol. I, pp. 38-47.
3. Ibid., vol. I, p. 45.
4. Ibid., vol. I, p. 69.
5. Ibid., vol. I, pp. 8-9.
6. G.S. Lokhande, *Bhimrao Ramji Ambedkar: A Study in Social Democracy*, New Delhi, 1977, pp. 198-9.
7. *BAWS*, vol. I, pp. 47, 88-9.
8. Ibid., *Riddle*, no. 22, vol. IV, pp. 281-7.
9. Dhananjay Keer, *Dr Ambedkar: Life and Mission*, Bombay, 1987, p. 502.
10. Ibid., Chaps. XIV, XXII, XXVI; *BAWS*, vol. III, Chap. 18.
11. Ibid., p. 421, 502; *BAWS*, vol. III, p. 442.
12. *BAWS*, vol. IV, *Riddles*.
13. Eleanor Zelliot, 'The Social and Political Thought of B.R. Ambedkar', *Political Thought in Modern India*, eds. Thomas Pantham and Kenneth L. Deutsch, New Delhi, 1986, pp. 172-3.
14. Rosalind O'Hanlon, *Caste, Conflict and Ideology: Mahatma Jyotirao Phule and Low Caste Protest in Nineteenth-century Western India*, Cambridge, 1985.

11
Beyond the Torturing Times: Dr Ambedkar and the Dalit Future

Anand Teltumbde

Discussion of a future for Dalits would not be possible without reference to Babasaheb Ambedkar for at least a couple of centuries to come. The imprint of that colossus of rebellion is written so large upon every aspect of Dalit life that it is impossible to conceive a Dalit future without its influence. Babasaheb devoted his entire life to a struggle for the deliverance of Dalits from inhuman bondage and the draconian clutches of the caste system throughout the millennia perfected itself into a unique and effective instrument of perpetuating the comprehensive exploitation of one segment of society for the benefit of another, by means of a remarkable continuum of hierarchies. He attacked the citadel of this devilish system from many directions and left a hazy track behind him, the extrapolation of which might constitute the building of a Dalit future. Considering the enormity of the problem, which had eaten deep into Indian life, that he ventured to face it head-on despite being utterly without resources, and the kind of impact he could create in the lives of so many people, one can find few parallels to his phenomenal contribution to the cause of human emancipation in the course of history.

Dr Ambedkar single-handedly shook the foundations of that monolithic structure of the caste system and encouraged millions of its victims to completely overthrow it, in order to usher in an era of human liberty, equality and fraternity. Over the years, directly or indirectly as a result of the movement Dr Ambedkar launched, the resources of this multi-million army of his torch-bearers expanded many times in terms of money, power and education. It was expected that this enormous force would accelerate the pace of the Ambedkarian movement and soon inaugurate an era of revolution, demolishing the fossilized socio-economic structure of society in India. Looking back at the decades after the death of Dr Ambedkar, one cannot but be disappointed to see the state of the so-called Ambedkarian movement in this country. This kind of value-judgement might offend the sensibilities of many who out of sheer devotion to Babasaheb would not like to hear so much as a whisper of failure associated with their saviour, or their great movement. There are many vested interests, moreover, who play upon the sentiments of gratefulness of the Dalit masses towards Dr Ambedkar in order to thwart the process of candid evaluation of the movement and rational analysis of its development, lest they themselves be exposed. Notwithstanding the innocence and ignorance of the Dalit masses, for whom indeed Ambedkar was no less a god, such meticulous playing upon sentiments and deliberate deification of Ambedkar is largely responsible for preventing people from knowing what went wrong with the Ambedkarian movement.

The proud symbols of the movement have all been reduced to miserable ruins at the hands of people who claimed his legacy. The political movement launched by Dr Ambedkar, which once promised the Indian proletariat its liberation from all kinds of shackles, has turned into a process of generating political pimps. They trade Dalit sentiments, aspiration and faith and earn their brokerage. The educational institutions which Dr Ambedkar had fondly built to provide Dalit boys and girls with the means to reach a standard of excellence, and which during their founding had attracted many stalwarts to associate themselves with the process of epoch-making change, have been reduced to dens of corruption and storehouses of incompetence. The religio-cultural movement that Babasaheb had launched by renouncing caste-ridden Hindusim and embracing Buddhism, reformulating the latter in consonance with the rationalist ethos of modern times, fell into the hands of ignoramuses who hardly cared to know Buddhism as it was, not to mention the radical form of his conception. They have left no stone unturned to reduce it to useless mumbo-jumbo, quite like that of the Hinduism which they despised. The socio-cultural aspects of the Dalit movement which had reached a zenith in the wake of its struggle for self-emancipation, are today in a shambles and struggling to survive. The uncompromising struggles that had become the hallmark of the Ambedkarian movement are today conveniently relegated and confined to books and archives, their place being taken by shameless compromises for petty self-gain. While there is so much noise being made in eulogizing Babasaheb, all that he lived and died for is being trampled upon by the very people who claim to carry on his legacy.

The establishment once shaken and scared by his powerful blows and steadfast determination today appears to be adopting Dr Ambedkar and sponsoring the deafening din in his name. While the innocent followers of Dr Ambedkar are made to rejoice at this glorification of their saviour, these widespread festivities and celebrations have completely obscured the spirit and identity of Ambedkarian struggle. Right from the multi-fractured Republican Parties to the communalist Bhartiya Janata Party; from every den of Dalit Panthers to the rabid Rashtriya Swayamsevaka Sangha; from the most ardent and fire-brand Naxalites to right-inclined parliamentary Communist parties; from Congress to the Janata Dal to the BSP: in short almost all organizations in the country—political and apolitical—variously uphold Ambedkar. In the ensuing confusion, it has become increasingly difficult to understand what in essence constituted the Ambedkarian movement, which is meant to steer the Dalit future.

The subtle stratagems of the establishment, operating through vested interests of various types, are bound to separate Dalits from the true Ambedkarian essence and slacken the process of their emancipation. It is high time that Dalits understood the mechanics blocking the paths to their liberation. Only then will they be able to smash it and recover their weaponry to relaunch their true struggle. The basic part of this process is firstly to conceptualize what exactly Ambedkarism is. It would involve detailed reconstruction of the context in order to comprehend the essential meaning of Ambedkar's words and deeds. Dr Ambedkar is indeed an enigma of modern Indian history, who, while pursuing the values of his goals, would not care at all about any consequence or label. His belief in the rightness of his mission was so strong that he would often shift his position, depending on the surrounding objective conditions and simply reason that consistency was the virtue of an ass. He spoke and wrote volumes, which invariably bore the compound imprint of his academic and research bias; heavy polemics and his labyrinthine tactics and emotional rage were inevitable in the turbulent times in which he, as an activist, found himself. Words perhaps never failed more miserably than they did in his case.

It is a task of gigantic proportions, therefore, to decipher the core-meaning of his words, analyse them and reconstruct the composite body of the thought that he lived. This write-up merely touches upon some salient issues without going into their analytical aspects and ventures certain approaches so as to provoke reflection and discussion among the activist-scholars of the Ambedkarian movement.

The terms 'Ambedkarian', Ambedkarism', and 'Ambedkarite', etc., have become so commonplace in Dalit life that we hardly realize how greatly they are abused. For instance, anyone belonging to the Scheduled Castes, having picutres of Dr Ambedkar and/or Buddha hung in his house and chanting concern for his community, qualifies to be called Ambedkarite. Social identities of this kind do crystallize around certain symbols, but when these identities constitute an important role in social movements they need an ideological vigilance for warding off distorting factors. In the case of the Ambedkarian movement, this ideological vigilance has been effected through sectarian dogma, a little constrained by the low political consciousness of Dalits, even more so by conscious engineering by vested interests, which made these social identities increasingly puerile.

A singular misfortune of the Ambedkarian movement is that it did not have a theoretician of first-class calibre, required to chart out its path through the labyrinths of the fast-changing world. After the disappearance of Dr Ambedkar from the scene, it started groping in the past to seek support in his words and deeds for its sustenance. Without a dialectical perspective, a commensurate level of political consciousness and information base, it was not easy to link together those scattered words and deeds. Before the Dalit community came of age, the social charlatans and political pimps hijacked the Ambedkarian movement and confounded the whole fabric of Ambedkar's thought. Dalits repeatedly mistook trees for the wood and strayed away from the true direction. Many in vanguard positions chose to have their field-day in the ensuing ideological confusion and accelerated quite wantonly the pace of aberration. For many, their greed and betrayal were the main factors responsible for the current state of the Ambedkarian movement. For many, as a corollary of this, the gullibility, ignorance, resourcelessness, cultural inertia and extremely low-level of political consciousness of the Dalit masses were equally responsible. Many, relatively more perceptive, found the vicious machinations of the Congress party—party from the days of Gandhi's blackmailing Dr Ambedkar into signing the Poona Pact and doing away with the equation between political separation and social segregation granted by the Communal Award—responsible for its plight. Some blamed Ambedkar's later spiritual inclinations and reading too much into a 2,500 years-old Buddhism, or shunning the path of real struggle and adopting constitutionalism. Those subscribing to a Marxist methodology saw his Fabian leanings, utterly non-class programme, bourgeois liberalism, unprincipled pragmatism, and recessive sectarianism as responsible for the pitiful state of his movement today. Some even held the containment process, represented by the reservation policy, responsible for the growing emasculation and neutralization of educated Dalits which eventually bore upon the Dalit movement. To these one can also add more factors which are considered responsible for the decay of the Dalit movement, by the people depending upon their respective orientation and political beliefs. They are: Dr Ambedkar's dissociation from the national mainstream; his opposition to communists; his idealism; his deification, and the formation of a cult after his death. This spectrum of varied reasons for the miserable plight of the Dalit movement, practically does not exclude anything, sounds strangely plausible and containing some truth to a wide variety of people. It is as easy for the Dalits to lay blame on the Congress party or some other agency and externalize the problem. Those initiated into the theories of scientific socialism and inured to measure peoples and situations with the help of its set moulds, are frustrated by the broad tendencies of dialectical idealism that Dr Ambedkar's responses to situations reflect. They hasten to attribute most of the ills suffered by the Dalit movement to this ideological flaw. In total contrast to this, an increasing number of Dalits see the non-adherence of the Dalit leadership of Ambedkarism, which is assumed to be perfect, to be responsible for their plight.

Regarding the accusation of non-adherence to Ambedkarism, interestingly, none of the Dalit leaders, irrespective of whether they belong to professedly Dalit outfits like the RPI, Dalit Panthers, Bhim Sena, BSP and the variously named Dalit Liberation Movements; or the non-Dalit organizations like the mainstream political parties of the ruling classes (Congress, Janata Dal, Bhartiya Janata Party); or the Communist parties including the Marxist-Leninist ones; or even the people who have somehow managed to reach positions of power, none of these even remotely seek to disclaim Ambedkar. Each one of these factions has its own conception and interpretation of Ambedkarism and with competitive zeal will defend it from the criticism of the others.

While Dalit women were being paraded naked on the streets,

Dalit workers being brutally blinded and Dalit children burnt alive, we sang long *Mangal Gathas* in incomprehensible Pali in our Buddha Viharas for hours, enjoying caning the dead serpents in Hindu scriptures with the stick of impotent intellect. The islands created by reservations and political prostitution, placed Dr Ambedkar in the position of the Hindu goddess of wealth—Lakshmi. Adherence to Ambedkar or Ambedkarism was apparently aplenty. What was strikingly lacking was its identity. The struggle against oppression shunned, the concept of mass-organizations ruined, the value of enlightenment negated, the so-called Ambedkarites of all hues hurry to cash in on Ambedkarism.

The question that naturally arises in this confusing situation is what exactly Ambedkarism is. Can that be first of all conceived in a composite body of thought? Many answer in the affirmative and attempt to define it along the lines of Ambedkar's leanings towards dialectical idealism, his Fabian tendencies, his love for parliamentary democracy, constitutionalism, Buddhism and so on, depending upon their own predispositions. All are therefore sectarian and superficial. A fundamental departure from these previous approaches, that is, the fitting of Dr Ambedkar's words into pre-established moulds, is needed if we want Ambedkarism to be the guiding philosophy for the Dalit movement. The only viable way of concentrating on an Ambedkarian essence with this new approach is through a genuine empathy for the cause he chose to be his life's objective. It is then alone that one can comprehend why his concern for landless peasants and workers had to be subdued in favour of his wider community, why he had to go against the Communists or Gandhi, why he had to sit as Labour member of the Viceroy's Executive Council, accept the Law ministership in Nehru's cabinet, or write India's Constitution and later, disown it. In his apparent inconsistencies one would probably find more valuable material than may appear at first sight. He would be more understandable by the questions he raised than by the anwers he seems to provide. The antithesis might hold forth more promise than the thesis. The unsaid might prove more truth-bearing than what is said, for, if not by anything else, his expressions were clouded by his own familiarity.

The essence of Ambedkarism springs from Dr Ambedkar's concept of human beings having certain inalienable rights which ought to be safeguarded by socio-political organizations at all times. Basic in his vision is to so create an organization of society as to enable human beings to live life fully in unison with the world, without any feeling of alienation. It radically opposed anything other than this—any kind of exploitation that anything entailed. In the Indian context, the caste-based organization of society represented an extreme form of exploitation, the experience of which provided him with the motive-force to wage a lifelong battle against it. Taking into account any myth-ridden history of the country, the resources available to him, the formidable characteristics of the enemy, and his own life-span as the only available time, he just plunged into the fray and fought against the enemy camp with all his armoury, and with steadfast determination. His main concern was not to philosophize or interpret the surrounding world, but to change it; his acute awareness of the time actually granted to him for this, heavily constrained the tactical methodology for bringing about this change. His concern was nothing less than to bring about a revolution which would maximize harmony between man and the world. But, confronted with the strange objective reality around him, he saw the process of history creating revolutionary nodes, a little differently from the prophets of scientific socialism in the Western world. His concern was also socialism, but it was not divorced from his basic value premise linked with the concept of human being, which many may find not to be different from Marx's concept of man (see Erich Fromm). As modern thought on socialist experience would corroborate, his socialism represented a social constitution, a relationship of human beings with each other (Otto Ulrich). Socialism for him was not a society of regimented, automatized individuals merely seekig increasing satisfaction of their material and so-called cultural needs through a constant growth of socialist production. His reading of history revealed that revolutions were always preceded by socio-cultural movements, which need not be taken as being at variance with the process of political conscientization as it is understood in revolutionary circles. His utterances vis-a-vis Communism are deceptive, as are perhaps many others, inasmuch as they are construed to be anti-Marxist. They are certainly opposed to the dogmatic notions then held in Communist circles, particularly so in India. The mechanistic approach has prevailed and still prevails, though on a diminishing scale. It considers the material (economic) aspect as the only reality and ignores everything else as an illusive reflection of his excessive idealistic leaning on man's conscience and society's ethical foundations, devoid of their material base. Despite his early spiritual socialization and formative influences from the idealistic, bourgeois liberal environment and despite uncongenial experiences at home with the dogmatic Communists, he did recognize all through his life the revolutionary efficacy of the Marxist approach and prophesied its eventual success. His greatest reservations about it were related with the actual process of its achievement, as reflected in the world of his time. He never discussed it systematically at a level commensurate with the degree of complexity of the philosophical foundation of Marxist theory, though, there always appears to be its tacit acceptance behind the veneer of criticism. This criticism itself centred around the classic debate of the relationship between base and superstructure and some kind of transient mode of achieving revolutionary change, such as the dictatorship of the proletariat. Dogma apart, the validity of doubts about these concepts cannot be easily denied.

Many of his occasional utterances, like the denunciation of violence, rejection of extremes and adoption of a middle path, the antipathy to any kind of dictatorship, have perhaps been misconstrued and taken by devout Dalits as definitive doctrines. In an exploitative set-up violence is integrated with its very being, and any kind of opposition to it, even seemingly most bloody in its form, ought always to be directed to eliminating that violence itself, possibly by removing its very cause. Even the non-violence of Buddha, conceived millennia ago, pre-empted absolute conceptions of violence. When a landlord or a capitalist sucks the blood of large numbers of his landless peasants or factory workers, violence is committed throughout the whole of this process. But, if in order to counteract this violence, the workers take up arms with a revolutionary consciousness and spill the blood of a few of their exploiters, the violence merely performs the role of midwife in bringing about change.

Nobody can deny that the former is much more vicious than the latter. When human history is replete with violence and directly indicative that revolutions each time reduce its potential for violence, any talk of non-violence should be qualified with value-premises. The middle-path controversy, likewise, is mechanically developed. It represents a dialectical concept which aims at following the eternal conflict of thesis and antithesis. Babasaheb would never bless this kind of naivete. The reaction to the phraseology about the dictatorship of the proletariat can also be understood in line with the argument about the violence.

Thus a viable formulation of Ambedkarism for dealing with the Dalit future is possible neither through the many indications he left behind, nor even through his words, dependent as they are on their context, but only through uncovering the core of the revolutionary concerns behind them. Ambedkarism thus conceived, could alone be capable of evolving into a systematic revolutionary theory and tool of analysing human situations. And it is the only way of understanding it if we mean to be concerned with its emancipatory potential for Dalits henceforth. It alone would be able to indicate a workable strategy and tactics in the increasingly complex situation that Dalits find themselves in. It alone would delineate our allies and adversaries in the battles we fight.

Today the leadership of the Ambedkarian movement has fallen completely into the hands of those who have reduced it either to a club-like forum engaging continually in festivities in the name of Ambedkar, or to an amateur stage for rehearsing expression of sterile wrath against the Brahmins and their ism, but unashamedly at the same time eulogizing the rulers, thereby obscuring everything and dubiously consecrating everything the state represents. Today Ambedkarism is mired deeply in parliamentarianism, so much so that it has become its be all and end all, when tragically, Parliament itself is becoming increasingly out of reach. By design, no one can be elected on their own strength unless they compromise and take a tail-end approach behind a main political party representing the Establishment.

The containment strategy adopted by the Indian ruling classes so far has vast resilience and in essence is an extension of caste itself. Caste, as an instrument of perpetuating exploitation, has displayed enough resilience in the distant past and has done so as well in recent years. Although its feudal moorings are weakening owing to the changes in objective conditions and anti-caste movements built up in the wake of those changes, the post-independence institutions and electoral politics cunningly made use of it quite effectively, as if giving it a new lease of life. In such circumstances, if the anti-caste movement relied solely on the caste idiom, it would only lend strength to the strategy of the exploiters and there could be continual cauldrons of caste and communal strife.

The crux of the Dalit problem today is rooted in the socio-economic structure of the Indian village and in turn could be traced to the land question. The genius of Babasaheb had realized this even before he had formally launched his movement, and he lamented at the end of his life that he had not been able to do anything about it. Until this structural problem is resolved, the superstructure will never be effectively dealt with. This is not to ignore the existence of global caste-prejudices which even materially well-off Dalits suffer everywhere, even among the emigrant communities in Europe and America. But to root out this cultural evil can only be possible through pioneering a cultural and conscientization movement and not through strengthening of the existing caste divisions. Sadly, the Ambedkarian movement has become extremely sectarian even the various castes of Dalits are vying with each other to safe-guard their purity. The guiding ethos, if we examine it carefully, is strikingly Brahmanic, as reflected in these Dalit attitudes. This has resulted in a deadlock, whereby only one or two castes in each state have come into the Ambedkarian movement, others choosing to stay away and enjoying its successes.

Caste prejudice becomes manifested and assumes material form invariably through those who have some vested interests. If we adopt an analytical and rational approach to the problem, the probability of reaching its roots would increase and we would be in a better position to strike at them, rather than beating around the bush in the abstract. The people who normally fall prey to the machinations of vested interests would also realize the folly of their behaviour and might choose to side with us, once they are convinced of their long-term interests being served by us. In any struggle it is a basic requirement to correctly recognize friends and foes. It is axiomatic that we cannot wage a viable war with so many foes and such few friends. It would be imperative that we re-draw our battle lines along the systematic analyses of the situation. Ambedkarism has all the potential to help in our rational approaches and ensure our ultimate success, provided we free it from obscuration, and liberate it from the clutches of charlatans, ignoramuses and vested interests. Perhaps this would be the Dalits' most immediate battle.

APPENDIX 1

*Not the British Raj, but Swaraj could Solve Dalit Problem: Dr Ambedkar at the RTC, London, 1930**

Arun Shourie believes, and he wants his readers, too, to believe that Dr Ambedkar was not for Indian Independence. The Dalit leader, he opines, wanted the British rule to continue so that he could get some benefits from it for himself in particular and Dalits in general.

Was Ambedkar really like this? Had he no taste for India's Independence? I think the following excerpts from a speech of Dr Ambedkar would answer these queries and settle many confusing points. —Editor

Dr B.R. Ambedkar: Mr. Chairman, my purpose in rising to address this conference is principally to place before it the point of view of the depressed classes, whom I and my colleague, Rao Bahadur Srinivasan, have the honour to represent, regarding the question of constitutional reform. It is a point of view of 4,30,00,000 people, or one-fifth of the total population of British India. The depressed classed form a group by themselves which is distinct and separate from the Muhammadans and, although they are included among the Hindus, they in no sense form an integral part of that community. Not only have they a separate existence, but they have also assigned to them a statute which is invidiously distinct from the status occupied by any other community in India. There are communities in India which occupy a lower and subordinate position; but the position assigned to the depressed classes is totally different. It is one which is midway between that of the serf and the slave, and which may, for convenience, be called servile with this difference, that the

**Proceedings of the Round Table Conference* (First Session, Fifth Sitting, 20 Nov. 1930), Government of India, Central Publication Branch, Calcutta, 1931, pp. 123-9.

serf and the slave were permitted to have physical contact, from which the depressd classes are debarred. What is worse that this enforced servility and bar to human intercourse, due to their untouchability, involves, not merely the possibility of discrimination in public life, but actually works out as a positive denial of all equality of opportunity and the denial of those most elementary of civic rights on which all human existence depends. I am sure that the point of view of such a community, as large as the population of England or of France, and so heavily handicapped in the struggle for existence, cannot but have some bearing on the right sort of solution of the political problem, and I am anxious that this Conference should be placed in possession of that point of view at the very start.

The point of view I will try to put as briefly as I can, it is this that the bureaucratic form of government in India should be replaced by a government which will be a government of the people, by the people and for the people. This statement of the view of the depressed classes I am sure will be recieved with some surprise in certain quarters. The tie that bounds the depressed classes welcomed the British as their deliverers from age-long tyranny and oppression by the orthodox Hindus. They fought their battles against Hindus, the Mussalamans and the Sikhs and won for them this great Empire of India. The British, on their side, assumed the role of trustees for the depressed classes. In view of such an intimate relationship between the parties. this change in the attitude of the depressed classes towards British Rule in India is undoubtedly a most momentous phenomenon. But the reasons for this change of attitude are not far to seek. We have not taken this decision simply because we wish to throw in our lot with the majority. Indeed, as you know, there is not much love lost betweeen the majority and the particular minority I represent. Ours is an independent decision.

1 We have judged of the existing administration solely in the light of our own circumstances and we have found it wanting in some of the most essential elements of a good government. When we compare our present position with the one which it was our lot to bear in Indian society of the pre-British days, we find that, instead of marching on, we are only marking time. Before the British, we were in the loathsome condition due to our untouchability. Has the British Government done anything to remove it? Before the British, we could not enter the temple. Can we enter now? Before the British, we were denied entry into the Police Force. Does the British Government admit us in the Force? Before the British, we were not

allowed to serve in the Military. Is that career now open to us? To none of these questions can we give an affirmative answer. That the British, who have held so large a sway over us for such a long time, have done some good we cheerfully acknowledge. But there is certainly no fundamental change in our position. Indeed, so far as we were concerned, the British Government has accepted the social arrangements as it found them, and has preserved them faithfully in the manner of the Chinese tailor who, when given an old coat as a pattern. produced with pride an exact replica, rents, patches and all. Our wrongs have remained as open sores and they have not been righted, although 150 years of British rule have rolled away.

2. We do not accuse the British of indifference or want of sympathy. What we do find is that they are quite incompetent to tackle our problems. If the case was one of indifference only it would have been a matter of small moment, and it would not have made such a profound change in our attitude. But what we have come to realize on a deeper analysis of the situation is that is not merely a case of indifference, rather it is a case of sheer incompetence to undertake the task. The depressed classes find that the British Government in India suffers from two very serious limitations. There is first of all an internal limitation which arises from the character, motives and interests of those who are in power. It is not because they cannot help us in these things but because it is against their character, motives and interests to do so. The second consideration that limits its authority is the mortal fear it has of external resistance. The Government of India does realize the necessity of removing the social evils which are eating into the vitals of Indian society and which have blighted the lives of the downtrodden classes for so many years. The Government of India does realize that the landlords are squeezing the masses dry, and the capitalists are not giving the labourers a living wage and decent conditions of work. Yet is is most painful thing that it has not dared to touch any of these evils. Why? Is it because it has no legal powers to remove them? No. The reason why it does not intervene is because it is afraid that its intervention to amend the existing code of social and economic life, will give rise to resistance. Of what good is such a Government to anybody? Under a Government, paralysed between two such limitations, much that goes to make life good must remain held up.

3. We must have a government in which the men in power will give their undivided allegiance to the best interest of the country. We must have a government in which men in power, knowing where

obedience will end and resistance will begin, will not be afraid to amend the social and economic code of life which the dictates of justice and expediency so urgently call for. This role the British government will never be able to play. It is only a government which is of the people, for the people and by the people that will make this possible.

There are some of the questions raised by the depressed classes and the answers which in their view these questions seem to carry. This is therefore the inevitable conclusion which the depressed classes have come to: namely, that the bureaucratic Government of India, with the best of motives, will remain powerless to effect any change so far as our particular grievances are concerned.

4. We feel that nobody can remove our grievances as well as we can, and we cannot remove them unless we get political power in our own hands. No share of this political power can evidently come to us so long as the British Government remains as it is. It is only in a Swaraj Constitution that we stand any chance of getting the political power into our own hands, without which we cannot bring salvation to our people.

There is one thing, Sir, to which I wish to draw your particular attention. It is this. I have not used the expression Dominion Status in placing before you the point of view of the depressed classes. I have avoided using it, not because I do not understand its implication nor does the omission mean that the depressed classes object to India's attaining Dominion Status. My chief ground for not using it is that it does not convey the full content of what the depressed classes stand for. The depressed classes, while they stand for Dominion Status with safeguards, wish to lay all the emphasis they can on one question and one question alone. And that question is, how will Dominion India function? Where will the centre of political power be? Who will have it? Will the depressed classes be heirs to it? These are the questions that form their chief concern. The depressed classes feel that they will get no shred of the political power unless the political machinery for the new constitution is of a special make. In the construction of that machine certain hard facts of Indian social life must not be lost sight of. It must be recognized that Indian society is a gradation of castes forming an ascending scale of reverence and a descending scale of contempt—a system which gives no scope for the growth of that sentiment of equality and fraternity so essential for a democratic form of government. It must also be recognized that while the intelligentsia is a very important part of India society, it is drawn from its upper strata and although it speaks in the name of the country and leads the political movement, it has not shed the narrow particularism of the class from which it is drawn. In other words what the depressed classes wish to urge is that the political mechanism must take account of and must have a definite relation to the psychology of the society for which it is devised. Otherwise you are likely to produce a constitution which, however symmetrical, will be truncated one and a total misfit to the society for which is designed.

There is one point with which I should like to deal before I close this. We are often reminded that the problem of the depressed classes is a social problem and that its solution lies elsewhere than in politics. We take strong exception to this view. We hold that the problem of the depressed classes will never be solved unless they get political power in their own hands. If this is true, and I do not think that the contrary can be maintained, then problem of depressed classes is, I submit, eminently a political problem and must be treated as such. We know that political power is passing from the British into the hands of those who wield such tremendous economic, social and religious sway over our existence. We are willing that it may happen, though the idea of Swaraj recalls to the mind of many of us the tyrannies, oppressions and injustices practised upon us in the past and fear of their recurrence under Swaraj. We are prepared to take the inevitable risk of the situation in the hope that we shall be installed, in adequate proportion, as the political sovereigns of the country along with our fellow countrymen. But we will consent to that on one condition and that is that the settlement of our problems is not left to time. I am afraid the depressed classes have waited too long for time to work its miracle. At every successive step taken by the British Government to widen the scope of representative Governments the depressed classes have been systematically left out. No thought has been given to their claim for political power. I protest with all the emphasis I can that we will not stand this any longer. The settlement of our problem must be a part of the general political settlement and must not be left over to the shifting sands of the sympathy and goodwill of the rulers of the future. The reasons why the depressed classes insist upon it are obvious. Every one of us knows that the man in possession is more powerful than the man who is out of possession. Everyone of us also knows that those in possession of power seldom abdicate in favour of those who are out of it. We cannot therefore hope for the effectuation of the settlement of our social problem. If we allow power to slip into the hands of those who stand to lose by settlement unless we are to have another revolution to dethrone those, whom we today help to ascend the throne of power and prestige. We prefer being despised for too anxious apprehensions, than ruined by too confident a security, and I think it would be just and proper for us to insist that the best guarantee for the settlement of our problem is the adjustment of the political machine itself so as to give us a hold on it, and not the will of those who are contriving to be left in unfettered control of that machine.

What adjustments of the political machine the depressed classes want for their safety and protection I will place before the Conference at the proper time. All I will say at the present moment is that, although we want responsible Government, we do not want a government that will only mean a change of masters. Let the Legislature be fully and really representative if your Executive is going to be fully responsible.

I am sorry Mr. President I had to speak in such plain words. But I saw no help. The depressed classes have had no friend. The Government has all along used them only as an excuse for its continued existence. The Hindus claim them only to deny them or, better still, to appropriate rights. The Muhammadans refuse to recognize their separate existence, because they fear that their privileges may be curtailed by the admission of a rival. Depressed by the government, suppressed by the Hindu and disregarded by the Muslim, we are left in a most intolerable position of utter helplessness to which I am sure there is no parallel and to which I was bound to call attention.

Regarding the other question which is set down for discussion I am sorry it was decided to tag it on to a general debate. Its importance deserved a session for itself. No justice can be done to it in a passing reference. The subject is one in which the depressed classes are deeply concerned and they regard it as a very vital question. As members of a minority, we look to the Central Government to act as a powerful curb on the provincial majority to save the minorities from the misrule of the majority. As an Indian, interested in the growth of Indian nationalism, I must make it plain that I am a strong believer in the Unitary form of Government and the thought of disturbing it I must confess does not please me very much. This Unitary Government has been the most potent influence in the building up of the Indian nation. That process of unification which has been the result of a unified system of Government has not been completed and I should be loathed to withdraw this most powerful stimulus in the formative period and before it has worked out its end.

However, the question in the form in which it is placed is only an academic question and I shall be prepared to consider a federal form, if it can be shown that in it local autonomy is not inconsistent with central unity.

Sir, all that I, as a representative of the depressed classes, need say on their behalf I have said. May I crave your indulgence to permit me as an Indian to say a word or two generally on the situation which we have to meet. So much has been said regarding its gravity that I shall not venture to add a word more to it, although I am no silent spectator of the movement. What I am anxious about is to feel whether we are proceeding on right lines in evolving our solution. What that solution should be rests entirely upon the view that British delegates choose to take. Addressing myself to them I will say, whether you will meet the situation by conciliation or by applying the iron heel must be a matter for your judgement for the responsibility is entirely yours. To such of you as are particular to the use of force and believe that a regime of *Letters de Cachet* and the Bastille will ease the situation, let me recall the memorable words of the greatest teacher of political philosophy, Edmund Burke. This is what he said to the British nation when it was faced with the problem of dealing with the Americal colonies:

> The use of force alone is but temporary. It may endure for a moment, but it does not remove the necessity of subduing again: a nation is not governed which is perpetually to be conquered. The next objection to force is its uncertainty. Terror is not always the effect of force, and an armament is not a victory. If you do not succeed, you are without resource; for conciliation failing, force remains, but force failing, no further hope of reconciliation is left. Power and authority are sometimes brought by kindness, but they can never be begged as alms by an impoverished and defeated violence. A further objection to force is, that you impair the object by your very endeavours to preserve it. The thing you fought for (to wit the loyalty of the people) is not the thing you recover but depreciated, sunk, wasted and consumed in the contest.

The worth and efficacy of this advice you all knew. You did not listen to it and you lost the great continent of America. You followed it to the lasting good of yourself and the rest of the Dominions that are with you. To such of you as are willing to adopt a policy of conciliation I should like to say one thing. There seems to be prevalent an impression that the Delegates are called here to argue for and against a case for Dominion Status and that the grant of Dominion Status will be dependent upon which side is the victor in this battle of wits. With due deference to all who are sharpening their wits, I submit that there can be no greater mistake than to make the formula of logic govern so live an issue. I have no quarrel with logic and logicians. But I ward them against the disaster that is bound to follow if they are not careful in the selection of the premises they choose to adopt for their deductions. It is all a matter of temper whether you will abide by the fall of your logic, or whether you will refute it, as Dr Johnson did the paradoxes of Berkeley by trampling them under his feet. I am afraid it is not sufficiently realized that in the present temper of the country, no constitution will be workable which is not acceptable to the majority of the people. The time when you were to choose and India was to accept is gone, never to return. Let the consent of the people and not the accident of logic be the touchstone of your new constitution, if you desire that it should be worked.

APPENDIX 2

*Dangers to the Indian Democracy: Dr Ambedkar's Warning**

Looking back on the work of the Constituent Assembly it will now be two years, eleven months and seventeen days since it first met on the 9th of December, 1946. During this period the Constituent Assembly has altogether held eleven sessions. Out of these eleven sessions, the first six were spent in passing the Objectives Resolution and the consideration of the Reports of Committees on Fundamental Rights, on Union Constitution, on Union Powers, on Provincial Constitution, on Minorities and on the Scheduled Areas and Scheduled Tribes. The seventh, eighth, ninth, tenth and the eleventh sessions were devoted to the consideration of the Draft Constitution. These eleven sessions of the Constituent Assembly have consumed 165 days. Out of these, the Assembly spent 114 days for the consideration of the Draft Constitution. Coming to the Drafting Committee, it was elected by the Constituent Assembly on 29th August 1947. It held its first meeting on the 30th August. Since August 30th it sat for 141 days during which it was engaged in the preparation of the Draft Constitution. The Draft Constitution, as prepared by the Constitutional Adviser as a text for the Drafting Committee to work upon, consisted of 243 Articles and 13 Schedules. The first Draft Constitution as presented by the Drafting Committee to the Constituent Assembly contained 315 Articles and 8 Schedules. At the end of the consideration stage, the number of Articles in the Draft Constitution increased to 386. In its final form, the Draft Constitution contains 395 Articles and 8 Schedules. The total number of amendments to the Draft Constitution tabled was approximately 7,635. Of them, the total number of amendments actually moved in the house were 2,473.

I mention these facts because at one stage it was being said that

*Speech delivered in the Constituent Assembly of India, on the eve of the adoption of the Constitution, 25 November 1949

the Assembly had taken too long a time to finish its work, that it was going on leisurely and wasting public money. It was said to be a case of Nero fiddling while Rome was burning. Is there any justification for this complaint? Let us note the time consumed by Constituent Assemblies in other countries appointed for framing their Constitutions. To take a few illustrations. The American Convention met on May 25th, 1787 and completed its work on September 17,1787, i.e. within four months. The Constitutional convention of Canada met on the 10th October 1864 and the Constitution was passed into law in March 1867 involving a period of two years and five months. The Australian Constitutional Convention assembled in March 1891 and the Constitution became law on the 9th July 1900, consuming a period of nine years. The South African Convention met in October 1908 and the Constitution became law on the 20th September 1909 involving one year's labour. It is true that we have taken more time than what the American or South African Conventions did. But we have not taken more time than the Canadian Convention and much less than the Australian Convention. In making comparisons on the basis of time consumed two things must be remembered. One is that Constitutions of America, Canada, South Africa and Australia are much smaller than ours. Our Constitution as, I said contains 395 Articles while American has just seven Articles, the first four of which are divided into sections which total up to 21, the Canadian has 147, Australian 128 and South African 153 sections. The second thing to be remembered is that the makers of the Constitutions of America, Canada, Australia and South Africa did not have to face the problem of amendments. They were passed as moved. On the other hand, this Constituent Assembly had to deal with as many as 2,473 amendments. Having regard to these facts the charge of dilatoriness seems to me quite unfounded and this Assembly may well congratulate itself for having accomplished so formidable a task in so short a time.

Turning to the quality of the work done by the Drafting Committee, Mr. Naziruddin Ahmed felt it his duty to condemn it outright. In his opinion, the work done by the Drafting Committee is not only not worthy of commendation, but is positively below par. Everybody has a right to have his opinion about the work done by the Drafting Committee and Mr. Naziruddin is welcome to have his own. Mr. Naziruddin Ahmed thinks of himself as a man of greater talents than any member of the Drafting Committee. The Drafting Committee does not wish to challenge his claim. On the other hand, the Drafting Committee would have welcomed him in their midst if the Assembly had thought him worthy of being appointed to it.

If he has had no place in the making of the Constitution it is certainly not the fault of the Drafting Committee.

Mr. Naziruddin Ahmed has coined a new name for the Drafting Committee evidently to show his contempt for it. He calls it a Drifting Committee. Mr Naziruddin must no doubt be pleased with his hit. But he evidently does not know that there is a difference between drift without mastery and drift with mystery. If the Drafting Committee was drifting, it was never without mastery over the situation. It was not merely angling with the off chance of catching a fish. It was searching in known waters to find the fish it was after. To be in search of something better is not the same as drifting. Although Mr. Naziruddin Ahmed did not mean it as a compliment to the Drafting Committee, I take it as a compliment to the Drafting Committee. The Drafting Committee would have been guilty of gross dereliction of duty and of a false sense of dignity if it had not shown the honesty and the courage to withdraw the amendments which it thought faulty and substitute what it thought was better. If it is a mistake, I am glad the Drafting Committee did not fight shy of admitting such mistakes and coming forward to correct them.

I am glad to find that with the exception of a solitary member, there is a general consensus of appreciation from members of the Constituent Assembly of the work done by the Drafting Committee. I am sure the Drafting Committee feels happy to find this spontaneous recognition of its labours expressed in such generous terms. As to the compliments that have been showered upon me both by the members of Assembly as well as by my colleagues of the Drafting Committee. I feel so overwhelmed that I cannot find adequate words to express fully my gratitude to them. I came into the Constituent Assembly with no greater aspiration than to safeguard the interests of the Scheduled Castes. I had not the remotest idea that I would be called upon to undertake more responsible functions. I was therefore greatly surprised when the Assembly elected me to the Drafting Committee. I was more than surprised when the Drafting Committee elected me to be its Chairman. There were in the Drafting Committee men bigger, better and more competent than myself, such as my friend Sir Alladi Krishnaswami Iyer. I am grateful to the Constituent Assembly and the Drafting Committee for reposing in me so much trust and confidence and to have chosen me as their instrument and given me this opportunity of serving the country.

The credit that is given to me does not really belong to me. It belongs partly to Sir B.N. Rau, the Constitutional Adviser to the Constituent Assembly who prepared a rough draft of the Constitution for the consideration of the Drafting Committee. A part of the credit must go to the members of the Drafting Committee who, as I have said, have sat for 141 days and without whose ingenuity to devise new formulae aid capacity to tolerate and to accommodate different points of view. The task of framing the Constitution could not have come to so successful a conclusion. Much greater share of the credit must go to Mr. S.N. Mukerjee, the Chief Draftsman of the Constitution. His ability to put the most intricate proposals in the simplest and clearest legal form can rarely be equalled, nor his capacity for hard work. He has been an acquisition to the Assembly. Without his help, this Assembly would have taken many more years to finalise the Constitution. I must not omit to mention the members of the staff working under Mr. Mukerjee. For, I know how hard they have worked and how long they have toiled sometimes even beyond midnight. I want to thank them all for their effort and their co-operation.

The task of the Drafting Committee would have been a very difficult one if this Constituent Assembly had been merely a motely crowd, a tassellated pavement without cement, a black stone here and a white stone there, in which each member or each group was a law unto itself. There would have been nothing but chaos. This possibility of chaos was reduced to nil by the existence of the Congress party inside the Assembly which brought into its proceedings a sense of order and discipline. It is because of the discipline of the Congress Party that the Drafting Committee was able to pilot the Constitution in the Assembly with the sure knowledge as to the fate of each Article and each amendment. The Congress Party is, therefore, entitled to all the credit for the smooth sailing of the Draft Constitution in the Assembly.

The proceedings of this Constituent Assembly would have been very dull if all members had yielded to the rule of party discipline. Party discipline, in all its rigidity would have converted this Assembly into a gathering of yesmen. Fortunately, there were rebels. They were Mr. Kamath, Dr. P.S. Deshmukh, Mr. Sidwa, Prof. Saxena and Pandit Thakurdas Bhargava. Along with them were Prof. K.T. Shah and Pandit Hridaynath Kunzru. The points they raised were mostly ideological. That I was not prepared to accept their suggestions, does not diminish the value of their suggestions nor lessens the service they have rendered to the Assembly in enlivening its proceedings. I am grateful to them. But for them, I would not have had the opportunity which I got for expounding the principles underlying the Constitution which was more important than the mere mechanical work of passing the Constitution.

Finally, I must thank you Mr. President for the way in which you have conducted the proceedings of this Assembly. The courtesy and the consideration which you have shown to the members of the Assembly can never be forgotten by those who have taken part in the proceeding of this Assembly. There were occasions when the amendments of the Drafting Committee were sought to be barred on grounds purely technical in their very nature. There were very anxious moments for me. I am, therefore, specially grateful to you for not permitting legalism to defeat the work of constitution-making.

As much defence as could be offered to the Constitution has been offered by my friends like Sir Alladikrishnaswamy Ayyar and Mr. T.T. Krishnamachari.

I shall not therefore enter into the merits of the Constitution. However good a Constitution may be, it is sure to turn out to be bad because those who are called to work it, happen to be a bad lot. However bad a Constitution may be, it may turn out to be good if those who are called to work it, happen to be a good lot. The working of a Constitution does not depend wholly upon the nature of the Constitution. The Constitution can provide only the organs of State such as the Legislature, the Executive and the Judiciary. The factors on which the working of those organs of the State depend are the people and the political parties they will set up as their instruments to carry out their wishes and their politics. Who can say how the people of India and their parties will behave? Will they uphold constitutional methods of achieving their purposes or will they prefer revolutionary methods of achieving them? If they adopt the revolutionary methods, however good the Constitution is, it requires no prophet to say that it will fail. It is, therefore, futile to pass any judgement upon the Constitution without reference to the part which the people of India and their parties are likely to play.

The condemnation of the Constitution largely comes from two quarters, the Communist Party and the Socialist Party. Why do they condemn Constitution? Is it because it is really a bad Constitution? Not, at all. Communist Party wants a Constitution based upon the principle of the Dictatorship of Proletariat. They condemn the Constitution because it is based upon parliamentary democracy. The Socialists want two things. The first thing they want is that if they come in power, the Constitution must give them the freedom to nationalize or socialize all private property without payment of compensation. The second thing that the Socialists want is that the Fundamental Rights mentioned in the Constitution must be absolute and without any limitations so that if their Party fails to come into power, they would have the unfettered freedom not merely to criticize but also to overthrow the state.

These are the main grounds on which the Constitution is being condemned. I do not say that the principle of parliamentary democracy is the only ideal form of political democracy. I do not say that the principle of no acquisition of private property without compensation is so sacrosant that there can be no departure from it. I do not say that Fundamental Rights can never be absolute and limitations set upon them can never be lifted. What I do say is that the principles embodied in the Constitution are the views of the present generation or if you think this to be an over-statement, I say they are the views of the members of the Constituent Assembly. Why blame the Drafting Committee for embodying them in the Constitution? I say why blame even the members of the Constituent Assembly? Jefferson, the great American statesman who played so great a part in the making of the American Constitution, has expressed some very weighty views which makers of Constitution can never afford to ignore. In one place, he has said:

> We may consider each generation as a distinct nation, with a right, by the will of the majority to bind themselves, but non to bind the succeeding generation, more than the inhabitants of another country.

In another place, he has said:

> The idea that institutions established for the use of the nation cannot be touched or modified, even to make them answer their end, because of rights gratuitously supposed in those employed to manage them in the trust for the

public, may perhaps be a salutary provision against the abuses of a monarch, but is most absurd against the nation itself. Yet our lawyers and priests generally inculcate this doctrine, and suppose that preceding generations held the earth more freely than we do: had a right to impose laws on us unalterable by ourselves, and that we in the like manner, can make laws and impose burdens on future generations, which they will have no right to alter; in fine, that the earth belongs to the dead and not the living.

I admit that what Jefferson has said is not merely true, but is absolutely true. There can be no question about it. Had the Constituent Assembly departed from this principle laid down by Jefferson. It would certainly be liable to blame even to condemnation. But I ask, has it? Quite the contrary. One has only to examine the provision relating to the amendment to the Constitution. The Assembly has not only refrained from putting a seal of finality and infallibility upon this Constitution by denying to the people the right to amend the Constitution as in Canada or by making the amendment of the Constitution subject to the fulfilment of extraordinary terms and conditions as in America or Australia, but has provided a most facile procedure for amending the Constitution. I challenge any of the critics of the Constitution to prove that any Constituent Assembly anywhere in the world has in the circumstances in which this country finds itself, provided such a facile procedure for the amendment of the Constitution. If those who are dissatisfied with the Constitution cannot obtain even a two-thirds majority in the Parliament elected on adult franchise in their favour, their dissatisfaction with the Constitution cannot be deemed to be shared by the general public.

There is only one point of constitutional importance to which I propose to make a reference. A serious complaint is made on the ground that there is too much of centralizations and that the States have been reduced to Municipalities. It is clear that this view is not only an exaggeration, but is also founded on a misunderstanding of what exactly the Constitution contrives to do. As to the relation between the Centre and the States, it is necessary to bear in mind the fundamental principle on which it rests. The basic principle of Federalism is that the Legislative and Executive authority is partitioned between the Centre and the States not by any law to be made by the Centre but by the Constitution itself. This is what Constitution does. The States under our Constitution are in no way dependent upon the Centre for their legislative or executive authority. The Centre and the States are co-equal in this matter. It is difficult to say how such a Constitution can be called centralism. It may be that the Constitution assigns to the Centre too large a field for the operation of its legislative and executive authority than is to be found in any other federal Constitution. It may be that the residuary powers are given to the Centre and not to the States. But these features do not form the essence of federalism. The chief mark of federalism as I said lies in the partition of the legislative and executive authority between the Centre and the Units by the Constitution. This is the principle embodied in our Constitution. There can be no mistake about it. It is, therefore, wrong to say that the States have been placed under the Centre. Centre cannot by its own will alter the boundary of that partition, nor can the Judiciary. For as has been well said:

> Courts may modify, they cannot replace. They can revise earlier interpretations as new arguments, new points of view are presented. They can shift the dividing line in marginal cases, but there are barriers, they cannot pass; definite assignments of power they cannot reallocate. They can give a broadening construction of existing powers, but they cannot assign to one authority powers explicitly granted to another.

The first charge of centralization defeating federalism must therefore fall.

The second charge is that the Centre has been given the power to override the States. This charge must be admitted. But before condemning the Constitution for containing such overriding powers, certain considerations must be borne in mind. The first is that these overriding powers do not form the normal features of the Constitution. Their use and operation are expressly confined to emergencies only. The second consideration is, could we avoid giving overriding powers to the Centre when an emergency has arisen? Those who do not admit the justification for such overriding powers to the Centre even in an emergency do not seem to have a clear idea of the problem which lies at the root of the matter. The problem is clearly set out by a writer in that well-known magazine, 'The Round Table', in its issue of December, 1935 that I offer no apology for quoting the following extract from it. Says the writer:

> Political systems are a complex duties resting ultimately on the question, to whom, or to what authority, does the citizen owe allegiance. In normal affairs the question is not present, for the law works smoothly, and a man goes about his business obeying one authority in this set of matters and

another authority in other. But in a moment of crisis, a conflict of claims may arise, and it is then apparent that ultimate allegiance cannot be divided. The issue of allegiance cannot be determined in the last resort by a juristic interpretation of statutes. The law must conform to the facts of so much the worse for the law. When all formalism is stripped away, the bare question is, what authority commands the residual loyalty of the citizen. Is it the Centre or the Constituent States?

The solution of this problem depends upon one's answer to this question which is the crux of the problem. There can be no doubts that in the opinion of the vast majority of the people, the residual loyalty of the citizen in any emergency must be to the Centre and not to the Constituent States. For it is only the Centre which can work for a common end and for the general interests of the country as a whole. Herein lies the justification for giving to the Centre certain overriding powers to be used in an emergency. And after all what is the obligation imposed upon the Constituent States by these emergency powers? No more than this that in an emergency, they should take into consideration along side their own local interest, the opinion and 'interests of the nation as a whole. Only those who have not understood the problem, can complain against it.

Here I could have ended. But my mind is so full of the future of our country that I feel I ought to take this occasion to give expression to some of my reflections thereon.

On 26th January 1950, India will be an independent country. What would happen to her independence? Will she maintain her independence or will she lose it again? This is the first thought that comes to my mind. It is not that India was never an independent country. The point is that she once lost the independence she had. Will she lose it a second time? It is this thought which makes me most anxious for the future. What perturbs me greatly is the fact that not only India has once before lost her independence, but she lost it by the treachery of some of her own people. In the invasion of Sind by Mohammed-Bin-Kasim, the military commanders of King Dahar accepted bribes from the agents of Mohammed-Bin-Kasim and refused to fight on the side of their King. It was Jaichand who invited Mohammmed Ghori to invade India and fight against Prithvi Raj and promised him the help of himself and the Solanki Kings. When Shivaji was fighting for the liberation of Hindus, the other Maratha noblemen and the Rajput Kings were fighting the battle on the side of Moghul Emperors. When the British were trying to destory the Sikh Rulers, Gulab Singh their principal commander sat silent and did not help to save the Sikh kingdom. In 1857, when a large part of India had declared a war of independence against the British, the Sikhs stood and watched the event as silent spectators.

Will history repeat itself? It is this thought which fills me with anxiety. This anxiety is deepened by the realization of the fact that in addition to our old enemies in the form of castes and creeds we are going to have many political parties with diverse and opposing political creeds. Will Indians place the country above creed or will they place creed above country? I do not know. But this much is certain that if the parties place creed above country, our independence will be put in jeopardy a second time and probably be lost for ever. This eventuality we must all resolutely guard against. We must be determined to defend our independence with the last drop of our blood.

On the 26th of January 1950, India would be a democratic country in the sense that India from that day would have a government of the people, by the people and for the people. The same thought comes to my mind. What would happen to her democratic Constitution? Will she be able to maintain it or will she lose it again? This is the second thought that comes to my mind and makes me as anxious as the first.

It is not that India did not know what is Democracy. There was a time when India was studded within Republics and where there were monarchies, they were either elected or limited. They were never absolute. It is not that India did not know Parliaments or Parliamentary Procedure. A study of the Buddhist Bhikshu Sanghas discloses that not only there were Parliaments—for the Sanghas were nothing but Parliaments-but the Sanghas knew and observed all the rules of Parliamentary Procedure known to modern times. They had rules regarding seating arrangements, rules regarding Motions, Resolutions, Quorum, Whip, Counting of Votes, Voting by Ballot, Censure Motion, Regularization, Res Judicata, etc. Although these rules of Parliamentary Procedure were applied by the Buddha to the meetings of the Bhikshu Sangha, he must have borrowed them from the rules of the political assemblies functioning in the country in his time.

This democratic system India lost. Will she lose it a second time? I do not know. But it is quite possible in a country like India—where democracy from its long disuse must be regarded as something quite new—there is danger of democracy giving place to dictatorship. It is quite possible for this new born democracy to retain its form but give place to dictatorship in fact. If there is a landslide, the danger of the second possibility becoming actuality is much greater.

If we wish to maintain democracy not merely in form but also in fact, what must we do? The first thing in my Judgement we must do is to hold fast to constitutional methods of achieving our social and economic objectives. It means we must abandon the bloody methods of revolution. It means that we must abandon the methods of civil disobedience, non-co-operation and satyagarha. When there was no way left for constitutional methods for achieving economic and social objectives, there was some justification for unconstitutional methods achieving economic and social objectives. But where constitutional methods are open, there can be no justification for these unconstitutional methods. These methods are nothing but the Grammar of Anarchy and the sooner they are abandoned the better for us.

The second thing we must do is to observe the caution which John Stuart Mill has given to all who are interested in the maintenance of democracy, namely not 'to lay their liberties at the feet of even a great man, or to trust him with powers which enable him to subvert their institutions'.

There is nothing wrong in being grateful to great men who life-long services to the country. But there are limits to gratefulness. As has been well said by the Irish Patriot Daniel O'conel, 'no man can be grateful at the cost of his honour, no woman can be grateful at the cost of her chastity, and no nation can be grateful at the cost of its liberty. 'This caution is far necessary in the case of India than in the case of any other country. For in India, 'Bhakti' or what may be called the path of devotion or hero-worship, plays a part in its politics unequalled in magnitude by the part it plays in the politics of any other part of the world. 'Bhakti' in religion may be a road to the salvation of the soul. But in politics, 'Bhakti' or hero-worship is a sure road to degradation and to eventual dictatorship.

The third thing we must do is not be content with mere political democracy. We must make our political democracy a social democracy as well. Political democracy cannot last unless there lies at the base of it social democracy. What does social democracy mean? It means a way of life which recognizes liberty, equality and fraternity as the principles of life. These principles of liberty, equality and fraternity are not to be treated aas separate items in a trinity. They form a union of trinity in the sense that to divorce one from the other is to defeat the very purpose of democracy. Liberty cannot be divorced from equality, equality cannot be divorced from liberty. Nor can liberty and equality be divorced from fraternity. Without equality, liberty would produce the supermacy of the few over the many. Equality without liberty would kill individual initiative. Without fraternity, liberty and equality could not become a natural course of things. It would require a constable to enforce them. We must begin by acknowledging the fact that there is complete absence of two things in Indian Society. One of these is equality. On the social plane we have in India a society based on the principle of graded inequality which means elevation for some and degradation for others. On the economic plane, we have a society in which there are some who have immense wealth as against many who live in abject poverty. On the 26th January 1950, we are going to enter into a life of contradictions. In politics we will have equality and in social and economic life we will have inequality. In politics we will be recognizing the principle of one man one vote and one vote one value. In our social and economic life, we shall, by reason of our social and economic structure, continue to deny the principle of one man one value. How long shall we continue to live this life of contradictions? How long shall we continue to deny equality in our social and economic life? If we continue to deny it for long, we will do so only by putting our political democracy in peril. We must remove this contradiction at the earliest possible moment or else those who suffer from inequality will blow up the structure of political democracy which this Assembly has so laboriously built up.

The second thing we are wanting in is recognition of the principle of fraternity. What does fraternity mean? Fraternity means a sense of common brotherhood of all Indians, all Indians being one people. It is the principle which gives unity and solidarity to social life. It is a difficult thing to achieve. How difficult it is, can be realized from the story related by James Bryce in his volume on American Commonwealth about the United States of America. The story is—I propose to recount it in the words of Bryce himself that:

> Some years ago the American Protestant Episcopal Church was occupied at its triennial Convention in revising its liturgy. It was thought desirable to introduce among the short sentence Papers of prayers, a prayer for the whole people, and aneminent New England divine proposed the words. 'O

Lord, bless our Nation'. Accepted one after noon, on the spur of the moment the sentence was brought up next day for reconsideration, when so many objections were raised by the laity to the word 'nation', as importing too definite a, recognition of national unity, that it was dropped, and instead there were adopted the words 'O Lord, bless these United States'.

There was so little solidarity in the U.S.A. at the time, when this incident occurred that the people of America did not think that they were a nation. If the people of the United States could not feel that they were a nation, how difficult it is for Indians to think that they are a nation. I remember the days when politically-minded Indians resented the expression 'the people of India'. They preferred the expression 'The Indian nation'. I am of opinion that in believing that we are a nation, we are cherishing a great delusion. How can people divided into several thousands of castes be a nation? The sooner we realize that we are not as yet a nation in the social and psychological sense of the word, the better of us. For then only we shall realize the necessity of becoming a nation and seriously think of ways and means of realizing the goal. The realization of this goal is going to be very difficult, far more difficult than it has been in the United States. The United States has no caste problem. In India there are castes. These castes are anti-national; in the first place because they bring about separation in social life. They are anti-national also because they generate jealousy and antipathy and between caste and caste. But we must overcome all these difficulties if we wish to become a nation in reality. For fraternity can be a fact only when there is a nation. Without fraternity, equality and liberty will be no deeper than coats of paint.

These are my reflections about the tasks that lie ahead of us. They may not be very pleasant to some. But there can be no gainsaying that political power in this country has too long been the monopoly of a few and the many are not only beasts of burden, but also beasts of prey. This monopoly has not merely deprived them of their chance of betterment, it has sapped them of what may be called the significance of life. Those downtrodden classes are tired of being governed. They are impatient to govern themselves. This urge for self-realization in the downtrodden classes must not be allowed to devolve into a class struggle or class war. It would lead to a division of the House. That would indeed be a day of disaster. For, as has been well said by Abraham Lincoln, 'a House divided against itself cannot stand very long.' 'Therefore, the sooner room is made for the realization of their aspiration, the better for the few, better for the country, the better for the maintenance of its independence and the better for the continuance its democratic structure. This can only be done by the establishment of equality and fraternity in all spheres of life. That is why I have laid so much stress on them.

I do not wish to weary the House any further. Independence is no doubt a matter of joy. But let us not forget that this independence has thrown on us great responsibilities. By independence, we have lost the excuse of blaming the British for anything going wrong. If hereafter things go wrong we will have nobody to blame except ourselves. There is great danger of things going wrong. Times are fast changing. People including our own are being moved by new ideologies. They are getting tired of Government by the people. They are prepared to have Government for the people and are indifferent whether it is Government of the people and by the people. If we wish to preserve the Constitution in which we have sought to enshrine the principle of Government of the people and by the people, let us resolve not to be tardy in the recognition of the evils that lie across our path and which induce people to prefer Government for the people to Government by the people, nor to be weak in our initiative to remove them. That is the only way to serve the country. I know of no better.

Further Reading

S.K. Chahal

WRITINGS OF DR AMBEDKAR

Administration and Finance of the East India Company (M.A. dissertation, Columbia University, USA, 15 May 1915).

'Castes in India: Their Mechanism, Genesis and Development' (A paper read in 1916 in Prof. Goldenweiser's Anthropological Seminar. Later published in *Indian Antiquary*, May 1917).

'The National Dividend of India: A Historical and Analytical Study' (Ph.D. thesis, Columbia University, 1917. Later published under the title *Evolution of Provincial Finance in British India*, London: 1925).

A Review of Bertrand Russell's *Principles of Social Reconstruction* in *Journal of Indian Economic Society*, vol. 3: 1918.

'Evidence', submitted before the Southborough Committee on Franchise, Bombay: 1919.

'The Problem of Rupee' (thesis for D.Sc. in Economics at the University of London: 1923; Later *History of Indian Currency and Banking*, London: 1930).

'Responsibilities of Responsible Government in India' (A paper before the Students' Union, Bombay: 1923).

'Evidence', before the Hilton Young Commission on Indian Currency, Bombay: 1925.

'Statement concerning the State of Education of the Depressed Classes in the Bombay Presidency' (before the Simon Commission on behalf of the Bahiskrit Hitkarni Sabha, Bombay: 1928).

'Statement concerning the Safeguards for Protection of the Interests of the Depressed Classes as Minority in the Bombay Presidency and the Change in the Composition of the Guarantees from the Bombay Legislative Council necessary to ensure the same under Provincial Autonomy'. (Also submitted alongwith the previous statement to the Simon Commission, Bombay: 1929).

'Wanted: an Anti-Priestcraft Association' (An article published in the *Bombay Chronicle*, 8 November 1929).

Political Rights of the Untouchables (R.T.C., vol. III. Sub-Committee No. III (Minorities), London: 1930).

A Scheme of Political Safeguards for the Protection of Depressed Classes in the Future Constitution of Self-Governing India, *Round Table Conference*, Appendix I, pp. 168-76, vol. III, *Proceedings of the Minorities Sub-Committee* 1930.

A Letter in *The Second Annual Report of the League of Purity*, London: 1930.

Annihilation of Caste, Bombay: 1936.

Mahar ani tyanche Vatan (Marathi), Bombay: 1937.

Federation versus Freedom, Poona: 1939.

Thoughts on Pakistan, Bombay: 1940. (Later published as *Pakistan or the Partition of India*, Bombay: 1945).

Mr Gandhi and the Emancipation of the Untouchables, Bombay: 1942.

Ranade, Gandhi and Jinnah, Bombay: 1943.

What Congress and Gandhi have done to the Untouchables?, Bombay: 1945.

The Communal Deadlock and a Way to Solve it, Bombay: 1945.

Who were the Shudras? Bombay: 1946.

The Cabinet Mission and the Untouchables, Bombay: 1946.

States and Minorities, Bombay: 1947.

The Untouchables, Who Are They and Why They Became Untouchables? New Delhi: 1948.

Maharashtra as a Linguistic Province, Bombay: 1948.

The Buddha and the Future of His Religion, Bombay: 1950.

The Rise and Fall of Hindu Woman, Jalandhar: 1950.

Buddha Pujapatha (Marathi), Bombay: 1952.

The Buddha and his Dhamma, Bombay: 1956.

The Riddle of Rama, Bombay: 1982.

Slavery and Untouchability—Which is Worse?, ed. Bhagwan Dass, Jalandhar· 1989.

MANUSCRIPTS, PAPERS, ETC.

Source Material on Dr Ambedkar, Published by the Government of Maharashtra, Bombay: 1982.

Unpublished Private Papers of Dr Ambedkar, Siddhartha College Library, Bombay.

Ambedkar Collection, Bombay University Library, Bombay.

COLLECTED WORKS

Dr Babasaheb Ambedkar: Writings and Speeches, Government of Maharashtra, Bombay: d.d.

Volume I (1979)

1. *Caste in India.*

2. *Annihilation of Caste.*
3. *Maharashtra as a Linguistic Province.*
4. *Need for Checks and Balances.*
5. *Thoughts on Linguistic States.*
6. *Ranade, Gandhi and Jinnah.*
7. *Evidence before the Southborough Committee.*
8. *Federation versus Freedom.*
9. *Communal Deadlock and a Way to Solve It.*
10. *State and Minorities.*
11. *Small Holdings in India.*
12. *Mr. Russel and the Reconstruction of Society.*

Volume II (1982)

1. *Dr. Ambedkar in Bombay Legislature.*
2. *Dr. Ambedkar with the Simon Commission.*
3. *Dr. Ambedkar at the R.T.C.*

Volume III (1987)

1. *Philosophy of Hinduism.*
2. *Revolution and Counter-Revolution.*
3. *Buddha or Karl Marx.*

Volume IV (1987)

1. *Riddles in Hinduism.*

Volume V (1989)

1. *Untouchables or the Children of India's Ghetto.*
2. *Other Essays on Untouchables and Untouchability: Social, Political, Religious.*

Volume VI (1989)

1. *Administration and Finance of the East India Company.*
2. *The Evolution of Provincial Finance in British India.*
3. *The Problem of the Rupee.*

Volume VII (1990)

1. *Who Were the Shudras?*
2. *The Untouchables.*

Volume VIII (1990)

1. *Pakistan or the Partition of India.*

Volume IX (1991)

1. *What Congress and Gandhi have done to the Untouchables?*
2. *Mr. Gandhi and the Emancipation of Untouchables.*

Volume X (1991)

Dr. Ambedkar as Member of Governor–General's Council.

Volume XI (1992)

The Buddha and his Dhamma.

Volume XII (1992)

1. *Ancient Indian Commerce.*
2. *The Untouchables and Pax Britanica.*
3. *Lectures on the English Constitution.*

4. *The Notes on Acts and Laws, Writings for a Visa.*
5. *Other Miscellaneous Essays.*

Volume XIII

Dr. Ambedkar as the Principal Architect of the Constitution of India.

Volume XIV (2 parts)

Dr. Ambedkar and the Hindu Code Bill.

Volume XV

Dr. Ambedkar as Free India's First Law Minister and Member of Opposition in Indian Parliament (1947 to 1956).

Volume XVI

Dr. Ambedkar's

(i) *The Pali Grammar*

(ii) *The Pali Dictionary*

(a) *Pali into English*

(b) *Pali into English, Marathi, Hindi and Gujarathi*

(iii) *Bouddha Pooja Path*

Babasaheb Dr. Ambedkar: Sampurna Vangmaya

This multi-volume series is being published by Dr. Ambedkar Foundation, New Delhi, in Hindi and other Indian languages. The present volumes are the Hindi translations of volumes in English (*Writings & Speeches*), published by Maharashtra Government. Ten volumes have been released so far.

Thus Spoke Ambedkar, Selected speeches, comp. (ed.) Bhagwan Das, 4 vols., Jalandhar: d.d.

PROCEEDINGS & REPORTS

Bombay Legislative Council Debates—Official Reports, Bombay: 1927-37.
Bombay Legislative Assembly Debates—Official Reports, Bombay: 1938-9.
Constituent Assembly Debates, vols. I-XI, Delhi: d.d.
Montague-Chelmsford Reform Scheme, Calcutta: 1920.
Nehru Committee Report, Allahabad: 1928.
Report of the Indian Statutory Commission (Simon Commission), Calcutta: 1930.
First Round Table Conference, London: 1930.
Second Round Table Conference, London: 1931.
Third Round Table Conference, London: 1932.
Report of the Royal Commission on Labour, 1931.
Report of the Joint Committee on Indian Constitutional Reform, London: 1934.
The Sapru Committee Report, Delhi: 1935.
Sir Stafford Cripps Proposals, Delhi: 1942.
The Cabinet Mission, Delhi: 1946.
Report: Indian Labour Department, Standing Labour Committee, 1945.

Report of the Select Committee on Hindu Code Bill, Delhi: 1948.
Lok Sabha Debates, Delhi: 1947-51.
Rajya Sabha Debates, Delhi: 1952-6.
Report of the States Reorganisation Commission, Delhi: 1955.

GENERAL WORKS

Aggrawal, C.B., *The Harijans in Rebellion*, Bombay: 1934.
Aggarwal, S.K., *Dr Ambedkar on Muslim Fundamentalism*, New Delhi: 1993.
Ahir, D.C., *Buddhism and Ambedkar*, New Delhi: 1968.
———, *Gandhi and Ambedkar*, New Delhi: 1969.
———, *Dr Ambedkar and Indian Constitution*, Lucknow: 1972.
———, *Dr Ambedkar and Punjab*, Delhi: 1992.
Ajant, Surendra, *Buddha, Ambedkar Aur Dhammapada* (Hindi), Jalandhar: 1983.
Aum Prakash, *Bharat Men Jati, Jatiwad, Aur Sravamanya Ke Haq* (Hindi), Allahabad: 1991.
Bains, Ravinder Singh, *Reservation Policy*, Delhi: 1994.
Baisantry, D.K., *Dr. Ambedkar: A Pioneer of Labour Welfare*, Jalandhar: n.d.
———, *Ambedkar: The Total Revolutionary*, New Delhi: n.d.
Balley, L.R. (ed.), *Thoughts on Ambedkar*, Jalandhar: 1972.
Banerjee, A.C., *The Making of Indian Constitution*, Calcutta: 1948.
Bardhan, A.B., *Class, Caste, Reservations and Struggle Against Casteism*, New Delhi: 1990.
Behril, Chandra, *Social and Political Ideas of B.R. Ambedkar*, Jaipur: 1977.
Beidelman, Thomas O., *A Comparative Analysis of the Jajmani System*, New York: 1959.
Beteille, Andre, *Inequality and Social Change*, New Delhi: 1972.
———, *The Backward Classes and the New Social Order*, Delhi: 1988.
———, *The Backward Classes in Contemporary India*, Delhi: 1992.
Bhagat, M.G., *Untouchable Classes of Maharashtra*, Bombay: 1942.
Bhai, P. Nirmal, *Harijan Women in Independent India*, New Delhi: 1986.
Bharathi, K.S., *Foundations of Ambedkar's Thought*, Nagpur: 1990.
Bhatt, Anil, *Caste, Class and Politics: An Emprical Profile of Social Stratification in Modern India*, Delhi: 1987.
Bheema, S., *Strategies for the Removal of Social Inequalities*, Delhi: 1992.
Blakiston, Hillary, *But Little Dust, Life Amongst the Ex-Untouchables of Maharashtra*, Cambridge: 1990.
Borale, P.T., *Segregation and Desegregation in India*, Bombay: 1968.
Bose, Nirmal Kumar, *The Structure of Hindu Society*, (trans.) Andre Beteille, New Delhi: 1975.
Buhler, G., *The Laws of Manu*, Delhi: 1964.
Chagla, M.C., *Roses in December*, Bombay: 1968, 8th edn.
Chahal, S.K., *Doctor Ambedkar Aur Samajik Nyay* (Hindi), Gurgaon: 1996.

Chanchreek, K.L. (ed.), *Dr. B.R. Ambedkar: Patriot, Philosopher, Stateman*, A Century Volume Publication, Delhi: 1991.
Chandna, R.C., *Spatial Diamensions of Scheduled Castes in India*, New Delhi, n.d.
Chandran, E, *Issues in Reservations, Caste versus Economic Status*, New Delhi: 1990.
Chakarvarti, S.C. and S.N. Roy (eds.), *Brahmo Samaj, the Depressed Classes and Untouchabilitiy*, Calcutta: 1933.
Chauhan, B.R., *Scheduled Castes and Education*, Meerut: 1975.
Chavan, Sheshrao (ed.), *Bharat Ratna Dr Babasaheb Ambedkar*, Aurangabad: 1990.
———, *Bharat Ratna Dr. Babasaheb Ambedkar: Messiah of Untouchables*, Aurangabad, n.d.
Dangle, Arjun (ed.), *Poisoned Bread*, Delhi: 1992.
Diehl, Anita, *Periyar E.V. Ramaswami*, New Delhi: 1978.
Desai, I.P. (ed.), *Class, Caste, Conflict, and Reservations*, Surat: 1985.
Dhawan, Neeraj, *Brahmanism—A Political Concept*, New Delhi: 1990.
Dias, C.J., *The Quest of Equality: Protective Discrimination or Compensatory Justice*, Lexington: 1983.
Dongre, M.K., *Economic Thought of Dr. B.R. Ambedkar*, Nagpur: 1974.
Dr. Ambedkar Birth Centenary Souvenir, London: 1992.
Dube, S.C., *Indian Society*, New Delhi: 1990.
Dumont, Louis, *Homo Hierarchius: The Caste System and its Implications*, New Delhi: 1970.
Engineer, Ashgar Ali (ed.), *Mandal Commission Controversy*, Delhi: 1991.
Fanon, Frantz, *The Wretched of the Earth*, New York: 1968.
Freeman, James M., *Untouchables: An Indian Life History*, New Delhi: 1993.
Fuchs, Stephen, *At the Bottom of Indian Society*, Delhi: 1981.
Gaekwad, Fateh Singh Rao, *Sayajirao of Baroda*, London: 1989.
Gajendragadkar, P.B., *The Hindu Code Bill*, Dharwad: 1951.
Galanter, Marc, *Competing Equalities: Law and the Backward Classes in India*, Delhi: 1991.
Gandhi, M.K., *For Workers against Untouchability*, Ahmedabad: 1954.
———, *The Removal of Untouchability*, Ahmedabad: 1954.
———, *My Varnashrama Dharma*, ed. Hingorani T. Anand, Bombay: 1965.
Gangrare, M.F. (ed.), *Dr. Babasaheb Ambedkaranchi Bhashane* (Marathi), vols. I-VI, Nagpur: d.d.
Ganvir, Ratnakar (ed.), *Bahishkrit Bharatil Agralekh* (Marathi), Bhusawal: 1976.
———, *Vilayatehun Dr. Babasahebebachi Patre* (Marathi), Nagpur: 1984.
Gauba, O.P., *Dimensions of Social Justice*, New Delhi: 1983.
Ghosh, S.K., *Protection of Minorities and Scheduled Castes*, New Delhi: 1980.
Ghurye, G.S., *Caste and Class in India*, Bombay: 1957.

Glazer, Nathan, *Affirmative Discrimination: Ethnic Inequality and Public Policy*, New York: 1975.

Gokhale, Jayashree, *From Concession to Confrontation*, Bombay: 1993.

Gore, M.S., *Non-Brahman Movement in Maharashtra*, New Delhi: 1989

———, *The Social Context of an Ideology: Ambedkar's Political and Social Thought*, New Delhi: 1993.

Grover, Virender (ed.), *B.R. Ambedkar*, New Delhi: 1993.

Gwyer, Maurice Sir, A. Appadorai, *Speeches and Documents on the Indian Constitution* (vols. I and II) London: 1957.

Hardgrave, Robert, L. Jr., *The Dravidian Movement*, Bombay: 1965.

Harrison, Seligs, *India: The Most Dangerous Decades*, London: 1960.

Hatole, Shankarrao, *Dr. Babasaheb Ambedkar Yanche Aitihasik Bhasan* (Marathi), Aurangabad: 1984.

Haranur, L.G., *Specifying the Backward Classes without the Caste Basis*, Bangalore: 1965.

Hazari (pseud), *An Indian Outcaste: The Autobiography of an Untouchable*, London: 1951.

Hutton, J.H., *Caste in India*, London: 1969.

Inden, Ronald, *Imagining India*, London: 1990.

Isach, Harold R., *India's Ex-Untouchables*, Bombay: 1965.

Ishwari Prasad, *Reservation: Action of Social Equality*, Delhi: 1986.

Iyer, V.R. Krishna, *Dr. Ambedkar and the Dalit Future*, Delhi: 1990.

———, *Social Justice and the Undone Vast*, Delhi: 1991.

Jatav, D.R., *The Social Philosophy of B.R. Ambedkar*, Agra: 1965.

———, *The Political Philosophy of B.R. Ambedkar*, Agra: 1968.

———, *The Buddha and Karl Marx*, Agra: 1968.

———, *Dr. Ambedkar Ka Naitik Darshan* (Hindi), Agra: 1969.

———, *Dr. Ambedkar's Role in National Movement*, New Delhi: 1979.

Jenking, Iredell, *Social Order and the Limits of Law*, New Jersey: 1980.

Jha, M.L., *Untouchability and Education*, Meerut: 1973.

Jogdan, P.G., *From Discrimination to Movement—A Study of Dalit Movement in Maharashtra* (M.Phil. Dissertation, J.N.U., New Delhi: 1981.

——— (ed.), *Dalit Women: Issues and Perspectives*, New Delhi: 1995.

Joglekar, S.B., *A Reply to Ambedkar's Pakistan*, Bombay: 1941.

———, *Democracy in Search of Equality*, Delhi: 1982.

Joshi, Barbara R., *The Untouchable! Voices from the Dalit Liberation Movement*, London: 1986.

Juergensmeyer, Mark, *Religious Rebels in the Punjab*, Delhi: 1988.

Kadam, K.N., *Dr. Babasaheb Ambedkar and the Significance of His Movement, A Chronology*, London: 1991.

———, *Dr Ambedkar, The Rationalist and Humanist.*

———, *Currents and Counter-Currents in Ancient India: An Ambedkarite Approach.*

Kakkade, S.R., *Scheduled Castes and the National Integration*, New Delhi: 1990.

Kamble, B.C., *Samagra Ambedkar Charita* (Marathi) vols: I-VIII, Bombay: 1984-7.

Kamble, J.R., *Rise and Awakening of the Depressed Classes in India*, New Delhi: 1979.

———, *Pursuit of Equality in Indian History*, New Delhi: 1985.

Kamble, N.D., *Atrocities on the Scheduled Castes in Independent India*, Bangalore: 1979.

———, *Poverty Within Poverty*, New Delhi: 1979.

———, *The Scheduled Castes*, New Delhi: 1982.

———, *Deprived Classes and Their Struggle for Equality*, New Delhi: 1983.

Kannaikil, Jose (ed.), *Scheduled Castes and the Struggle Against Inequality*, New Delhi: 1983.

Kasabe, Raosaheb, *Ambedkar Aur Marx* (Marathi), Poona: n.d.

Kausalyayan, Anand, *Yadhi Baba Na Hote* (Hindi), Nagpur: 1968.

Keer, Dhananjay, *Dr. Ambedkar: Life and Mission*, Bombay: 1962.

———, *Mahatma Jotirao Phuley*, Bombay: 1964.

Khabde, Dinkar, *Dr. Ambedkar and Western Thinkers*, Pune: 1989.

Khan, Mumtaj Ali, *Scheduled Castes and Their Status in India*, New Delhi: 1980.

Kharat, Shankar Rao, *Dr. Ambedkaranchi Patre* (Marathi), Pune: 1961.

———, (ed.), *Dr Babasaheb Ambedkar Yanchi Amarkatha* (Marathi), Pune: 1987.

Klass, Morton, *Caste: Emergence of the South Asian Social System*, New Delhi: 1980.

Kosare, H.L., *Vidarbhateel Dalit Chalvalicha Itihas* (Marathi), Nagpur: 1984.

Kothari, Rajni (ed.), *Caste in Indian Politics*, Delhi: 1970.

Kshirsagar, R.K., *Bhartiya Republic Paksha* (Marathi), Aurangabad: 1979.

———, *Untouchability in India: Implementation of Law and Abolition*, New Delhi: 1986.

———, *Dalits and Constitutional Safeguards*, Deenapur: 1986.

———, *Political Thought of Dr. B.R. Ambedkar*, New Delhi: 1992.

Kuber, W.N., *Ambedkar: A Critical Study*, Delhi: 1973.

———, *B.R. Ambedkar*, New Delhi: 1989.

Kunte, B.C., *Source Material on Dr. Babasaheb Ambedkar*, Bombay: 1982.

Kuppaswamy, B., *Social Change in India*, New Delhi: 1990.

Kureel, J.P. (ed.), *Poona Pact* (Hindi), Lucknow: 1990.

Lander, Stephen, *'Backward Classes' in the Indian Constitution*, Chicago: 1965.

Lazarur, G., *A Brief Life Sketch of Dr. B.R. Ambedkar*, Deemapur: 1987.

Leach, E.R. (ed.), *Aspects of Caste in South India*, London: 1962.

Lederlay, M.R., *Philosophical Trends in Modern Maharashtra*, Bombay: 1976.

Limaye, Madhu, *A Self Liquidating Reservation Scheme: A Step to Social Justice*, New Delhi: 1992.

———, *Supreme Court Decision of Backward Class Reservation*, New Delhi: 1992.

Lockard, Duane, *Towards Equal Opportunity: A Study of Local and State Anti-Discrimination Laws*, New York: 1968.

Lohia, Rammanohar, *The Caste System*, Hyderabad: 1964.

Lokhande, G.S., *Bheemrao Ramji Ambedkar: A Study in Social Democracy*, New Delhi: 1982.

Lynch, Owen M., *The Politics of Untouchability*, New Delhi: 1974.

Madholia, Matadin, *Supreme Court on Reservation*, Delhi: 1988.

Magudkar, M.P. (ed.), *Dr. Ambedkar and Parliamentary Democracy*, Pune: 1976.

Mahar, Michael, J. (ed.), *The Untouchables in Contemporary India*, Tucson, Arizona: 1972.

Mali, M.G., *Krantijyoti Savitribai Phuley* (Marathi), Gargoti: 1981.

Malik, Suneila, *Social Integration of Scheduled Castes*, New Delhi: 1979

Marla, S., *Bonded Labour in India*, New Delhi: 1981.

Massery, James, *Dalits in India*, New Delhi: 1995.

Mattoo, Anita, *Buddha Dhamma Pradeep*, Nagpur: 1960.

Mehta, Ashok, *The Politics of Poverty*, New Delhi: 1995.

Moon, Vasant, *Buddha Dhamma Pradeep*, Nagpur: 1960.

——— (ed.), *Dr Babasaheb Ambedkar: Writings and Speeches*, vols. I-XIV, Bombay: 1979-96.

Mouli, V.C., *B.R. Ambedkar: Man and His Vision*, New Delhi: 1990.

Mukherjee, Hirendra Nath, *Gandhi, Ambedkar and Extirpation of Untouchability*, New Delhi: 1982.

Mukherjee, Prabhati, *Beyond the Four Varnas: The Untouchables in India*, Delhi: 1988.

Murthy, B.S., *Depressed and Oppressed*, New Delhi: 1972.

Murti, G.V., *Narayan Guru*, Bangalore: 1974.

Naik, T.B., *Chhatrapati Rajarshi Shahu Maharaj* (Marathi), Kolhapur: 1974.

Narayanrao, J.S., Somesekhar and K. Audiserhaiar (eds), *B.R. Ambedkar: His Relevance Today*, Delhi: 1994.

Nath, Trilok, *Politics of the Depressed Classes*, Delhi: 1987.

Natrajan, Swaminath, *A Century of Social Reform in India*, London: 1959.

Nim, Hoti Lal (Comp.), *Thoughts of Dr. Ambedkar*, Agra: 1969.

Nirmal, Arvind P. and V. Devashayam, *Dr B.R. Ambedkar: A Centenary Tribute*, Madras: 1991.

O' Malley, S.S., *Indian Caste Customs*, Delhi: 1974.

Omvedt, Gail, *Cultural Revolt in a Colonial Society: The Non-Brahman Movement in Western India, 1873-1930*, Pune: 1976.

——, *Dalits and the Democratic Revolution: Dr. Ambedkar and the Dalit Movement in Colonial India*, New Delhi: 1994.

Padmanabhan, A., *Mandal Commission Judgement and the Scheduled Castes and Scheduled Tribes*, New Delhi: 1993.

Panikkar, K.M., *Hindu Society at Cross-Roads*, New York: 1961.

Pantawane, Gangadhar, *Patrakar Dr Babasaheb Ambedkar* (Marathi), Nagpur: 1987.

Patwardhan, S., *Change Among India's Harijans: A Case of Maharashtra*, New Delhi: 1973.

Phadke, B.D., *Dr Babasaheb Ambedkar* (Marathi), Pune: 1985.

Pilchick, Terry, *Jai Bheem! Despatches from a Peaceful Revolution*, Glasgow: 1988.

Phillips, Godfrey, *The Untouchable's Quest*, London: 1936.

Pradhan, Atul Chandra, *The Emergence of the Depressed Classes*, Bhubneshwar: 1986.

Prasad, Anirudh, *Reservation Policy and Practices in India: A Mean to an End*, Delhi: 1991.

Pyarelal, *The Epic Fast*, Ahmedabad: 1933.

Rajagopalachari, C., *Ambedkar Refuted*, Bombay: 1946.

Rajah, M.C., *The Oppressed Hindus*, Madras: 1925.

Rajshekhar, V.T., *Ambedkar and His Conversion*, Bangalore: 1980.

Rajashekhariah, A.M., *B.R. Ambedkar: The Politics of Emancipation*, Bombay: 1971.

———, *B.R. Ambedkar: The Quest for Social Justice*, New Delhi: 1989.

Ram, Nandu, *The Mobile Scheduled Castes: Rise of a New Middle Class*, Delhi: 1988.

Ramaswami, Periyar E.V., *Untouchability: History of Vikom Agitation*, Madras: 1981.

Rameteke, S.N., et al., *Nayay Murti B.R. Bhole*, Madad: 1982.

Ramgopal, *Dr Ambedkar Ka Samajik Chintan* (Hindi), Jodhpur: 1994.

Ranapise, A.S., *Dalitanche Vripattre* (Marathi), Bombay: 1962.

Rao, C.H., *Indian Caste System—A Study*, New Delhi: 1931.

Rao, K. Raghavendra, *Babasaheb Ambedkar* (Makers of Indian Literature Series), New Delhi: 1993.

Rao, M.S.A., *Social Movements and Social Transformation*, Delhi: 1978.

Rattu, Nanak Chand, *My Days With Babasaheb* (unpublished).

Robb Peter (ed.), *Dalit Movements and Meanings of Labour in India*, Oxford: 1993.

Rodge, Srirang, *Ramji Ambedkar* (Marathi), Wardha: 1989.

Rudolph, Llyod J. and S.H. Rudolph, *The Modernity of Tradition: Political Development in India*, Chicago: 1957.

Sandanshiv, D.N., *Reservations for Social Justice—A Socio- Constitutional Approach*, Bombay: 1986.

Sangharakshita, Ven, *Ambedkar and Buddhism*, England: 1986.

Sangwan, Om Prakash, *Dalit Society and the Challenge of Development*, New Delhi: 1996.

Sanjana, J.E., *Caste and Outcast*, Bombay: 1946.

Santhanam, K., *Ambedkar's Attack*, New Delhi: 1945.

———, *The Fight Against Untouchability*, New Delhi: 1946.

Satyamurthy, T.V. (ed.), *Region, Religion, Caste, Gender and Culture in Contemporary India* (3 vols.) Oxford: 1996.

Shah, G., *Social Movements in India—A Review of the Literature*, New Delhi: 1990.

Shahare, M.L. and Nalini Anil, *Dr Babasaheb Ambedkar Ke Teen Guru—Mahatma Buddha, Mahatma Kabir Evam Mahatma Phuley* (Hindi), New Delhi: 1994.

Shamsul Islam, *Arakshan Kyon Zaruri Hai?* (Hindi), Delhi: 1991.

Shanti Deva and G.M. Wagh, *Dr. Ambedkar and Conversion*, Hyderabad: 1965.

Sharma, B.A.V. and M.K. Reddy, *Reservation Policy in India*, New Delhi: 1982.

Sharma, B.D., *Dalits Betrayed*, New Delhi: 1994.

Sharma, K.L. (ed.), *Social Inequality in India: Profiles of Caste, Class, Power and Social Mobility*, New Delhi, n.d.

Sharma, R.S., *Shudras in Ancient India: A Survey of the Position of the Lower Orders*, Delhi: 1958.

Sharma, R.S. and Vivekanand Jha (eds.), *Indian Society: Historical Probings*, New Delhi: 1977.

Sharma, S.K., *Social Movements and Social Change*, Delhi: 1985.

Shashi, S.S. (ed.), *Ambedkar and Social Justice*, New Delhi: 1992.

Shastri, S., *My Memories and Experiences of Dr. B.R. Ambedkar*, Ghaziabad: 1989.

Shetty, K.P.K., *Fundamental Rights and Social and Economic Justice in Indian Constitution*, Bombay: 1969.

Shourie, Arun, *Worshipping False Gods: Ambedkar and the Facts which have been Erased*, Delhi: 1997.

Sinha, D.N., *Dr. Ambedkar*, Poona: 1963.

Shinde, V.R., *Bhartiya Asprishyatecha Prashna* (Marathi), Bombay: 1976.

Shukla, J.J., *Dr. Babasaheb Ambedkar on Hinduism*, Ahmedabad: 1993.

Sinder, Leon, *Caste Inequalities in Moghal India*, Seoul: 1961.

Singh, Parmanand, *Equality, Reservation and Discrimination in India*, New Delhi: 1985.

Sinha, Jogendra, *Dr. B.R. Ambedkar—A Critical Study*, Patna: 1993.

Srinivas, M.N., *Caste in Modern India and Other Essays*, London: 1962.

———, *Strategies for Removal of Social Inequality*, Delhi: 1992.

Tagore, Rabindranath, *Mahatma Gandhi and the Depressed Humanity*, Vishva Bharti: 1932.

Thapar, Ramesh, *Tribe, Caste and Religion*, New Delhi: 1977.

Thomas, Daniel, *Sri Narayan Guru*, Bangalore: 1965.

Triloknath, *Politics of Depressed Classes*, Delhi: 1987.

Tripathy, R.B., *Dalits—A Sub-Human Society*, New Delhi: 1994.

Vakil, A.K., *Gandhi-Ambedkar Dispute*, New Delhi: 1990.

Varale, B.H., *Dr. Ambedkar Anchya Sangati* (Marathi), Pune: 1988.
Venkatraman, S.R., *Harijans Through the Ages*, Madras: 1946.
Verma, G.P., *Caste Reservations in India*, Allahabad: 1980.
Verma, P.S., *Reservation for Whom and Why?*, Delhi: 1991.
Vivekanand, Swami, *Caste, Culture and Socialism*, Calcutta: 1955.
Wilkinson, T.S. and M.M. Thomas (eds.), *Ambedkar and the Neo-Buddhist Movement*, Madras: 1972.
Wilson, John, *Indian Caste*, Delhi: 1985.
Wiser, W.H., *The Hindu Jajmani System*, Lucknow: 1958.
Yadav, K.C., *India's Unequal Citizens: A Study of Other Backward Classes*, New Delhi: 1994.
Yuvolva, E.S., *Scheduled Castes in India*, New Delhi: 1990.
Zelliot, Eleanor, 'Ambedkar and Mahar Movement,' Ph.D. thesis, University of Pennsylvania, USA.
———, *Gandhi and Ambedkar: A Study in Leadership*, New Delhi: 1973.
———, *From Untouchable to Dalit*, Delhi: 1992.
Zeanath, Robin, *Dr. Ambedkar and his Movement*, Hyderabad: 1964.
Zinkin, Taya, *Caste Today*, London: 1962.

Contributors

UPENDRA BAXI, former Vice-Chancellor, University of Delhi, is Professor of Law at the University of Delhi.

S.K. GUPTA is Professor of History and Vice-Chancellor of Himachal Pradesh University, Shimla.

GOPAL GURU is Mahatama Gandhi Professor of Political Science at the University of Pune.

RAOSAHEB KASBE is Professor of Political Science at the University of Pune.

BEVERLEY NICHOLAS was correspondent of allied newspapers in India during the Second World War, 1939-45.

GAIL OMVEDT, writer and social activist is a Visiting Professor of Sociology at the University of Pune.

ANAND TELTUMBDE, a scholar and Dalit activist, is grand-son-in-law of Dr Ambedkar.

K.C. YADAV, former Professor of History and Director, Centre for Ambedkar Studies at Kurukshetra University, is Director of the Indian Institute of Social Justice (IISJ), Gurgaon.

YOGENDRA YADAV is Fellow at the Centre for Study of Developing Societies (CSDS), Delhi.

ELEANOR ZELLIOT is Laird Bell Professor of History at Carleton College, Northfield, Minnesota, USA.

Contributors

Index

9788173042768